VOICES WITHIN AND WITHOUT

Responses to long-term unemployment in Germany, Sweden and Britain

Jochen Clasen, Arthur Gould and Jill Vincent

The POLICY PRESS

First published in Great Britain in 1998 by
The Policy Press
University of Bristol
Rodney Lodge
Grange Road
Bristol BS8 4EA, UK
Telephone +44 (0)117 973 8797
Fax +44 (0)117 973 7308
e-mail tpp@bristol.ac.uk
Website http://www.bristol.ac.uk/Publications/TPP/

British Library Cataloguing-in-Publication Data
A catalogue entry for this book is available from the British Library

ISBN 1 ~~86134 090 7~~ 1861341083.

Jochen Clasen is Senior Lecturer in Social Policy at the Department of Applied Social Science, Stirling University. **Arthur Gould** is Senior Lecturer in Social Policy at the Department of Social Sciences, Loughborough University. **Jill Vincent** is Senior Research Fellow at the Centre for Research in Social Policy, Loughborough University.

Front cover: Photograph supplied by Raissa Page of Format Photographers, London.
Cover design: Qube Design Associates, Bristol.

The Policy Press works to counter discrimination on grounds of gender, race, disability, age and sexuality.

Printed in Great Britain by Hobbs the Printer Ltd, Southampton.

Contents

Acknowledgements

We would like to thank: the Joseph Rowntree Foundation for funding the research on which this book is based; the members of the steering committee who gave us useful advice and support throughout the project (Len Dawes of the Employment Service; Arthur Fleiss of the Department of Social Security; Eithne McLaughlin of Queens University, Belfast; John Philpott of the Employment Institute; Carolyn Vogler of City Univeristy; Gary Watson of the Department for Education and Employment); and Derek Williams of the Joseph Rowntree Foundation for his administrative support.

We also wish to acknowledge the cooperation and support we received from our colleagues in Germany (Hubert and Sylvia Heinelt of Hannover University) and Sweden (Rolf Stål of Örebro University and Olle Bursell of Örebro Kommun). They not only helped us to plan the whole project but were instrumental in making the arrangements for the interviews with the long-term unemployed and sending us the transcriptions.

We also owe thanks to a number of colleagues in Loughbrough University's Centre for Research in Social Policy (CRSP): Robert Walker who played a key role in the early stages of the project; Mary Hart and Karen Kellard who conducted and analysed many of the British interviews; Sue Middleton for her coordinating work at a crucial time; Rosie Woolley (secretary) and Nigel Bilsborough (executive officer).

We are very grateful to all those who agreed to take part in the 'policy' interviews: politicians, civil servants, trade union officials, business people and professional workers. Last but by no means least, we would like to thank the long-term unemployed people in each of the three countries for giving us the opportunity to convey their experiences to a wider audience.

The responsibility for the analysis and views expressed in this book rests entirely with the authors.

Jochen Clasen
Arthur Gould
Jill Vincent

Glossary

German

DM	German Mark
ABM	Job creation schemes
AFG	Labour Promotion Act
Arbeitslosengeld	Unemployment insurance benefit
Arbeitslosenhilfe	Unemployment assistance
BDA	Association of German Employers
Beschäftigungsgesellschaften	Employment enterprises
BHI	Programme for long-term unemployed
BMAS	Ministry of Labour and Social Affairs
CDU	Christian Democratic Union
CSU	Christian Social Union
DAG	White collar worker trade union
DGB	Association of German Trade Unions
FDP	Liberal party
FLO	Federal Labour Office
GDR	German Democratic Republic
Gymnasium	Upper secondary school
Länder	German federal states
Soziale Betriebe	Social companies
Sozialhilfe	Social assistance

Swedish

SKr	Swedish Krona
Af	Public Employment Service
A-kassa	Earnings-related unemployment benefit
AKU	Labour Force Survey
ALU	Job creation programme
AMK	Labour Market Office
AMS	National Labour Market Board
AMU	Labour Market Training

API	Workplace introduction
Arbetslinjen	The work line
Ds	Department of Employment
FHS	Folk high schools
Grundskola	Primary and lower secondary school
Gymnasium	Upper secondary school
KAS	Flat-rate unemployment benefit
KOMVUX	Education grants for adults
Kronofogden	Crown baillif
LO	Federation of manual trade unions
ÖBO	Local government housing office in Örebo
RAS	Direct recruitment support
Riksdag	Parliament
ROT	Repair and reconstruction project
SA	Social assistance
SAF	Employers Federation
Social utslagning	Social exclusion
Stuga	Country cottage
SVUXA	Study assistance for unemployed adults
TCO	Federation of service sector unions
Tryggetsråd	Employment Security Council

British

£	Pound sterling
AMA	Association of Metropolitan Authorities
CBI	Confederation of British Industry
CSE	Certificate of Secondary Education
DfEE	Department for Education and Employment
DSS	Department of Social Security
HP	Hire-purchase
JIG	Job Interview Guarantee
JSA	Jobseeker's Allowance
LEC	Local Enterprise Company
MP	Member of Parliament
MSC	Manpower Services Commission
NVQ	National Vocational Qualification
O-level	Ordinary level examination

TEC	Training Enterprise Council
TfW	Training for Work
TUC	Trades Union Congress

International

EC	European Community (now the EU)
EU	European Union
GDP	Gross domestic product
ILO	International Labour Organisation
OECD	Organisation for Economic Co-operation and Development

Currencies

At the time this research was being carried out £1 was worth about DM2.5 and SKr10.

List of tables

Introduction

It can be argued that in a capitalist society employment is an essential feature of citizenship for those of employable age. While occasional bouts of unemployment are acceptable, the implications of long-term unemployment on being and feeling part of society are very significant. Long-term unemployment, for those who experience it, is a deprivation rather than an opportunity. Among politicians, pundits and professional observers, long-term unemployment can provoke fears of social decay and crime and memories of fascism in the 1930s. It can also inspire new terminologies for conceptualising the problem, such as 'the two thirds/ one third society', 'the underclass' and 'social exclusion'. The dilemma in Western Europe is that while everybody is aware of the individual and collective dangers of long-term unemployment, few are sure they have the answers.

This book considers long-term unemployment in three European countries: Germany, Sweden and Britain. It discusses the problem from three perspectives – that of existing literature on the subject; that of people who are part of the policy-making process or who contribute to it, and that of the long-term unemployed themselves – in an attempt to find out whether there is any common ground between these points of view. Are the concerns of and criticisms made by academics, administrators and politicians who write about and discuss existing policy and provision similar to those at the receiving end of policy? What can be learned from the views of long-term unemployed people themselves? And is there anything to be learned from the ways in which different countries respond to long-term unemployment?

On a more theoretical level, the book aims to contribute to two current debates within social policy analysis: one on welfare state typologies or regimes (Esping-Andersen, 1990) and the other on the nature of social exclusion and marginalisation. This introduction begins with a brief discussion of both of those debates in relation to the problem of long-term unemployment and then gives statistical information about the unemployment situation and long-term unemployment in the three countries. It concludes with an account of the methodology used in the study.

Welfare regimes and long-term unemployment

The three countries selected for this study represent what are generally regarded as different social and political traditions. In the latter half of the 20th century, German politics has been dominated by the conservative alliance between the Christian Democratic Union (CDU) and the smaller Bavarian Christian Social Union (CSU). The CDU/CSU has favoured a corporatist approach to a range of issues and has helped to create and support institutions which involve a partnership between the state and the representatives of employers and employees. Swedish politics have been dominated by a social democratic government which has been equally supportive of corporatism, but has given considerable influence to the trade union movement. Britain's postwar corporatist consensus between Conservative and Labour governments began to crumble after the oil crisis of the 1970s. The aim of Conservative governments from 1979 was to restructure the welfare state along distinctly neo-liberal lines.

As far as their respective welfare systems are concerned, the three countries could be seen as corresponding to three different types of welfare regimes identified by Esping-Andersen (1990) as prevalent in industrialised countries – the liberal (Britain), the conservative–corporatist (Germany) and the social democratic (Sweden). Briefly, liberal regimes were characterised by means-tested assistance, modest universal transfers and modest social insurance plans; an emphasis is placed upon the work ethic, a targeting of welfare spending and the encouragement of private welfare. Recent policies included an even further shift towards deregulation of market principles via a deregulation of labour markets, downward pressure on wages and cut-backs in welfare rights (Myles, 1996).

Conservative–corporatist welfare regimes were characterised by Esping-Andersen as preserving status differentials through earnings-related and distinct social insurance transfers, a readiness of the state to act according to the principles of subsidiarity and a consequential reinforcement of the role of mothers and an unwillingness to provide daycare and family services. This strong corporatism between employers and trade unions, a relatively underdeveloped service sector and the tendency towards promoting forms of labour market exit via early retirement and other types of reduction of labour supply combine to create a situation increasingly characterised by labour market insiders and outsiders (Esping-Andersen, 1996).

The social democratic or Nordic model of welfare extended "the principles of universalism and decommodification" (Esping-Andersen, 1990, p 27) to embrace the new middle classes through providing high quality comprehensive welfare benefits and services for all. Egalitarian ideas were based on the notion of full employment, equal access to the labour market for women and the minimisation of welfare dependency.

Since his seminal work published in 1990, Esping-Andersen's attempt to categorise advanced national welfare states into three types has provoked a number of criticisms focusing on, for example, the conceptualisation of welfare rights and social citizenship (Taylor-Gooby, 1991), the neglect of the role of unpaid work in relation to welfare states (Lewis, 1992) or the operationalisation of decommodification and the redistributive capacity of welfare states (Castles and Mitchell, 1992). As a consequence, a number of reclassifications, extensions and alternative typologies have been proposed (for an overview see Kvist and Torfing, 1996). More recently, the intellectual gain in attempting to categorise welfare states as a way to account for cross-national differences has been questioned (Baldwin, 1996).

Whatever the merit of these and other criticisms, for the purpose of this study it has been assumed that Scandinavian welfare states differ from continental European welfare states as well as those of the Anglo-Saxon world if not in all respects (and the attempt to encapsulate entire welfare states might be the problem here) at least in crucial aspects, including the ways in which unemployed people are supported. On the basis of this assumption, our aim was to test whether welfare regimes can be identified from within and outside the policy making system, that is, rather than conceptualising worlds of welfare 'from within' (based on either a description of salient policy instruments or an analysis of aggregate policy outcomes), we wanted to see whether responses from both groups of interviewees (policy communities and long-term unemployed) would justify a conceptualisation of three distinct worlds of welfare or, more precisely, worlds of unemployment support for those out of work for a long time.

As will be discussed in more detail in Chapters One, Three and Five (and illustrated in the Appendix), the three countries under consideration differ considerably in the way in which they support unemployed and long-term unemployed people and could thus be seen as adopting three different systems. For example, Germany and Sweden can be conceptualised as adopting 'insurance-oriented' models of unemployment support which emphasise the link between earnings and benefits by providing wage replacement transfers and which maintain accustomed living standards at least for some time, while Britain can be seen as a 'welfare-oriented' model which is aimed at preventing poverty by providing moderate or low, and often means-tested benefits only (Reissert, 1994; Schmid and Reissert, 1996).

When considering further aspects in relation to benefit generosity and universality, three distinct systems emerge: 'selective', 'comprehensive' and 'residual' forms of unemployment benefit regimes (Kvist and Ploug, 1996; Ploug and Kvist, 1996). To illustrate briefly, Germany can be regarded as favouring the selective model since benefits are generous for some unemployed, modest for others and exclude some claimants from primary and secondary unemployment support altogether. What is more, earnings-related insurance benefits are relatively generous not only for some groups of unemployed but also those participants on labour market programmes with a previously strong labour market attachment. Others have to resort to the lower unemployment assistance system which is generally still regarded as less stigmatising than the local social assistance scheme.

Sweden, by contrast, adopts a more comprehensive or universalistic model, and has achieved a more egalitarian treatment of claimants due to a relatively easy access to benefits, wide coverage, high wage replacement levels (especially for low income groups) and the right (but also expectation) to participate in labour market programmes. The British system of unemployment support is egalitarian on a residual level. Training programmes often provide little more than a small supplement to benefits and replacement rates of unemployment benefit (as the system was called at the time) are among the lowest in Europe, making application for additional social security support almost inevitable. A recent study demonstrated that even if wider public support programmes (housing benefits, family allowances) for the unemployed are taken into account, the UK can still be classified as providing residual support in comparison with most other European countries (Fawcett and Papadopoulos, 1997).

However, how far does such a classification based on a broad description of social security and labour market support reach? Systematic differences outlined above can be assumed to apply to the prime clientele for mainstream unemployment support programmes, that is, to those who have been out of a job for a relatively short period. But what about long-term unemployed people? To what extent does their perception of national support mechanisms correspond with the notion of different welfare regimes? For example, does the idea that earnings-related social insurance benefits provide a strong work orientation also hold true for long-term unemployed in Germany? Do long-term unemployed people in Sweden regard themselves as socially included in the supposedly 'comprehensive' welfare regime? What about those involved in devising policies? Do they consider the link between long-term unemployment and poverty or marginalisation in the 'residual' British welfare regime to be more pronounced than that in the 'comprehensive' Swedish system? It is hoped that this study will provide at least some answers to these and other questions, which will then allow the idea of welfare regimes 'from within and without' to be addressed.

Unemployment and long-term unemployment

In order to set both the description of national policy instruments and responses from policy communities in context, it is important to present briefly some facts and figures on the unemployment situation in the three countries leading up to the mid-1990s, which was the time of the interviews.

In both Britain and Germany, unemployment had begun to rise from the mid-1970s. In the former, it rose to more than 12%, in the latter to around 8%. However, Swedish governments throughout the 1980s successfully maintained a commitment to full employment with rates of around 3%. While Germany and Sweden continued to pursue an *active labour market policy* throughout the 1980s, Britain abandoned its own labour market board – the Manpower Services Commission (MSC) – by the end of the decade.

All three countries suffered a worsening economic situation from 1989. The reunification of Germany initially prolonged an economic boom in the former West Germany which had started in the late 1980s but the implications soon added to the depth of two recessions in the early and mid-1990s. By 1995 more than two and a half million people, or 9.3% of the labour force, were out of work in the western half of the country while the destruction of jobs in the eastern half resulted in an official unemployment rate of 16%. It would have been twice as high but for a battery of job creation, retraining and other labour market programmes. The employment situation continued to deteriorate during the next few years with unemployment rates approaching the historical mass unemployment of the 1930s (Sozialpolitische Umschau, 1996:9).

The Swedes, who had maintained full employment and a generously-funded welfare state throughout the 1980s, found it increasingly difficult to do so after 1989. The consequent inflationary pressures resulted in the abandonment of full employment. From 1991-94, Sweden was governed by a four party centre-right coalition elected on a neo-liberal manifesto. By 1993, the official unemployment rate stood at more than 9% with a further 6% on labour market schemes (Arbetsmarknadsverket, 1994, pp 10-11). At the same time, the public sector deficit stood at 14% of GDP and the national debt at 80% of GDP. Attributing part of the cause of their economic difficulties to not being part of the European Union (EU), the Swedes finally became members in 1995. Having reached levels of unemployment similar to those of other European countries, there is little prospect of them being substantially reduced in the near future.

Britain's unemployment rates remained higher than those of most other Organisation for Economic Co-operation and Development (OECD) countries throughout the 1980s (Gallie et al, 1994). They rose again in 1989 and did not begin to fall until 1993. However, many of the new jobs which have been created in recent years cannot be compared to the full-time jobs lost in the manufacturing industry. Most of them are temporary and/or part time (Shaw and Walker, 1996).

Comparable figures for 1993-95 (see Table 1) show that unemployment rates were very similar by the time this study was under way. The main differences were in the composition of unemployment. The unemployment rate for women in Germany tends to be higher than that of men whereas in the other two countries it is the other way round. The unemployment rate for women is also higher in Germany than for Sweden and Britain. However, young people in Germany are much less likely to experience unemployment than their counterparts in the other two countries.

During the 1980s, in the former West Germany one third of all unemployed people were out of a job for more than 12 months. There was a slight drop in the figures towards the end of the decade but they have risen again in the 1990s. Particularly problematic was that in September 1996 there were about 450,000 people (more than half of all long-term unemployed) who had been out of a job for more than two years (ANBA, 1997). Of those unemployed in the east, 27% were long-term unemployed, with about 40% of these out of work for two years (ANBA, 1997). However, these figures are likely to be underestimates since many of those seeking employment are not included in national

Table 1: Annual rates of unemployment in Germany, Sweden and Britain (1993-95)

		Unemployment (%)		
		Germany	Sweden	Britain
Whole population	1993	7.9	9.5	10.4
	1994	8.4	9.8	9.6
	1995	8.2	9.2	8.8
Males	1993	6.6	11.1	12.3
	1994	7.2	11.2	11.3
	1995	7.1	10.1	10.1
Females	1993	9.6	7.7	8.1
	1994	10.1	8.2	7.5
	1995	9.8	8.2	7.0
Under 25 years	1993	7.9	22.6	17.9
	1994	8.7	22.6	17.0
	1995	8.8	19.4	15.9

Source: *Eurostatistics* (1997)

statistics (Wagner, 1995a). Kronauer et al (1993) estimated that the proportion of people out of work for more than two years was twice as high as the official figures suggested. It is not surprising to find that internationally comparable data tends to adjust Germany figures in an upwards direction (Gaß et al, 1995).

In Britain, Employment Service responses to long-term unemployment are initiated at six months but the most widely used measure of long-term unemployment is people out of work for more than 12 months. The percentages rose steadily from 25% of the unemployed in the mid-1970s to 40% by the end of the 1980s (White and Lakey, 1992) falling slightly to 39% by 1996 (ONS, 1996). However, these figures are based on a 'claimant count' and do not include people not claiming Unemployment Benefit or unemployment-related Income Support. This means that unemployed single parents, workers aged above 60 and those with caring responsibilities are not represented. The Unemployment Unit has argued that this "significantly undercounts the totals out-of-work" (Unemployment Unit, 1995, p 4).

Long-term unemployment in Sweden, in contrast to both Germany and Britain, is defined as those unemployed for more than *six months*. In 1984, it rose to 30% of all those unemployed and then *fell* to 15% in 1989 before returning to 30% of a much higher level of unemployment in

1993 (*Social Rapport*, 1994:10, p 45). These figures, based on statistics from AMS (the National Labour Market Board) tend to understate unemployment compared with those produced by the Central Bureau of Statistics' Labour Force Survey (AKU). The former are based on those actively seeking work while the latter are a consequence of a sample survey of the labour force carried out monthly. AKU, according to a report published by the National Board for Health and Social Affairs, states that 40% of the unemployed are long-term unemployed (*Social Rapport*, 1994:10). If figures for the unemployed and the long-term unemployed are understated by AMS, they are also complicated by the fact that the long-term unemployed are much more likely to receive a disability pension than others in the workforce (Diderichsen, 1994, pp 99-100).

When comparisons are made with the other two countries, in terms of those unemployed for more than 12 months, Sweden comes off very well (see Table 2). However, while long-term unemployment in Sweden may *officially* seem to be quite low, it is known to be a growing and understated problem. Even the Department of Employment admits that the real level of long-term unemployment in Sweden is much closer to European levels. In April 1994, when 100,000 were officially long-term unemployed, 645,000 (15.2 % of the labour force) had been registered with Employment Offices for more than six months (Ds, 1994:108, p 61). The Department examined this phenomenon by saying that many of them were on a benefits/schemes 'merry-go-round'. As the unemployed began to exhaust their Unemployment Benefit entitlement, so they were placed on labour market schemes, after which they were entitled to a further period of benefit.

Table 2: Annual rates of long-term unemployment (12 months and more) as a percentage of unemployment in Germany, Sweden and Britain (1995) (rates in %)

	Germany	Sweden	Britain
All unemployed	48.7	20.2	43.6
Unemployed males	45.9	23.4	49.6
Unemployed females	51.3	15.9	32.3
15-24 years	26.8	12.7	27.2
25 years and more	51.7	22.8	50.3

Source: *Eurostat* (1997)

However, the Department claims that the main difference between the position of long-term unemployed people in Sweden and EU countries is not so much in actual numbers or percentages but in the scale and quality of labour market measures and, as a result, the greater likelihood of the long-term unemployed finding employment.

Who are the long-term unemployed?

Age is the most crucial factor associated with long-term unemployment in the old Länder of Germany. National statistics show that workers older than 45 are less likely to become unemployed than younger people. However, once made redundant, the likelihood of them returning to employment is significantly lower. In 1996, the average unemployment spell for those between 45 and 65 was more than 20 months – more than twice as long as for those between 25 and 45 (ANBA, 1997). Almost two thirds of those out of work for more than one year were older than 45 (ANBA, 1997). By contrast, the level of long-term unemployment among younger people in Germany is low in comparison with many countries. Perhaps also less so than elsewhere, instability of previous employment does not seem to be closely associated with long-term unemployment (Andreß, 1989).

Women are disproportionately affected. In 1996, the female labour force participation rate in Germany was just below 60% compared with 81% for men, yet women constituted almost half of those in unemployment and long-term unemployment (ANBA, 1997).

Other risk factors associated with long-term unemployment are a lack of vocational qualifications or a medical condition. When combined with age, these three factors are likely to increase the length of unemployment quite considerably (ANBA, 1997, p 124). During the 1980s, a new group of long-term unemployed emerged. These were relatively young, qualified and fit. According to Klems and Schmid, they constituted 20% of all long term unemployed and 35% of those aged less than 55 (1992, p 451). International comparisons confirm that groups who previously had been relatively unaffected by unemployment, such as graduates and skilled workers, were increasingly out of work for long periods during the 1980s (Commission, 1992).

In Sweden, people between the ages of 55 and 64 are the most vulnerable to long-term unemployment. According to the Department of Employment, half of those unemployed in this age group in 1993 were unemployed for more than six months – double the percentage for 16-24 years old (Ds, 1994:108, p 57).

Unemployed males in Sweden are more likely to be long-term unemployed (34%) than unemployed women (27%) (*Social Rapport*, 1994:10). Until recently the sex differences between the young long-term unemployed were minimal but by 1994 41% of young unemployed males (16-24) were long-term unemployed compared to only 24% of young unemployed women (Ds, 1994:108).

Unemployment rates among non-Nordic foreign citizens living in Sweden tend to be twice the rate of the rest of the population (*Social Rapport*, 1994:10, p 41). The percentage of the unemployed in both groups who experienced long-term unemployment was not that great. However, the gap is now beginning to widen (Ds, 1994:108, p 59).

In Britain, the recession of the early 1980s created many redundancies in traditional industries such as textiles, mining and heavy engineering (Walker et al, 1995). The people affected tended to be male, older workers who were either unskilled or whose skills had become outdated. They found it difficult to take advantage of the jobs being created which were typically in the services sector, part time, and requiring higher or different skills (OECD, 1988).

Overall, the risks of long-term unemployment fell mainly on those who were poorly qualified and unskilled, those who were young and inexperienced, those older than 50, workers with poor health or with a disability and people from ethnic minorities (Convery, 1997a).

Table 2 provides us with the first set of Eurostat figures for which long-term unemployment can be compared for the three countries. The Swedish rates for long-term unemployment *as a percentage of total unemployment* are significantly lower than for Germany and Britain. Again we find that the position of women in Germany is inferior to that of men whereas for Britain and Sweden it is the reverse. In all three countries long-term unemployment is much more severe for older than for young workers.

Table 3: Annual rates of long-term unemplyment as a percentage of the labour force in Germany, Sweden and Britain (1995)

	Germany	Sweden	Britain
Whole population	4.0	1.9	3.8
Males	3.3	2.4	5.0
Females	5.0	1.3	2.3
Under 25 years	2.4	2.5	4.3

Source: Adapted from *Eurostat* (1997) and *Eurostatistics* (1997)

When we use the figures from Tables 1 and 2 to work out *the percentage of the workforce* which is unemployed for more than 12 months (see Table 3), the rate for Sweden is half that of Germany and Britain. German women are in a much worse position that their counterparts in the other two countries as are young people in Britain.

Causes of these cross-national differences in the social structure of long-term unemployment are beyond the scope of this study, which is primarily concerned with the cross-national differences in responses to the problem. Reasons would include: variations in national labour market structures and regulations; employers' recruitment strategies; patterns of vocational training; types and scope of active and passive labour market programmes; and demographic structures (see Adnett, 1996).

Social exclusion

In conducting interviews in each of the three welfare state regimes, it was necessary to address the issue of the consequences of long-term unemployment. This could be done at one level simply by focusing on the material and social disadvantages people suffered. How best to refer to the cumulative impact of these disadvantages presented a number of problems.

At the outset, it was thought that that the term *social exclusion* might be preferable to that of the *underclass*. The use of the underclass by Charles Murray – to denote those who had dropped to the bottom of the social pile because of their own fecklessness and who were encouraged to live on welfare benefits by a social system which had forgotten how to express disapproval of anti-social behaviour – did not appeal initially to many social scientists (C. Murray, 1990; 1994). Gallie felt that data from the British Social Change and Economic Life Initiative gave little support to the idea that the long-term unemployed in particular developed a distinctive underclass subculture (Gallie, 1994, p 737). After exhaustive analysis of the concept, Morris concluded that while it might have some validity in describing a particular status, it had little explanatory value (Morris, 1994, p 165). She also said that the concept of the underclass underestimated the "internal heterogeneity and likely diversity of interests of long-term unemployed people" (Morris, 1994, p 108). Commentators who have considered that the concept of the underclass might have some utility and need not be linked with a politics of the right have also concluded that it was too clumsy to do justice to the "different groups of people within the underclass [who faced] different problems and barriers"

(Robinson and Gregson, 1992, p 49). Yet they were happy to argue that unemployment in a post-Fordist economy had created a "surplus population" which had become "socially and economically excluded" (Robinson and Gregson, 1992, p 48). Similarly, Rodger, in his discussion of the underclass, claimed that his paper illuminated "the social processes of structuring marginality without becoming embroiled in a semantic discussion about the term 'underclass'". He then went on to talk about types of exclusion (Rodger, 1992, p 48).

In contrast, the term 'social exclusion' seemed to offer the opportunity to focus more on the dynamic process by which people became marginalised within a society, rather than on the static concern with the characteristics of an underclass, while at the same time offering the possibility of subsequent inclusion or integration. Unlike the term 'underclass', social exclusion implies that society has done the excluding and that the excluded person is a victim. Linguistically, the concept is French in origin and is embedded in "a particular interpretation of French revolutionary history and republican thought" denoting a set of mutual rights and responsibilities which citizens possessed in solidarity with each other (Silver, 1994/95, p 537). It was the state's task to ensure that citizens did not become excluded from their society. While the term is not used in Germany, *soziale Ausgrenzung* is a reasonable translation. The Swedish term *social utslagning* is Sweden's official translation of social exclusion within the EU, but its origins and meaning are not exactly the same. In Britain, where poverty and deprivation have been used to describe the situation of the long-term unemployed, the concept of social exclusion is relatively novel. Silver (1994/95) has quoted an EC document which states that the concept has been used to describe, in addition to the situation of the long-term unemployed, that of migrant workers, those on low incomes, drug users and child labour. He concluded:

> ... [the] cultural embeddedness of the concept ... makes the development of legitimate cross-national indicators more difficult than those ... for measuring poverty or unemployment.... Choosing one's definition means accepting the theoretical and ideological 'baggage' associated with it. (Silver, 1994/95, p 544)

While the term social exclusion was adopted initially, it quickly became apparent that its different ideological uses and the difficulties of finding a precise comparative definition meant that it would have to serve as no more than a starting point in the investigation. For example, in the policy interviews it was a useful way to elicit a broader, more philosophical response than was obtained from people when asked about the cumulative individual and social consequences of long-term unemployment. What was important, however, was that in both the policy interviews and the interviews with long-term unemployed people the experiences people went through, the processes which they underwent and the way in which they reacted and coped with their situation, were explored.

Methodology

This study of long-term unemployment was carried out through an examination of existing literature, interviews with a number of actors in the policy field and interviews with long-term unemployed people. From the outset, the research team in Britain was aided by collaborators in Sweden and Germany who gave useful advice at each stage of the project.

Literature reviews were carried out in the three countries prior to embarking on the empirical part of the study. These gave a picture of the unemployment situation both past and present. Studies of long-term unemployment, policy provision and contemporary issues and debates were also examined. Subsequently, interviews were conducted with a range of 'policy experts' – researchers, business, trade union and interest group representatives, local and national politicians, administrators and civil servants. Around 25 of these were carried out, in each of the countries, between September 1995 and January 1996. A rough comparability between the different categories was achieved (as can be seen from Chapters Two, Four and Six). Interviewees were asked to comment upon the nature of the problem in their own country; the adequacy of existing measures to deal with it; the consequences of long-term unemployment for the individuals concerned and society as a whole; what obstacles prevented the unemployed from gaining employment; what incentives were provided to help people find work; and whether realistic alternatives to present policies existed.

Following these, qualitative interviews with samples of long-term unemployed people and their unemployed partners (except in the case of Britain) were carried out between November 1995 and February 1996 by indigenous interviewers. This study does not claim to describe in a representative way the situation of the long-term unemployed in the three countries; with only about 25 people from each country selected the number of interviews is far too small to do this. Instead, the aims were to conduct an illustrative, explorative and, as far as possible, comparative study, although different constraints in each of the countries made strict comparability difficult to achieve.

As previous research had tended to focus on older and younger groups of long-term unemployed (for example, White and McRae, 1989), the aim of this study was to concentrate on those aged between 30 and 45, a group for whom there are relatively few labour market entry and exit programmes. To get at a broad range of experiences, we interviewed four groups of long-term unemployed people: single people without children; lone parents; married or cohabiting parents; and married or cohabiting couples without children. Of the latter two groups we only interviewed those where both members were out of work. Where interviewees had a partner, efforts were made to interview both members of that couple.

Individuals were selected from three medium-sized cities which were broadly comparable in terms of the level of unemployment in relation to the national average and labour market structures (for example, no city was affected by a rapid decline of a major industry). The towns selected were: Hildesheim (in the western part of Germany); Örebro (Sweden); and Lincoln (Britain). In Örebro, the selection of long-term unemployed to be interviewed was made by the social services department and the employment agency and, similarly, in Hildesheim by the social assistance office and a training agency, all of whom were familiar with the local employment situation. An industrial dispute among civil servants prevented a similar strategy in Lincoln. Selection was therefore carried out through Job Clubs and house-to-house calling in areas which were known to have high levels of unemployment.

Respondents were interviewed for between 60 and 90 minutes on the following topics: personal background, education and work history, current spell of unemployment, finances, jobsearch activities, employment services, perceived obstacles to employment, policy options and alternatives. The interviews were transcribed. The subsequent analysis in their language of origin, using a software package for analysing qualitative data, NUD*IST (Non-numerical Unstructured Data by supporting process of Indexing, Searching and Theorising), was carried out by Jochen Clasen (German interviews), Arthur Gould (Swedish interviews) and Jill Vincent and colleagues in Loughborough University's Centre for Research in Social Policy (British interviews). A common coding frame was devised, tested and agreed by those involved in the analysis.

Comparing three countries

One method of writing up results often used by comparativists, namely devising chapters according to particular themes with comparisons (in this case, between Britain, Sweden and Germany) throughout the chapter, was rejected for this study because of a concern that it would lead to a fragmented sense of each country's unique situation and pattern of its policy responses. It was decided instead to structure the substantive material of the study by country supplemented by a comparative introduction, comparative concluding chapters to each of the two main parts and a comparative concluding chapter in the third section.

Each of the authors took special responsibility for one of the countries. Care was taken to ensure that they addressed similar issues and followed a consistent structure and format. This should make it relatively easy for readers who wish to explore particular issues and make their own comparisons, to do so. However, no attempt was made to create an artificially 'uniform' style of writing. As each country had its own idiosyncrasies which required appropriate expression and emphasis, so each author had a personal style which it was felt should not be unnecessarily restricted. It is hoped that the combination of the individuality of the countries and their authors will add to the readability and interest of the book.

Outline of this book

Part One begins with a literature review and policy interview chapters for Germany (Chapters One and Two), Sweden (Chapters Three and Four) and Britain (Chapters Five and Six) in turn. This will enable the reader to gain a clear idea of long-term unemployment in each country; how the problem is perceived and dealt with; and the nature of existing debates. It concludes with a chapter comparing the findings in each of the three countries (Chapter Seven). **Part Two** presents the results of the interviews with long-term unemployed people (Chpaters Eight to Ten) – the findings are compared in a concluding chapter (Chapter Eleven). **Part Three** consists of a final chapter which relates the outcomes of the previous two parts.

Part One

The policy context

ONE

German context

Introduction

Despite some convergence, an analysis of unemployment and long-term unemployment in Germany requires separate investigations for the old and the new Länder (the former West Germany and GDR) respectively. In the former, unemployment has to be regarded against a backdrop of relatively high economic output for most of the postwar period, coupled with long-term structural change and increasingly 'jobless growth' since the mid-1970s. By contrast, unemployment in the new Länder is a consequence of a sudden and complete collapse of the former economic system and labour market after German unification. The characteristics of long-term unemployment differ considerably between the two parts of the country. For example, in 1996 more than 60% of all long-term unemployed in the western part of the country were older than 45 while almost three quarters of all long-term unemployed in the new Länder were women (ANBA, 1997).

The town selected for the interviews with long-term unemployed people is situated in the western part of the country and the policy interviews were conducted with officials and other respondents in the old Länder: the focus is on west German responses to the problem of long-term unemployment. However, the discussion of income maintenance programmes and active labour market schemes applies to Germany in general since regional differences are minimal in purely administrative and institutional terms (for more details on the situation in the new Länder, see Kress et al, 1995). This chapter begins by outlining the social security support available for unemployed people, then discusses the active labour market programmes at both the federal and local levels before reflecting briefly on empirical research into consequences of long-term unemployment. It concludes with a summary of some of the major obstacles, as well as opportunities for returning to the world of work long-term unemployed people face.

Social security

About two thirds of all registered unemployed people in Germany receive one of the two main types of unemployment benefits administered by the Federal Labour Office (FLO) in Nuremberg, an agency governed by tripartite boards with representatives from unions, employer organisations and public authorities. While being a separate body outside of the federal government it has some autonomy from the Ministry of Labour and Social Affairs, which determines relevant policy changes. Both so-called active labour market programmes (vocational training, retraining, job creation schemes and so on) and benefits (for example, unemployment benefits and short-time working allowances) are jointly funded out of earmarked contributions to the FLO (see Clasen, 1994a). Calculated on the basis of monthly gross wages, contributions are paid in equal parts by insured employees and their employers. In 1996 the combined contribution rate was equivalent to 6.5% of gross wages.

Provided contributions have been paid for at least one year, claimants are entitled to unemployment insurance benefit (*Arbeitslosengeld*) equivalent to 67% (60% for claimants without children) of previous net earnings. However, because the basis for benefit calculation is 'adjusted' net earnings (excluding overtime pay or regularly paid bonuses), benefit levels are normally lower. Bäcker (1995) estimated actual rates to be about 61%, and 54% for claimants without children. The standard benefit duration for receipt of Arbeitslosengeld is 12 months. However, dependent on the length of individual contribution records, benefit receipt is extended for those who are at least 45 years of age. The maximum of 32 months is granted to claimants older than 57 years of age who have paid contributions for five out of seven years prior to becoming unemployed.

Unemployment assistance *(Arbeitslosenhilfe)* is the more typical form of income maintenance especially for younger long-term unemployed. There are two ways to access this benefit: either exhausting eligibility to unemployment insurance benefit or having had insured employment for at least six months prior to becoming unemployed. For the former group of claimants, unemployment assistance is, in principle, paid for an indefinite period. For the latter, eligibility is restricted to one year. Benefit levels reflect former net earnings, representing 57% for claimants with children (53% for others), with actual rates having been calculated to be equivalent to 52% and 48% respectively (Bäcker, 1995). However, eligibility to unemployment assistance is subject to a means test. A further aspect, important for policy making in social security (see Clasen, 1994a), is that unemployment assistance is funded out of general taxation rather than from contributions.

About one in three of all registered unemployed in the old Länder did not receive any insurance-related benefits in 1995 (Wagner, 1995a). Insurance benefits are not always sufficient to prevent the need to apply for additional support. About 3% of unemployment benefit recipients and about one in seven unemployment assistance claimants received additional means-tested social assistance (*Sozialhilfe*) in 1994 (ISA, 1995). Unlike the British income support scheme, Sozialhilfe is the responsibility of local authorities who both administer and fund the system (see Clasen, 1994b). As a 'last safety net', it is intended to support people for only temporary and exceptional periods of life rather than to cover 'standard risks' which are supposed to be met by insurance and other benefits. However, in 1993 almost 600,000 recipients stated 'loss of employment' as the main cause for claiming social assistance (Wagner, 1995a). While this is a considerable increase compared with the 1980s, longitudinal research shows that many claimants receive social assistance for relatively short periods of time, not least because they are waiting for insurance claims to be cleared (Leibfried et al, 1995).

There are regulations in all three types of income maintenance which allow unemployed people to retain some income from paid work. Recipients of Arbeitslosengeld or Arbeitslosenhilfe have the option to pursue part-time work for up to 19 hours per week without becoming ineligible for benefit receipt so long as hourly wages remain below a ceiling. According to complex calculations a certain amount of monthly earnings (about one quarter of individual benefit levels) remains entirely disregarded. Any earnings above that level are deducted at a rate of 50%. For recipients of Sozialhilfe any type of other income, including earnings, will normally reduce the level of benefit on a DM for DM basis. However, a certain amount of earnings are disregarded to take account of specific work expenses and to provide a work incentive. The level of these disregarded earnings depends on local, and partly discretionary, rules but disregarding earnings equivalent to between 20-25% of individual benefit level are not uncommon. According to the scarce literature on work incentives and disincentives, while family benefits and the tax system have been found to have some effect on labour supply, there is little evidence that unemployment compensation increases the level of unemployment in Germany (Zimmermann, 1994).

Labour market programmes

Federal Labour Office

Both unemployment benefits and labour market policies, such as training and retraining schemes, job creation programmes, wage subsidies and other 'active' measures, are financed out of contributions to the Federal Labour Office (FLO) which implements programmes through its network of regional and local employment offices in accordance with the Labour Promotion Act (AFG).

In 1994, a total of 226,000 people participated in training and retraining schemes in the old Länder (ANBA, 1995 p 36). The long-term unemployed have not constituted a specific target group and as a proportion of all participants this group has decreased in size since the mid-1980s to 9% in 1993 (Schmid and Gaß, 1995, p 188). In part, this low rate can be explained by entitlement criteria. For example, long-term unemployed people who have not received unemployment insurance benefits within the past three years are ineligible to claim a maintenance allowance which would enable them to participate in training schemes.

The FLO is also responsible for job creation schemes (ABM). Although those out of work for more than one year without having made prior contributions to the FLO can, in principle, participate in ABM, places are targeted at those unemployed for at least six months who have paid previous contributions. Schemes are generally located within the public and voluntary sector and employment has to be of 'public interest' and 'additional', that is, it would not have materialised without public subsidies. In the past, wages for ABM participants were equivalent to regular wages paid to non-subsidised employees. However, in the mid-1990s, the government has lowered ABM wages to 90%, and more recently to 80%, of equivalent wages paid to non-subsidised employees.

Towards the end of the 1980s, up to 120,000 people participated in ABM at any one time. With unification the number decreased in the old Länder to about 80,000 while ABM in the new Länder were extensively used as a mechanism by which to cushion the collapse of the economy and employment. In the first half of 1992 there were more than 400,000 participants in the east (*Employment Observatory*, 1995).

The number of ABM places taken up by long-term unemployed people remained fairly stable in the old Länder during the early 1990s with about 50,000 participants. It amounted to more than 60% of the total in 1994 (Gröbner et al, 1995). However, it appears that for many participants, and especially those without qualifications, job creation schemes represent little more than an interruption of unemployment (Hardes, 1988). Only one quarter of those who have been unemployed for less than six months remain in work after leaving ABM compared with 18% of long-term unemployed who have been out of work for more than two years (Schmid and Gaß, 1995, p 190).

Within the AFG framework there are three different types of wage subsidies paid to employers taking on unemployed people. Legislation was altered several times since the 1980s, leading to significant fluctuations in the level of subsidies paid and consequently in the number of participants. There are no exact figures for specific groups, but the total number of places and take-up has been relatively low. It can be assumed that the long-term unemployed do not benefit much from these schemes, with employers preferring to take on those with shorter periods out of work. However, one programme has had some success. It is targeted at those older than 55 who are either long-term unemployed or have participated in ABM. In 1994, about 18,000 jobs were promoted with the help of this scheme (ANBA, 1995, p 113).

In the spring and autumn of 1995 the FLO asked local employment offices to focus pro-active placement efforts on the long-term unemployed and those 'threatened' by long-term unemployment. Employment offices approached local employers directly, irrespective of whether vacancies had been notified or not. Out of a total of 750,000 claimants who were suggested for work contracts, about 260,000 long-term unemployed found new jobs through these special 'placement initiatives' (Sozialpolitische Umschau, 1996:7). The majority of these placements occurred without inducements of BHI wage subsidies (see below), which were granted in only 54,000 cases.

Employment aids for the long-term unemployed

While the FLO is responsible for the bulk of active labour market measures, there are 'special' programmes not funded by contributions. Most important for the long-term unemployed is the tax-funded 'employment aids' programme for long-term unemployed (BHI). This began in 1989 and initially ran until 1994. However, in January 1995 the government decided to continue the programme until 1999 (Gröbner et al, 1995). There was mass advertising in the press appealing to employers to make use of the subsidies. As its 1989 predecessor, the new BHI scheme provides wage subsidies for employers for a maximum of one year if long-term unemployed people are being appointed on a non-fixed-term basis. The level of the subsidy is determined by the length of unemployment, representing between 40% and 80% of earnings. Endowed with a total of DM3 billion, the scheme was expected to lead to work contracts for 'at least' 180,000 long-term unemployed people (Sozialpolitische Umschau, 1995:60).

The government claims that two thirds of the 130,000 long-term unemployed taken on with the help of BHI between 1989 and the end of 1993 were still with the same employer 18 months later (Gröbner et al, 1995). Early indications show that the new round of the programme will be just as successful as far as take-up is concerned. However, the initial programme coincided with an economic upturn which would have led to the appointment of many long-term unemployed even without wage subsidies. Research shows that the programme has contributed to selection processes within the pool of long-term unemployed which have proved to be beneficial for those without any restrictions except for lack of paid work and especially for men aged between 25 and 45 (Klems and Schmid, 1992). In the late 1980s this group represented 33% of all long-term unemployed but 60% of those on the BHI programme (Klems and Schmid, 1992). By assisting 'creaming' effects, the programme has been counterproductive in some respects, leaving behind those with one or more 'problematic attributes'.

Project funding

The limited success of traditional labour market policies during the 1980s contributed to the launch of a programme in 1989 for particularly disadvantaged unemployed and 'hard to place long-term unemployed' people (those out of work for at least two years and with at least one 'problematic' attribute). Unlike conventional AFG schemes, this programme did not support individuals but projects. These projects could receive up to 80% of costs for investments, for overheads and for wages to pay instructors and people guiding participants. They combined diverse support mechanisms such as employment and qualification elements as well as mentoring and 'social guidance', providing psychological support with, for example, personal and familial problems, drug addiction and debt management. The latter aspects had previously not been part of the AFG framework.

This emphasis on project funding marked a diversion from traditional German labour market policy which is dominated by individual support for unemployed contributors to the FLO. It was also exceptional in that recognising the importance of mixing different types of support for particular groups of long-term unemployed it breached the institutional gap between labour market policy (codified in the AFG) on the one hand and welfare policy (codified in the Federal Social Assistance Law) on the other. The programme also intended to bring together relevant local actors (such as local labour market offices, municipalities, welfare associations, churches, employers and unions) to form 'round tables'. Reflecting EU discussions about the effectiveness of targeted programmes and local labour market policies (Dyson, 1989; Commission, 1992), the adoption of a 'holistic' labour market policy approach was believed to foster new ideas and to 'tailor' projects to regional and local needs. In conjunction with this new programme, eight local labour market offices were selected and given wider discretionary power to test 'new ways' of labour market policy (see Schmid et al, 1994a).

Research shows that the inclusion of 'social guidance' elements and the combination of different support mechanisms such as training and employment proved fairly successful, leading to significant improvements in labour market integration rates of the 'hard to place' unemployed (Schmid et al, 1994b). However, even within this programme selection processes were noticeable since older unemployed people, women and those with medical conditions remained underrepresented. Other negative aspects identified were a lack of involvement of private companies in the programme and problems of coordination between local agencies.

Based on the experience of this new type of support, institutional funding has now become an established element within the AFG. However, funds remain limited. In 1994, the FLO supported 360 new projects with 8,800 unemployed people in total (ANBA, 1995, p 66). This suggests that this type of labour market policy is unlikely to herald a new paradigm in German labour market policy. Instead, entitlement-based 'individual' schemes such as job creation and training programmes will continue to dominate, supplemented by 'institutional' support within tight constraints.

Local authorities and the 'second labour market'

With the persistence of mass unemployment in Germany, the role of local authorities and municipalities has changed substantially. As a consequence of an increased number of unemployed without any or with insufficient entitlement to insurance benefits, local authorities witnessed an increasing share of their budget being diverted towards unemployed social assistance claimants. Responses to this process of the so-called 'communalisation' of the problem of mass unemployment (Blanke et al, 1987) have been two-fold. While local authorities have attempted to secure ABM places, funded by the FLO, they also initiated active labour market programmes for their clientele, that is, unemployed social assistance recipients (see Blanke et al, 1986; 1987; Jaedicke et al, 1991; Huebner et al, 1992).

Already in the 1980s local authorities had started to provide some unemployed social assistance claimants with employment contracts. While this strategy is more expensive than simply paying out social assistance, in the long run it can be more cost-effective since contracts are generally temporary, allowing participants to build up entitlement to insurance benefits which can be claimed once contracts run out. In this way, the financial burden can be transferred back from the local level to the FLO. This institutional aspect is crucial for an understanding of German labour market policy and its inherent difficulties. On the one hand, there are those unemployed who fulfil entitlement criteria for unemployment benefits and, after some time in unemployment, are likely to participate in one of the labour market programmes for which the FLO is responsible. On the other, there are those who are, or have become, entirely dependent on social assistance and are a problem primarily for local authorities and their welfare offices.

Local welfare offices can make use of various options of so-called 'help-to-work' programmes as stipulated in the Federal Social Assistance Law (Huebner et al, 1992, p 35). Normal employment contracts might be offered to unemployed social assistance recipients. Alternatively, regular wages might be paid for jobs which have to be 'socially useful' and 'additional' according to social welfare legislation. Both options constitute employment in accordance with labour law and social insurance regulations. By contrast, claimants might merely be paid a small supplement to social assistance which would also mean that they would remain without entitlement to social insurance benefits. Local authorities have the freedom to 'test' claimants' willingness to work by requiring them to do certain types of activities. The latter two possibilities cited above can be regarded as workfare options which some local authorities made fairly extensive use of during the 1980s (see Albert, 1989). Nowadays local authorities appear to prefer the option of regular, but temporary, work contracts which lead to either employment elsewhere or, more likely, receipt of unemployment insurance benefits.

Survey data reveals that in 1993 local authorities offered employment to about 120,000 unemployed social assistance claimants (ISA, 1995). While this is a considerable effort, the bulk of employment policy in Germany remains firmly located within the AFG framework. This can be illustrated with reference to expenditure data: in 1993, local authorities spent a total of DM3.1 billion on employment for social assistance claimants compared with FLO expenditure of DM13 billion on job creation schemes alone and DM19 billion on training programmes (Jacobs, 1995).

Hildesheim, the city selected for interviews with long-term unemployed people for this study, is not atypical in this respect. In 1995, the welfare office offered work contracts to 40 social assistance claimants for 'additional' jobs of 'public interest' in the voluntary sector. Types of employment included laundry, kitchen help, secretarial, social care and landscape gardening work. Hildesheim is situated within the Land of Lower Saxony which agreed to take over some of the costs – but by mid-summer no funds had been forthcoming for 1995. In the previous year there were also about 100 places jointly financed by the social welfare and the local employment office. Such cooperation is politically desired and encouraged. However, it is not mandatory and the degree of cooperation depends on local circumstances and funds available from within employment offices. By mid-1995 no joint funding places had begun in Hildesheim.

Given local authorities' limited resources the demand for placements far outweighs the number of available 'help-to-work' places (Deutscher Städtetag, 1994). Programmes appear to be biased in favour of those who already have some work experience and possess at least basic qualifications. Half of this group leave 'help-to-work' programmes to start regular work (ISA, 1995). By contrast, other participants, such as drug and alcohol addicts, those with criminal records, people in hostels and those who have been in receipt of social assistance for lengthy periods, are not only underrepresented in communal 'help-to-work' schemes but also less likely to complete placements successfully or to find employment thereafter (Klein et al, 1992). Some local authority programmes target these specifically disadvantaged groups and might offer elements of training or qualifications within their schemes. However, in general programmes have been criticised by participants for the short period of the placement, the absence of training and other support mechanisms and the failure to take account of personal circumstances and individual needs (Klein et al, 1992).

However, some attempts are made to tailor support and to combine different types of assistance. For example 'employment enterprises' (*Beschäftigungsgesellschaften*) were founded by mainly larger cities in the 1980s to provide a combination of employment, training and social guidance. In the early 1990s about 20 of these 'enterprises' existed in the old Länder, some of which supported a large number of social assistance claimants. The 'employment enterprise' in Hamburg, for example, employs about 1,000 social assistance claimants who receive training for a period of up to three years (Häntsch and Mirbach, 1994). After unification, 'employment enterprises' in the new Länder were introduced in much larger numbers as one way to respond to the collapse of employment. In 1994, there were about 400 of those enterprises, employing about 110,000 people (Bosch, 1995).

Adequate funding is invariably a problem for local employment initiatives. As indicated above, 'help-to-work' programmes might receive subsidies from additional sources such as Länder or the FLO, which might fund job creation schemes for project personnel. The Catholic and, even more so, the Protestant church provide funds for local employment projects or even organise them directly (see Krömmelbein et al, 1995). Large welfare organisations run projects and the European Social Fund (one of the three main EU Structural Funds) has become another important source of finance for local initiatives. Depending on particular circumstances, projects provide work experience, qualification and training courses, social guidance and mentoring or simply paid work. Activities range from recycling and energy conservation to 'alternative' party services but also include traditional forms of work such as carpenting or bricklaying. While welfare offices organise some local employment directly, the majority of projects receive funding from a variety of sources and are run by one of a multitude of non-governmental organisations.

Collectively, such types of publicly subsidised employment have been referred to as the 'second labour market'. Projects within the second labour market differ as to their particular target groups and funding arrangements. However, what they have in common is their focus on groups of unemployed people with reduced chances of reintegration into regular work, such as long-term unemployed, older people, people with disabilities, ethnic minorities, drug and alcohol addicts and ex-convicts. Schemes aim to give these groups a chance to participate in employment for a limited time, to acquire or to maintain skills and, more generally, to prevent processes of social marginalisation and deprivation (Wagner, 1995b).

Compared with conventional labour market schemes run by the FLO, the scope of the second labour market has remained relatively limited. However, pointing to the inability of traditional labour market policy to reduce unemployment to any significant degree, recent proposals envisage a gradual expansion and firm establishment of publicly subsidised employment to about one million jobs (Bergmann, 1993; 1994). Such a move would be welcomed by some but has been strongly criticised by others. More generally, arguments about the appropriate role, size and future of the second labour market in Germany have become crucial in the political debate about the problem of unemployment (see Chapter Two).

A further initiative started in the Land of Lower Saxony in 1991 involves establishing a number of so-called 'social companies' (*soziale Betriebe*). This initiative has subsequently spread to other Länder such that in 1994 there were about 70 'social companies' employing about 1,500 exclusively long-term and other 'hard to place' unemployed people. To compensate for the assumed lower productivity of these employees, companies receive public subsidies for a 'kick-start' period of five years, after which they are supposed to be independent of any public support. Unlike most second labour market programmes, participants are offered permanent contracts, given the opportunity to gain further qualifications and, most importantly, are employed in companies which operate in fields which are deliberately not 'additional'. Social companies are supposed to compete for business, to establish themselves and, after five years, operate without public support. Early indications are that these companies do well economically but the aim of becoming entirely independent has proved too ambitious for most of them (Christe, 1995).

Consequences of long-term unemployment

Studies into psychological and social effects of unemployment in the former West Germany reach back to the 1970s and 1980s (Brinkmann, 1984). A detailed discussion of these and later investigations would go beyond the scope of this chapter. However, two key aspects to note are that while there appears to be no single pattern of coping with unemployment or long-term unemployment, factors which have been singled out as most likely to impinge on the psychological well-being of those involuntarily out of work include the reduction of social contacts, repeated rejections of job applications and a general insecurity about future prospects (Bach et al, 1994). Also, whether and to what extent these factors influence individuals depends on a range of other conditions such as personal employment biography, length and frequency of unemployment, availability of alternative roles to gainful employment, financial situation, general attitude towards waged work and social support within families and other networks (Brinkmann and Wiedemann, 1994).

A study of 400 unemployed married men in two German cities distinguished three groups which coped with unemployment differently (Hess et al, 1991). A total of 20% of the sample perceived unemployment as not entirely negative as it allowed them to spend more time with the family and on other activities. The group consisted of a disproportionately high number of skilled workers and middle class employees who had some recourse to additional income from other family members. A total of 50% of respondents were characterised as the 'socially isolated' group who suffered during unemployment owing largely to the loss of contacts with their colleagues and friends, and because of the financial restrictions. On average, members of this group were less qualified and in receipt of lower benefits, or none at all. The remaining 'depressed' group (30%) comprised of people whose self-esteem was significantly lower than that of other interviewees. On average, this group included people with few or no qualifications, longer individual cumulative unemployment, and who were generally pessimistic about finding another job.

Based on interviews with unemployed men and their partners, the study illustrates that implications of unemployment are neither directly nor solely dependent on changes in the material situation nor on the length of unemployment. Instead, the three most important influences on the degree of psychological and social well-being were found to be individual attitudes towards waged work, personal employment biographies and family relationships. Demonstrating how unemployment affects daily family routines, the study indicates that families are often not a stabilising element or factor in improving the chance of reintegration into the labour market. Instead, family relationships, and traditional gender roles in particular, were found to be an additional psychological and social burden associated with unemployment.

As far as financial implications of unemployment are concerned, a representative survey in 1989 revealed that almost half of all unemployed had postponed planned purchases, 37% had used up savings partially or entirely and 17% had taken up loans (Rosenbladt, 1991). A survey commissioned by the Ministry of Labour and Social Affairs (BMAS) in 1990 showed that unemployed people relying on social assistance in particular are prone to be in financial debt and have problems with paying their rent (BMAS, 1990). However, linking unemployment with processes of deprivation, marginalisation or social exclusion is perhaps misleading. Kronauer (1993; 1995) has suggested that the connection between long-term unemployment and processes of marginalisation or even social exclusion is perhaps weaker in Germany than elsewhere due to institutional arrangements such as vocational training and comparatively generous social security support. Instead, the term 'labour market exclusion' has been proposed as a more appropriate description of the immediate problems some groups of long-term unemployed face, especially since German society continues to identify itself strongly as a 'work society', with institutional arrangements centred around gainful employment (Kronauer et al, 1993).

Obstacles and opportunities

While most of the discussion in this chapter has centred around income maintenance programmes and mechanisms to reintegrate long-term unemployed people into work, there is little doubt that the main problem unemployed people face in Germany today is an insufficient demand for labour. The 'employment gap' in Germany has widened after each economic recession since the mid-1970s and the current lack of jobs has been calculated to be between six and seven million, based on those registered as unemployed and others who are seeking employment but, for a number of reasons, either do not register or are not counted as unemployed. What is more, the number of long-term unemployed has risen since the mid-1990s. Out of this group there are now more people out of work for more than two years than for between one and two years (ANBA, 1997). There is little prospect that this job gap will be closing much during the next decade or so merely because of economic growth. Thus, labour market programmes will always be an insufficient response to unemployment and long-term unemployment if they are not accompanied by economic policies which foster the growth of employment opportunities and address the allocation of existing employment in society.

Experiences of some countries such as Sweden (see Chapters Three and Four) show that high levels of unemployment do not necessarily have to be accompanied by high levels of long-term unemployment. In Germany, there is considerable movement in and out of unemployment and the majority of those becoming unemployed return to the labour market after a relatively short spell out of work. However, the lack of overall demand for labour pushes those with few or no qualifications, those with medical impairments and women looking for part-time work into disproportionately long periods of unemployment. Long-term unemployment in Germany is concentrated on older people in particular. In September 1996, more than 60% of all long-term unemployed were aged 45 and over (ANBA, 1997). Yet there does not seem to be a strong association between long-term unemployment and unstable work histories. In the mid-1990s almost two thirds of all long-term unemployed had become jobless for the first time at the average age of 51 after an average 27 years in employment (Bogai et al, 1994; BMAS, 1995).

The large number of long-term unemployed people with lengthy employment histories and good qualifications indicates a relatively rigid labour market in Germany with employers apparently not inclined to give job applicants who have been away from the labour market for relatively long periods a chance. As one way of changing this a government commission proposed to deregulate labour laws in general and more specifically to allow employers to appoint long-term unemployed people on a wage rate below the one agreed in collective bargaining (Deregulierungskommission, 1991). However, explorative empirical survey data suggests that low wages would not entice employers to appoint long-term unemployed people (Klems et al, 1992). On the other hand, the same study found that wage subsidies was the most favoured incentive for employers to appoint long-term unemployed people. As discussed, wage subsidies have figured as an option to tackle long-term unemployment in Germany for some time. Legislation in 1997 re-emphasised the focus on influencing employers' recruitment strategies with the introduction of a new 'integration contract' (see Sozialpolitische Umschau, 1997:16). Employers willing to take on long-term unemployed people on a trial basis for six months are to be compensated with the suspension of certain labour law regulations, such as redundancy restrictions, and also with the transfer of costs to the FLO such as the continuation of wages paid to employees who are sick, on a training course or on holiday.

However, there are other obstacles discussed in this chapter which need to be overcome in order to tackle long-term unemployment more effectively. One of these is the realisation that despite some concentration on certain social groups, long-term unemployment affects a wide and heterogeneous spectrum of society. Accordingly, a range of policy responses are needed. While some lack nothing but a job, others would be best supported with access to training or a period of work experience after a long spell out of work. Others still are in need of a combination or 'chain' of support programmes best provided by projects which involve advice, counselling, the chance to acquire qualifications and skills, followed by employment. However, institutional fragmentation of labour market policy in Germany with responsibilities for different groups of long-term unemployed going to different bodies means that those who are younger, easier to place and with recent employment records are target groups for the FLO. Eligibility for maintenance allowances for participating in training, job creation and other federal labour market programmes has still to be linked to prior contributions. Also, institutional conditions continue to induce local employment officers to focus efforts on claimants of unemployment compensation or at least on those who are most likely to leave the unemployment register.

Conclusions

Increased discretionary powers for local employment offices as well as a more regulatory framework for local labour market actors would go some way to improve the response to the problem of long-term unemployment in Germany. Recent legislation has given employment offices more autonomy (Sozialpolitische Umschau, 1997:12) but has stopped short of meeting demands for more substantial institutional reforms for labour market policy (see Arbeitskreis AFG Reform, 1994; Kühl, 1995). The AFG remains top-down and restrictive, leaving insufficient discretion to local outposts of the Federal Employment Office to spend resources on innovative programmes which would take account of local labour market situations. At the same time, a closer and less ad hoc cooperation between local labour market offices and social assistance authorities, as well as other local groups involved in creating employment opportunities, would remove some uncertainties, not least regarding the continuity for funding, which appear to hamper a more sustained attempt to help many long-term unemployed to regain access to the world of work.

TWO

Policy interviews in Germany

Interviews

A total of 29 interviews were carried out with German 'policy experts' between August and September 1995. Four of these were MPs, who together represented the two parties in government (the conservative CDU/CSU and the liberal FDP as the junior party in government) as well as the two opposition parties (the social-democratic SPD and the Green Party). All four are also members of the parliamentary select committee on social affairs. Five employees of employment offices were interviewed at three administrative levels; the FLO, Land and local employment office. Two trade union interviewees represented the Association of German Trade Unions (DGB) and the Trade Union of white-collar workers (DAG). The employer representative is a member of the Association of German Employers (BDA). Other interviewees include five social scientists and economists who have conducted research on different aspects of long-term unemployment in Germany, one BMAS civil servant and another one at the equivalent Ministry at Land level. At the local level, interviews were conducted with two people involved in projects for long-term unemployed and a representative of an unemployment initiative. In Hildesheim, the town selected for interviews with long-term unemployed people, interviews were conducted with an employment officer, a representative of an unemployment initiative, four social welfare officers and one person involved in projects for long-term unemployed in the voluntary sector. Table 4 gives a summary breakdown of those taking part.

Assessment of the situation

Only towards the end of the last decade did the long-term unemployed, together with other so called hard-to-place unemployed – that is, older

Table 4: Policy actors interviewed in Germany

Members of Parliament	4
Employment office	6
Employers	1
Trade union	2
Social scientists and economists	5
Civil servants	2
Local projects and initiatives	5
Social welfare officers	4
Total	29

workers, those with disabilities and those with low or no qualifications – become a central focus in the debate on unemployment. New labour market policy programmes were introduced to tackle the problem of reintegrating members of these groups.

In the second half of the 1980s, which saw a high level of long-term unemployment, there was a growing awareness that younger people as well as those quite highly qualified were being affected. Focusing on long-term unemployment, the Protestant church issued a public statement in 1987 which some respondents believed sparked off a wider debate about the problem. Other factors mentioned were the possible threat of political radicalisation among the unemployed (the neo-fascist Republican Party was gaining support at the time) but also the debate on long-term unemployment in other European countries and attempts to respond to it at European Community (EC) level.

The reduction in the level and rate of long-term unemployment in the early 1990s was widely regarded as being due to special programmes and efforts made by the FLO. However, many respondents stressed that all could not be attributed to labour market policies. The economy was in upswing due to a surge in demand in the eastern part of the country which decreased unemployment and long-term unemployment in the West.

Causes and incidence of long-term unemployment

Causes of long-term unemployment were widely associated with causes of mass unemployment generally. There was a consensus that the overall job shortage is of a structural nature, that is, unemployment is not expected to be significantly reduced simply by an economic upturn. Structural changes in the economy, with sectors such as steel and coal 'breaking away', combined with indications that Germany is becoming a less attractive location for investment, were singled out as the most significant obstacles for a return to higher employment levels. Such factors as the globalisation of capital movement, low wages paid in former Eastern bloc countries and the increased competitiveness of countries in South East Asia were mentioned as compounding the problem of unemployment in Germany. The politicians in the centre and to the right of the political spectrum, the employer representative, and the two civil servants among the interviewees all singled out what they regard as the 'excessive degree' of labour market regulation and the high wage-related costs as relevant factors inhibiting domestic investment and employment growth. Other interviewees acknowledged the fact that Germany is a high wage country but did not regard this to be a major cause for mass unemployment.

Long-term unemployment in particular was thought to be associated with changes in the economy which have led to selection processes within the pool of the unemployed, reducing the chances of re-entry into the labour market for older unemployed people and those without qualifications. A number of respondents claimed that the development of a floor of long-term unemployment in Germany has to be attributed to changes in production processes which have considerably reduced the number of jobs for non-skilled and low-skilled workers during the past decade or so. Many interviewees associated long-term unemployment among some groups of older workers with existing policies which allow them to retire early after a spell of unemployment and be financially supported by unemployment insurance benefits. The employer representative advocated a clearer statistical distinction between unemployed workers who aim to return to employment and others (especially older unemployed people) who are simply waiting until they are entitled to retirement.

A number of respondents pointed out that larger companies in particular are shedding labour in line with changes in production processes (such as computer-assisted work and new structures of work organisation) while concentrating human capital expenditure on training younger people. Both the researchers and employment officers pointed out that, compared with other countries, the German labour market is characterised by processes of social closure and segmentation, providing relatively secure positions for most of those who are in work but obstacles and prejudice for those who have been out for longer periods. This, according to the employer representative, applies especially to workers older than 45 who generally have a low redundancy risk but at the same time a small probability of returning to employment once they have been out of work for a longer period. Long-term unemployment in itself can become a reason for employers, who are making judgements about the likely productivity of job applicants, not to appoint particular jobseekers.

There was a general awareness among respondents that long-term unemployment in Germany is closely linked to three 'risk factors': disability, lack of qualifications and, in particular, age. The fact that a long period of joblessness is predominantly a problem for older workers is widely known and most respondents claimed that there was little chance of returning to work for those unemployed people who are 55 years of age or older. The employment office representatives pointed out that the 'critical' age threshold has come down over the past five years or so. Apparently, 45 years of age is now the crucial barrier beyond which the likelihood of returning to the labour market decreases considerably.

Asked which groups of long-term unemployed people received relatively little support, most respondents identified those who are outside the sphere of the AFG (the Labour Promotion Act), that is, individuals who have exhausted their rights to insurance-based unemployment benefits or who have never received them because of insufficient contribution records. As discussed in Chapter One, the FLO is responsible for unemployment insurance benefits and most active labour market programmes and, in principle, employment offices are responsible for all those registered as unemployed. However, in practice, conditions for access to many labour market programmes are often based on sufficient contribution records and/or receipt of insurance benefits. Also, it makes more sense for employment offices to concentrate placement efforts on recipients of insurance benefits rather than on social assistance claimants since the former receive contribution-based benefits while the latter are funded by local authorities.

As explained in Chapter One, the mismatch of different responsibilities, financial obligations and, consequently, rationales for action between employment offices and local authorities contributes to selection processes within the pool of the unemployed, leaving behind those with 'further problems' in addition to a lack of paid employment. This was echoed in conversations with respondents. The institutional structure of divided responsibilities for different sections of the unemployed was singled out by many as a significant factor for German labour market programmes being inefficient for regarding so-called 'problem groups' (that is, the long-term unemployed and other 'hard-to-place' unemployed).

Present policies and programmes

Social security benefits

As far as unemployment insurance is concerned, no respondent considered benefit rates to be too generous. Employment officers as well as union representatives pointed out that benefit rates of between 60-70% of former wages do not accurately reflect living standards since certain elements of earnings are disregarded for the calculation of benefit levels (such as overtime pay and other bonuses). A general perception was that benefit levels were "not comfortable" (according to a head of an employment office) but merely adequate or even too low due to cuts made in recent years. Even those who argue in favour of a deregulation of German labour markets and lower wage rates support current insurance benefit arrangements. The employer's representative argued that benefit rates were generally "okay" and the respondent from the free-market orientated FDP advocated a cut in benefit duration but not in the amount. At the other end of the spectrum, union and unemployment initiative representatives pointed out that with a prolonged duration of unemployment, benefits do not provide for an adequate standard of living. The material situation of people out of work deteriorates rapidly.

Possible adverse effects of insurance benefits on work incentives were generally dismissed as being marginal. Respondents from across the political spectrum said that the large majority of unemployed people were regarded as being keen to return to work since employment in German society is widely seen as something socially "desirable", enabling people to "participate in society" and acting as a "stabilising factor in daily life". However, when it comes to benefits based on principles of social assistance, the issue of work incentives becomes more controversial. Respondents can be divided into those who considered benefits to be too low and discriminating, and those who regarded the system as too generous and lenient for some claimants.

Federal Labour Office

Respondents generally acknowledged that unemployment needs a multifaceted response and broadly supported existing active labour market programmes provided by the FLO. However, specific criticisms were also made. Those on the left focused on recent cuts in the volume of funding and wages paid to participants in job creation schemes. More generally, the 'stop-go' policy regarding the overall number of schemes granted per year was singled out as preventing agencies involved in offering job creation places from being secure about funding. Representatives from across the political spectrum argued against making ABM "too extensive" because this might have adverse effects on regular types of employment in the so-called first (that is, the non-subsidised) labour market. Another criticism made, irrespective of political allegiance, was the problem of many schemes not leading to regular employment once participants leave. Instead, "cycles" or "revolving doors" of ABM and other active labour market programmes, interrupted by periods of unemployment, were identified and criticised as a counterproductive use of resources. According to an employment officer, ABM should always be a "bridge" to the first labour market.

Training and retraining courses were seen as useful for some long-term unemployed people but less so for others – researchers pointed out that many are already highly qualified. Older unemployed people were regarded as understandably reluctant to embark on lengthy retraining courses, realising that the prospect of employment would not improve considerably. Respondents from across the political spectrum pointed out that some training schemes seem to provide a "qualification for a qualification's sake" (employer representative), often benefiting training providers more than participants. Unlike ABM places which are now more targeted at the long-term unemployed than in the past, the proportion of the long-term unemployed within training schemes is disproportionate to its proportion of all unemployed.

Labour market policy administered by the FLO itself was mentioned as counterproductive in some senses since it prevents a more effective integration of the long-term unemployed. According to one of the agency's employees, the majority of programmes were targeted at benefit recipients and this concentration on, what she referred to as, "our clients" had increased even further after a complaint made by the Federal Audit Office about the proportion of non-contributors in some schemes. The issue of separate responsibility and accountability between the FLO and other actors such as local welfare agencies was identified as preventing a more effective labour market policy for some groups. Rather than cooperating more widely, these agencies tended to pursue their own agendas in line with the institutional structure within which they operate.

Employment aids for the long-term unemployed

Respondents regarded the BHI programme (see Chapter One), providing differential levels of wage subsidies for taking on long-term unemployed, as relatively successful although the researchers pointed out that high integration rates should be read cautiously since the beginning of the programme coincided with an upturn in the economy in the late 1980s and early 1990s. The current scheme is accompanied by a publicity campaign aimed at employers which points out the high proportion of well-qualified and younger people among the pool of long-term unemployed, many of whom had become jobless for the first time in their working life. This campaign was widely welcomed as an attempt to tackle employers' prejudices. However, respondents acknowledged that the programme was unlikely to be of much help to the less qualified and older unemployed and those who, in administrative terms, are referred to as "problem groups". Female immigrants or those with drug problems were mentioned in particular as those in need of more than mere wage subsidies in order to increase their chance of finding employment.

Some degree of creaming and windfall effects are apparently conceded as inevitable elements of the wage subsidy programme. According to a civil servant in the Ministry of Labour and Social Affairs these "have to be accepted" in the light of the overall success and popularity of the programme. Funds for 1995 had already been "booked up" by the middle of the year. Scepticism and criticism was raised by a representative of an unemployment initiative who feared that employers might use subsidies to reduce wage levels and a Green Party spokesperson who considered the government's publicity campaign as a "propaganda trick". She claimed that, while this scheme, which appeared to be doing something for the long-term unemployed, was being plugged, other labour market policies were simultaneously cut back.

Project funding

Allowing local employment offices to subsidise employment projects which offer a multitude of support for the long-term unemployed, known as 'project funding' (see Chapter One), has now become an integral part of the AFG. While it has remained only a small and supplementary element of German labour market policy because of its limited financial volume, it appears to be welcomed across the political spectrum. Trade unions and parties on the left advocated that a greater effort be made regarding integrated approaches or holistic 'support chains' which provide a combination of social guidance, training and work experience targeted on particular needs of individuals. Others are more cautious. A head of a Land employment office supported project funding, so long as funds remain limited and reserved for projects for unemployed people deemed to be "remote from the labour market", or, according to the employer representative, "very, very difficult cases".

Local labour market programmes

Local welfare offices frequently resented the need to take on a role of what has been called "ersatz", or substitute, employment offices. Often out of necessity, many local welfare offices have directly set up labour market initiatives or indirectly supported them. While these were discussed in Chapter One, two issues should be reiterated: in contrast to the insurance emphasis of federal programmes, local schemes are generally directed at recipients of social assistance; local schemes are merely 'additional and supplementary' when compared with federal labour market programmes. This latter aspect was illustrated by a civil servant at Land level who pointed out that in 1994 total expenditure on local and Land-funded schemes in Hesse amounted to less than 10% of what employment offices spent on their programmes in that particular Land.

Social assistance officers confirmed that, due to financial constraints, there are always more unemployed claimants than places available. Placements generally last only one year after which entitlement to unemployment insurance benefits will have been acquired, and the newly unemployed person will be able to claim this from the employment office. This "entitlement policy", as one employment officer called it, is compounded by employment office strategies to concentrate efforts on long-term unemployed who are "easier to place", rather than those who are considered as "labour market remote" (older workers and those with multiple disadvantages regarding employment prospects). This is because the former group is more likely to improve the rate of placement success. Social assistance officers claimed that they would "like" to offer more placements and for longer periods. However, financially this option would simply be "too expensive".

According to the AFG, local employment offices are encouraged to support social assistance offices in their endeavour to offer work experience and other programmes for unemployed social assistance claimants. However, while cooperation is supposedly "good in some places" (according to a Federal Ministry civil servant), there is no sanction for non-cooperation and little incentive for local employment offices to support social assistance offices. Consequently, employment places and projects jointly funded by these two public agencies are few and far between. It remains questionable whether this situation will change in the future. An employment officer at Land level claimed that so long as the size of 'problem groups' did not increase significantly, the target groups for employment offices would remain "their" clientele (insurance claimants) in general, and "those easier to integrate" in particular.

In Hildesheim, the town selected for interviews with unemployed people, welfare officers claimed that insufficient resources and a lack of external financial support prevented greater efforts in terms of employment initiatives. Consequently, as elsewhere, the number of unemployed social assistance claimants far outweighs the places available on employment programmes. On the other hand, welfare officers regarded many social assistance claimants, although registered as unemployed, as not being "fit to work". Rather than employment, the majority of those claimants were believed to be in need of supportive programmes, such as rehabilitation programmes, psychological help, counselling, and help with drug and alcohol addiction. Because such schemes are costly, in Hildesheim, as elsewhere, local authorities resort to offering little more than temporary employment to a limited number of claimants.

As outlined in Chapter One, there are a multitude of local projects run by different non-governmental organisations which rely on a variety of financial sources. The interviews revealed a deep ideological divide concerning publicly-subsidised employment known as the 'second labour market'. Respondents from the left of the political spectrum claimed that there was a need for a "permanently supported second labour market", with projects targeted only at market niches and local employers consulted before schemes were introduced to avoid "unhealthy competition". The representative of the Green Party pointed out that for many unemployed people there was no alternative to the schemes since a "first labour market orientation was illusory". Conservative and free-market politicians, as well as the employer representative, feared that publicly-subsidised employment adversely affects the 'first', non-subsidised labour market. The FDP spokesperson argued that there were no "harmless" projects and a distortion of market forces was inevitable. An expansion of the 'second labour market' would threaten to "squeeze out" non-subsidised employment.

A pragmatic middle position was represented by employment officers and trade union representatives who conceded that some publicly-subsidised employment might pose competition problems and that a substantial expansion of schemes was neither desirable nor financially possible. However, the 'second labour market' was a reality and so long as places functioned as 'bridges' to the 'first labour market', projects should be welcomed. A head of a municipal employment office (making a similar point to that of the Green Party representative cited above) claimed that for him the "second labour market was no longer an ideological topic", since there was "no alternative". It was 'needed' and his employment office was actively subsidising a number of projects which, for limited periods of time, offered long-term unemployed work in areas such as childcare, sale of second-hand clothing or recycling.

Similar controversies, although less in line with political persuasion, also surrounded specific initiatives. For example, the social companies (which receive public 'kick-start' funding from particular Länder for a five-year period after which they are supposed to become independent) were initially regarded by many as potentially a good support mechanism for many long-term unemployed. However, medium-term reports show that acquiring an autonomous status within markets appears to be proving very difficult for many projects. A civil servant at the FLO claimed that "kick-starting did not work", a trade union representative wondered how projects can survive at a time when 'normal' businesses have problems, and both the employer representative and the Green Party representative were "sceptical" about this particular scheme.

Consequences of long-term unemployment

Perceptions about consequences of long-term unemployment differed among respondents. Some interviewees associated long-term unemployment with processes of 'social marginalisation' or even 'social exclusion'. These effects were not believed to be widespread in Germany but there was a chance of them becoming more prevalent. The rise in the number of social assistance claimants, for example, was mentioned by respondents from the left as a sign of growing poverty and marginalisation. Younger unemployed and single mothers in particular were singled out as groups most prone to being cut off from access to the labour market and from participating in activities socially regarded as 'normal'. However, problems were believed to be hidden and occurring predominantly in cities rather than rural areas, and in places with low unemployment rates rather than regions where unemployment has been a reality for some time. This coincides with claims made by a number of respondents who argued that unemployment carried less stigma now than it did in the

1980s. Local welfare officers, for example, stated that unemployment has become "almost normal" for many people and so processes of 'social exclusion' would not really occur.

Irrespective of political persuasion, a majority of interviewees perceived the scope of the problem to be much worse and social marginalisation and exclusion to be more visible in other countries. The USA and Britain were singled out frequently. The situation in Germany was seen as comparatively better due to the existence of the 'social state' and the systems of educational and vocational training. Only a speaker for an unemployment initiative clearly associated long-term unemployment with a significant decline in material standards in particular and social exclusion in general. Consequently, he argued in favour of an introduction of a 'basic' or 'citizens' income guarantee. While the unemployed are not living comfortably, a number of interviewees pointed out that connecting long-term unemployment invariably with poverty or even an 'underclass' would be misleading. Often the problem is primarily one of labour market exclusion rather than social marginalisation or material deprivation. In that sense, the German situation was believed to be different from the one in the UK, as an employment officer stressed. A researcher emphasised that in Germany a distinction needs to be made between bigger cities where unemployed younger people and immigrants were more likely to experience social marginalisation, and smaller communities where long-term unemployed were often able to rely on informal support networks which kept them in contact with the world of work.

It was acknowledged that processes of 'self-exclusion' or 'cultural exclusion' might occur among some long-term unemployed. Having no access to the world of work can lead to 'retreat' from social and communal life due to feelings of 'worthlessness'. This has to be seen in conjunction with the continued importance of waged work in German society which many respondents believed to confer identity and self-respect. Interviewees from all backgrounds pointed out that paid employment continues to have a strong impact on self-esteem and dignity.

Obstacles, opportunities and incentives

There seems to be consensus about some types of barriers to employment within the policy community. For example, it is widely accepted that single parents often face a lack of childcare facilities, or associated high costs, and school sessions of sometimes less than half day. Regarding the 'risk factor' age, it is widely believed that some older long-term unemployed are "not really interested" in getting back into full-time work, but are interested in retirement. Other areas are more controversial. Some employment officers believed that many long-term unemployed lack the flexibility and motivation needed to change jobs, are not prepared to accept lower earnings or to undergo retraining. However, others regarded the long-term unemployed as generally highly motivated and willing to accept less attractive jobs, pointing to labour market regulations which prevent unemployed people to negotiate lower wages. As one researcher pointed out, many long-term unemployed find themselves in a dilemma. While being expected to be mobile in order to increase the chance of entering work, research has shown that the existence of local networks and contacts considerably improve the chance of finding a way back into paid employment.

Some groups of long-term unemployed are believed to face difficulties which go beyond the need for a job. According to a welfare officer, social assistance claimants in particular are often faced with a "huge mountain of debt". Incentives to take up paid work are lowered because earnings would be distrainable and employers would not be inclined to keep people whose wages are seized in that way. Other difficulties mentioned were family problems, drug and alcohol addiction and the inability to cope with the requirements of regular employment (such as punctuality and responsibility). In addition to paid employment, these groups are in need of training and other types of support. Yet companies are widely believed to be reluctant to meet these costs. Instead, given the current labour market situation, employers' recruitment policies – selecting better trained, younger and healthier workers – are regarded as rational and understandable. Trying to persuade employers to take on "social tasks" by appointing people from "problem groups" is unlikely to be an effective strategy. Rather than increasing costs, employers should be relieved of costs through wage subsidies.

These perceptions were widely shared by respondents. However, welfare officers in Hildesheim, as well as other respondents, also pointed to employers' prejudices. For example, many employers are apparently reluctant to recruit long-term unemployed people because of labour market regulations which employers believe make it difficult to 'sack' them once they have been given a contract. This perception, it was pointed out, was not accurate. Respondents from what might be considered opposite ends of the spectrum (unemployment initiatives and employer organisations) claimed employers harboured other misconceptions about long-term unemployed people, not realising that many of them are out of a job for the first time in their working life, are healthy and possess good vocational qualifications. The government's recent publicity campaign, pointing out these facts, was welcomed. However, it should be noted that even those on the left of the political spectrum considered employers' prejudices towards long-term unemployed as relatively "marginal" compared with other barriers to labour market integration mentioned above. Some respondents also pointed to the fact that large companies in particular appear to show little interest in employing people who have been out of work for longer periods, whereas smaller companies appear to be less reluctant to appoint especially younger long-term unemployed people.

Improvements and alternatives

Perceptions about effective policies for achieving reintegration into labour markets varied. What was generally agreed upon was that 'long-term unemployed people' do not conform to a generic type and so it is misleading to believe that there is a single policy which would adequately tackle the problem. Instead, as a researcher emphasised, different individual circumstances require "individualised" or tailored support. Many long-term unemployed are well qualified and lack "nothing but a job". Wage subsidies are potentially the most effective type of support here. Qualification and retraining programmes are certainly important for other groups and more efforts should be made on these, according to many respondents. Other existing labour market programmes were also believed to be important. If anything, job creation schemes were singled out by some as less valuable than other policies due to low reintegration rates of those who have been out of work for longer periods.

However, respondents pointed out that labour market policies can never be a sufficient response to the problem of mass and long-term unemployment. Instead, of primary importance are macroeconomic policies which focus on labour demand rather than supply – policies which lead to an increase in overall employment rather than programmes which improve the competitiveness of individual unemployed people. One option of combining labour demand and supply policies was made by the SPD. It proposed to focus labour market policies less on individual and more on regional support, combining labour market programmes most relevant for a particular region with economic regeneration programmes and regional planning. This idea was regarded positively by some researchers who pointed to the need for a thorough investigation of the particular nature of local labour supply and demand and of the "risk factors" regarding long-term unemployment. This could subsequently feed into specific restructuring programmes as well as labour market schemes such as training or wage subsidies tailored to specific and individual circumstances. However, the government rejected these plans not only because they would have significantly altered entitlement conditions to labour market programmes but also because of the commitment to fulfil the criteria for European Monetary Union which eclipsed any inclination to embark on policies which would require significant increases in public spending.

The importance of preventing long-term unemployment was widely emphasised. An employment officer argued in favour of stepping up and focusing existing job advice and placement activities. More specific suggestions related to reducing long-term unemployment among older workers via entitlements to partial retirement and making use of unemployment benefit to top up part-time wages. Trade unions argued that unemployed people should be entitled to an intensive job placement and advice activity after six months and, after two years, to participation in whatever would be the most appropriate type of labour market policy.

Two particular policies were widely perceived as meriting expansion. Firstly, respondents from as far apart as project providers in the 'second labour market' and the employer representative advocated a closer involvement of private companies in labour market programmes, such as trial periods and work experience. The general perception appears to be that "the closer a programme is to the company the better the chance of success". Secondly, even FLO employees acknowledged that the regulatory framework of German labour market policy needs to be assessed. The system should become more decentralised to take more account of local circumstances. Some attempts have been made in this respect: selected local employment offices have been allowed to make more discretionary decisions and have been provided with 'experimental funds' which they can use more flexibly (see ANBA, 1997). This needs to be intensified in order to become more effective, according to labour market researchers and officials.

Demands to relax entitlement criteria, widen access and extend the duration of FLO-run programmes were made by a number of respondents. Politicians on the left said that the FLO should be responsible for all unemployed people, irrespective of contribution records or benefit entitlement. If this was the case, social assistance recipients would have a right to participate in traditional labour market programmes. However, such a move would mean tackling the institutional separation between and different accountabilities of local welfare and employment offices. Financial implications as well as the entrenched traditional 'entitlement' principle of German labour market and social policy, which is staunchly defended by significant sections of both the government and the SPD (as well as trade unions), make any move towards universality unlikely.

A less wide-ranging suggestion made by many respondents was to improve the cooperation between employment offices, local authorities and alternative projects at the local level. This would assist local welfare officers who pointed out that programmes such as debt advice, rehabilitation, social counselling and guidance need to be pursued much more and be better funded to reach certain groups of long-term unemployed people. Another improvement would be to fund projects and programmes for longer periods than the norm of one year to allow for more stability and continuity in project planning. While such cooperation is already part of existing labour market regulation, it currently rests on a "dead letter paragraph" due to incentive structures which make a closer integration too expensive for local employment offices who would face increased costs. However, providing local employment offices with 'experimental' funds and allowing for more decentralised and discretionary decision making is likely to continue and might, within financial constraints, even be extended further.

More radical ideas are blocked not because of institutional but because of ideological and political reasons. For example, those on the political left, ecologists, local politicians and some academics argue in favour of an expansion of different types of publicly-subsidised employment. The 'second labour market' offers a much needed "plurality" and "creativity" in the response to long-term unemployment. It provides a "bridge" to the first labour market, gives a chance to those who are excluded from participating in traditional types of labour market programmes and is crucial for those with little hope of finding "regular paid employment". Employers, on the other hand, supported by conservatives, some academics and market liberals in particular, warn against any extension of the second labour market in any form.

A similar stalemate applies to demands for lower wages for long-term unemployed people, relaxed redundancy restrictions and, more generally, labour market deregulation. Market liberals in particular favour a lessening of the "appointment risk" for employers via a reduction of labour law regulations. For some time at least, the long-term unemployed should be paid "entry wages" which are below those agreed upon by collective bargaining. These and other ideas are frequently raised by employers and their political allies, the FDP, but strongly rejected by the majority of trade unions, the SPD and, so far at least, the government. However, in the light of pessimistic predictions regarding the employment situation, the government has started to become more sympathetic towards longstanding demands made by employers to 'deregulate' the labour market, including more scope for localised wage bargaining and the payment of lower wages, at least temporarily, for certain groups of job starters such as long-term unemployed people.

Conclusions

The interviews with the 'policy community' in Germany show a considerable degree of consensus regarding a number of issues. The causes of long-term unemployment are widely associated with a reduction in the number of jobs for unskilled and semi-skilled people in a labour market which is undergoing structural change. This is occurring within a global macroeconomic climate which itself is perceived to be changing and threatening the previously successful German model, associated with relatively high wages, high productivity and a high degree of labour market regulation. Similarly, there was agreement that the problem of long-term unemployment is multifaceted, affecting different groups to different degrees, and thus requires a range of policy responses. Even respondents from the conservative politicians and proponents of free markets did not seem to worry too much about possible disincentive effects of unemployment compensation, at least as far as insurance-based benefits were concerned. Similarly, possible windfall effects of wage subsidies to induce employers to appoint long-term unemployed people were generally regarded to be outweighed by the positive aspects of the programme, assisting some groups of unemployed people to reconnect with the world of work. There was also a shared perception that the institutional structure and separation of responsibilities of labour market policies and income maintenance disadvantages those long-term unemployed who, for whatever reason, remain outside of the AFG framework and entirely dependent on local public support.

When it comes to solutions, disagreements become visible. Some regard the persistence of unemployment as justification for their demands for labour market deregulation, introducing more flexibility and lowering wage rigidities. At the same time, they reject any expansion of 'second labour market' programmes which is proposed, in one form or another, by left and ecological groups inside and outside of the German Parliament. While there are indications that the government has heeded some of the ideas of the proponents of labour market deregulation, the expansion of the second labour market has so far been rejected for ideological as well as financial reasons.

Sweeping proposals, such as the SPD's idea to combine local regeneration policies with labour market programmes, have little prospect of success for similar reasons. However, small steps have been taken. Since the time of the interviews, various types of federal and local wage subsidy programmes have been extended or introduced. As part of a more general reform of labour market policy, some attempts have been made to decentralise labour market programmes, more scope for local decision making has been allowed, and local authorities have been asked to step up their efforts to offer employment or placement opportunities for long-term unemployed people in cooperation with local employment offices.

THREE

Swedish context

Introduction

Sweden's commitment to full employment and its pursuit of an active labour market policy in the decades prior to the recent recession are well known. In the early 1970s when there still existed an interventionist consensus in Britain, the Manpower Services Commission (MSC) was modelled on the Swedish Labour Market Board (AMS). Since that time the MSC has been abolished along with other forms of tripartite corporatism. However, in Social Democratic Sweden the AMS continues to play an important role in the economy. As unemployment has risen in the 1990s, it is appropriate to ask how well Sweden's social and labour market policies are working in general and how well they are serving the long-term unemployed.

After a brief description of social security arrangements and labour market measures for the unemployed, this chapter will continue with a consideration of the consequences of long-term unemployment, the difficulties facing attempts to alleviate the problem and some alternative proposals that have been put forward.

Social security

Unemployment insurance – *a-kassa* – is administered by the trade unions even though funded largely by contributions paid to the state. For those not members of trade unions, AMS administers a flat-rate benefit (KAS). During the 1980s, trade union members who became unemployed would, up to a certain income ceiling, receive a-kassa equivalent to 90% of their pay. Under the centre-right coalition (1991-94), this was reduced to 80% and, as a result of the new Social Democratic government's first budget, it had been further cut to 75%. (As a result of trade union pressure, the 80% level was restored in 1996 – see end of Chapter Four.) The 1995 social democratic budget also proposed that young people aged below 20 should not be able to receive unemployment benefit on the grounds that they should be in education, training or on a labour market scheme (*Riksdag och Departement*, 1995a).

A-kassa lasts for up to 300 days (450 days for those older than 55). A long-term unemployed worker, by Swedish definition, may still be receiving a-kassa. It is also possible for the unemployed to extend their period of benefit by joining a labour market scheme and subsequently claiming a further period of benefit.

> An unemployed individual can qualify for a 60-week spell of a-kassa by participating in a labour market programme.... As of 1986, five months' participation in practically any measure fulfils the work requirement. Furthermore, in 1983 insured individuals were given the right to relief work when their benefits were approaching termination; in 1993 this right to a placement in a programme was extended to include labour market training. (Agell et al, 1995, pp 106-7)

This is what is meant by those who use the term 'merry-go-round'.

When benefits and labour market schemes (see next section) run out, a means-tested social assistance (SA) can be claimed from the social services departments of local municipalities, or communes. Although the National Board for Health and Social Affairs suggests a minimum level for this benefit, many communes in recent years have set SA rates below this level. It is this benefit which large numbers of the long-term unemployed are likely to be receiving. In 1980, only 4% of the population had been living on SA; by 1992, this had doubled, largely due to unemployment (*Statistik Årsbok*, 1994). However, in recent years two thirds of the unemployed have received a-kassa, with a further 7-10% receiving KAS. Only around 25% are forced to claim SA (SOU, 1996:51). In Britain, these percentages are reversed (see Chapter Five).

Sweden may well be a country with a tradition of social democracy and a reputation for generosity in welfare matters, but the rules governing benefits in the past have been quite strict. *Arbetslinjen* is the term used to the describe the basis on which a-kassa is handed out. It literally means 'the work line'. It refers to the principle that cash support should only be given when all other possibilities have been exhausted. Applicants are expected to have explored the possibility of labour market measures before they rely on benefit. Beneficiaries are expected to keep in contact with the employment office and to seek work.

As mass unemployment and Sweden's economic difficulties have increased so pressures to limit the rights and sharpen the responsibilities of the unemployed have grown. Faced with the increasing costs of unemployment, the government took a tougher line over fraud and eligibility. A data register was to be set up under the auspices of AMS to prevent people claiming both sickness and unemployment benefit (*Dagens Nyheter*, 1994a). It was also proposed that those claiming unemployment benefit would be forced to keep in contact with the world of work and not just the form of employment they were previously used to but possibly something quite different from their normal line of work. The government claimed that it was concerned about the possibility of workers losing their 'competence'. The Labour Market Minister, according to a newspaper article, was also of the conviction that "rights and obligations must go hand in hand" (*Dagens Nyheter*, 1994b).

The committee investigating this proposal reiterated the minister's point and invoked the idea of a mutual "social contract" between society and the unemployed (SOU, 1995:7, p 17). In the past an individual's 'availability for work' had meant an obligation to accept "suitable work or labour market measures offered". This principle, it was now suggested, was now being abused through, for example, work on the black market. The report went on to say that at a time when unemployment was so high and both jobs and labour market measures were in limited supply, the meaning of the concept 'available for work' (the equivalent in English to what in Swedish translates literally as "to stand at the labour market's disposal"), had to be widened to prevent abuse on the one hand and passivity on the other. It was clear from the report that it was the long-term unemployed who were the chief cause for concern.

Active labour market policy

The administration of labour market policies in Sweden is the responsibility of AMS, the semi-autonomous administrative board accountable to the Department of Employment. Established in the 1940s, it was until recently run by a committee consisting largely of representatives of employer and employee organisations. This national organisation with a structure of regional and local offices has from the early 1960s implemented an *active labour market policy*, the chief characteristics of which were established by the economists Gösta Rehn and Rudolph Meidner. The Rehn–Meidner model gave AMS a crucial role in not only employment but also in economic policy. Aware that

Keynesian techniques of demand management could have inflationary consequences, the active labour market policy was intended to operate selectively. Not only would labour market measures such as training and job creation schemes be expanded as unemployment grew (to accommodate up to a maximum of 3% of the labour force), and be reduced as full employment was restored, but efforts would be made to identify and rectify sectoral, industrial and local deficiencies in terms of labour supply and demand (Hedborg and Meidner, 1984). AMS had the task of seeing that the labour market worked efficiently.

The corporatist assumptions of AMS have come under scrutiny in recent years with the international emphasis on free markets, flexibility and deregulation and (from 1991-94 with a centre-right government) a domestic version of the New Right. The Employers Federation (SAF) disengaged from the state's administrative boards in 1991 in protest against their domination by the interests of the labour movement. Subsequently, the centre-right coalition marginalised other board members by giving them a narrow supervisory role. As will be seen in this and the following chapter, AMS measures and the very existence of the institution have been under attack.

Labour market measures

A major *declared* aim of the public employment service in Sweden is to prioritise those who are long-term unemployed or whose position in the labour market is weak – the young, refugees and immigrants and the disabled. During 1993-94 the aim was to contain long-term unemployment (which according to official Swedish statistics included all those unemployed for *six months* or more) to less than 25% of the unemployed. This proved an impossible goal according to the AMS annual report (Arbetsmarknadsverket, 1994, p 18). However, the proportion of the long-term unemployed attending labour market schemes was on average higher than that of the unemployed generally (Arbetsmarknadsverket, 1994). Apart from that, the report made little mention of the long-term unemployed. This is not to imply that nothing special was being done for them but that it is impossible to glean from the range of activities on offer, which, if any, were of particular benefit for those out of work the longest. Much was done generally in terms of advice and information, jobsearch activities, and rehabilitation. Training, work experience for young workers and those straight out of university, relief work schemes for those older than 25, temporary replacements for

Table 5: Main categories of labour market measures and number of placements in Sweden (1993)

Involving work	
Schemes for the disabled	77,000
Relief work	14,000
Recruitment grant	9,000
Temporary replacements	10,000
Total	110,000
Not involving work	
Training	53,000
Youth training	58,000
Measures for the occupationally disabled	7,000
Job creation schemes (ALU)	35,000
Total	153,000
Overall total	263,000

Source: AKU (Labour Force Survey) as cited in *Social Rapport* (1994:10, p 33)

those on leave, job creation schemes (ALU), recruitment grants for firms employing immigrants, grants to unemployed people starting their own businesses and the financing of reparation, reconstruction and extension work (ROT), mainly in the public sector, to stimulate the building trade, were all on offer in theory to all unemployed people in receipt of unemployment benefit. The figures above (Table 5) indicate the relative size of the main programmes.

More recently, there has been some disagreement over a new measure introduced by the government. The direct recruitment support (RAS) reduced employers' social insurance contributions by SKr6,000 a month if they took on someone registered unemployed. The minister claimed that the long-term unemployed benefited from measures designed to reduce unemployment generally, while many economists insisted that the measure would be more effective if directed solely at the long-term unemployed (*Dagens Nyheter*, 1995a; 1995b). Support for the proposal from the Environment Party enabled the government to get the measure through Parliament despite opposition from the centre-right parties. The Left Party, which, like the economists already mentioned, thought that RAS should be directed at the long-term unemployed, also voted against the government (*Riksdag och Departement*, 1995b; 1995c).

In April 1995, a government proposal, called 'A more effective labour market policy', stated that:

> ... labour market measures ... should be directed in the first place to the long-term unemployed ... and other vulnerable groups. The Government, in its guidelines to AMS, will stress this clearly. People who have been unemployed for over six months must be over-represented on the different measures. Further recruitment subsidies will only be used for this group. ALU and API [workplace introduction – a new measure replacing a number of existing ones] must be reserved for the long-term unemployed and for immigrants and refugees who lack experience of the Swedish labour market. (Regeringens proposition, 1994/95:218, p 25)

Commune provision

Provision for the long-term unemployed is also made by local municipalities or communes. A major incentive for them to do this is to reduce the size of the social assistance budget, as 50% of this is attributable to unemployment (Klingensjö, 1994, p 13). Auer and Riegler (1994) describe legislation which has made it obligatory for communes to provide temporary employment for those unemployed for at least 14 months. It is also possible for communes to establish projects which are wholly or in part financed through AMS. Recipients of social assistance were provided with 7,000 placements in 1994 while an additional 56,000 placements were provided in collaboration with AMS (Ds, 1995:12).

A report into the efforts made by communes in the greater Stockholm area to alleviate unemployment is a clear indication that the problem is no longer of concern only to regions in economic decline. The report showed that open unemployment in the different communes varied between 3.3% and 7.8% (*Enheten för Regional Utveckling,* 1993, p 1) while expenditure per inhabitant varied between SKr50 and SKr1,027 (*Enheten för Regional Utveckling*, 1993, p 17). Nor was there much correlation between the two. Many communes with lower levels of unemployment were able to spend more than those with higher levels. Tyresö, for example, which led the league table of spenders, came 16th out of 22 in terms of unemployment rate.

The report dealt with a number of measures introduced to deal with employment generally but had a section which looked at schemes directed to the long-term unemployed in particular. At the time of the report, 24% of those unemployed in Greater Stockholm had been unemployed for six months or more – a figure not greatly different to the national average (*Enheten för Regional Utveckling*, 1993, p 30).

Solna commune, in cooperation with the Public Employment Agency and the local Chamber of Commerce, financed a project for 70 long-term unemployed which was further broken down into seven distinct sets of activities. One section combined the teaching of Swedish with skills in curtain-making and upholstery; another was concerned with organising study circles and jobseeking activities; bookkeeping and the use of personal computers was covered by a third; horticulture occupied a fourth; recreational activities were organised by another section; furniture repairs were carried out by another group; and lastly there was a retail outlet. According to the project leader each section was largely self-managed. A successful youth hostel had also been set up and run by the long-term unemployed in Solna (*Enheten för Regional Utveckling*, 1993, pp 30-1).

In Upplands-Väsby, those who were long-term unemployed and were not receiving any form of a-kassa attended a job club run by social services for three weeks and learned how to visit jobcentres, make job applications and manage interviews. Work experience was also provided and those attending receive an addition (stimulation allowance) to their social assistance of SKr25 a day. Non-attendance could result in individuals losing their right to social assistance (*Enheten för Regional Utveckling*, 1993, pp 31-3).

In Sollentuna, a centre was established by social services in cooperation with the Public Employment Agency for those who had lost, or were about to lose, their right to a-kassa. The centre had an office, a cafeteria, a sewing room, a woodwork room, a jobseeking corner and a group room. Up to 60 participants were involved in adult education, home services, and work with voluntary associations. As a result of this activity social assistance costs, it was claimed, had been reduced by 8.1% (*Enheten för Regional Utveckling*, 1993, pp 32-3).

In Sundyberg, a reduction in social assistance costs had been achieved by transferring the costs of the long-term unemployed to schemes for which a-kassa was paid. Work experience with a stimulation allowance and relief work for five months was provided. Those still without work could be placed on an ALU and be entitled to a-kassa as a result (*Enheten för Regional Utveckling*, 1993, p 32). Savings for the commune thus became a cost for AMS.

More than 60% of communes in other parts of the country were implementing schemes similar to those outlined above and most claimed that their social assistance costs had been reduced as a result (Klingensjö, 1994, p 11). However, it is not clear whether the savings were the result of workers gaining relatively permanent jobs or whether the costs were simply transferred from social services to the labour market authorities.

Effectiveness of labour market measures

An expert group of researchers, appointed by the government to examine the effectiveness of labour market policy, has stated that few adequate studies have been carried out and that the area is one seriously neglected by research (*Riksdag och Departement*, 1993, p 17). The work that had been done suggested that job creation schemes worked well, while pay subsidies and subsidies to industry and localities were fairly ineffective. For young people, recruitment grants seemed to work better than job creation schemes. The report concluded with the suggestion that labour market policy should be "comprehensive and directed towards *outsiders*" (that is, the long-term unemployed and vulnerable groups) since this would give the best return and would not be inflationary.

A 1986 study of long-term unemployment warned that the position of the long-term unemployed was only marginally affected by an upturn in the general economic situation (Nyberg, 1987, p 4). Selective measures were required to deal with long-term unemployment and these, in Nyberg's view (based on British research), were unlikely to have any inflationary effect (Nyberg, 1987, p 10).

Harkman (1994, p 10), in a paper written for the research section of AMS, claimed that his work shows that "a person who participated in labour market measures has a 40% better probability of finding employment after three years than a person who did not". He also claimed that "the temporary employment scheme and labour market training were substantially more beneficial for finding employment for the participant than [are job creation schemes] and relief work" (Harkman, 1994, p 11). His comments on relief work stand in sharp contrast to the evaluation of the expert group cited above. Harkman's conclusion was that "temporary interruptions of long periods of employment improve the probability of gaining employment" and that "those who have participated in ... [labour market measures] have thereby improved their position in comparison with those who have not" (Harkman, 1994, p 12).

This sort of conclusion was criticised in 1995 by the economist Lars Calmfors, who claimed that research which showed that AMS measures were effective was at best weak (*Dagens Nyheter*, 1995c). He insisted that AMS measures were directed at well-established *insiders* who represented the majority of voters rather than *outsiders* who faced the most difficult labour market situation. Since AMS was itself an "influential pressure group", and one with considerable trade union support, Calmfors argued that it should be abolished and replaced with independent, regionally-organised bodies.

Calmfors' conclusions seemed to gain support from the research of Susanne Ackum-Agell who investigated 4,000 participants on AMS programmes in 1994. Controlling for such factors as age, sex, education, nationality, Agell concluded that:

> Participants in the four active labour market programmes seem to exit to regular employment at a lower rate than non-participants. (Agell, 1995, p 92)

To be fair Agell did add that the sample might be biased by the fact that programme participants consisted of those who had the "most difficulties in finding a job ... in the first place". However, her results were widely commented on in the media as demonstrating the inadequacy of AMS measures.

These criticisms led the General Director of AMS to respond by arguing that AMS had not created the recession and mass unemployment which, in turn, had led the previous centre-right coalition to create a large number of places on low quality schemes against AMS' advice (*Dagens Nyheter*, 1995e). Labour market policy had been forced by events to adopt a social role. He added:

> Let us assume that a researcher presents a study which shows that people admitted to hospital have a greater risk of dying than those who are not admitted. And that an even greater risk is run by those taken into intensive care. How many would draw the conclusion that the hospital should be closed down as soon as possible, beginning with the intensive care unit? (*Dagens Nyheter*, 1995d)

Two months later, Agell had to apologise to everyone concerned. It was discovered that, through an accident, all those who had found jobs immediately following an AMS measure had "dropped out" of her statistics by mistake (*Dagens Nyheter*, 1995e). She admitted:

> It would have been terrible if the Government had acted on my statistics and abolished labour market policy or squeezed the budget.

However, as will be seen in the following chapter, Agell's original conclusions were uppermost in the minds of many of those interviewed about policy issues.

Consequences of long-term unemployment

Considering that until the 1990s Swedes experienced very low rates of unemployment – between 2% and 4% – it is not surprising that studies of the consequences of long-term unemployment should be limited. Inevitably, those who could not find work in a time of full employment were often those who had medical and social problems which made them difficult to employ. As far back as 1972, Berglind used the term 'utslagna' to describe those who could not "get or keep employment in the open labour market" (Berglind, 1972). The term came to be associated with psycho-social problems. 'Utslagna' means 'the rejected', 'those thrown out', 'outcasts'. Today, within the EU, 'utslagning' has become the Swedish translation of the term 'social exclusion'.

This concern with the possibility that long-term unemployment will result in people ceasing to be members of society, losing their place within it, is a familiar theme in the Swedish literature. One of the contributors to a recent seminar in Umeå entitled 'On the margins – to be put outside' said that, "To be placed outside working life is perhaps the most important way in which someone can be marginalised in today's society" (Furåker, 1995, p 5). He went on to say:

> If people are without a job for a long time with little likelihood of being admitted to the labour force, it is easy to give up. Alternatively, it can be a question of finding other ways of surviving: theft, prostitution and the drug trade. Subcultures may grow which Swedish society has seen little of hitherto. Moreover, a mistrust of their environment may develop amongst the unemployed with a different ethnic identity. (Furåker, 1995, p 18)

Soydan (1995), in the same seminar, used the term 'outsidership' in discussing the extent to which unemployed immigrants become marginalised. This term is also taken up by Nilsson, in a qualitative study of the long-term unemployed in the north of Sweden. She concluded that unemployment placed people outside "that which binds people together and which society sees as important" (1995). Those unemployed for a long period experienced a process of "disintegration"; they lacked "symbolic and social capital"; they felt guilty about being dependent even when they knew that their unemployment was due to "factors outside their control" (Nilsson, 1995, pp 44-6). This is probably related to the feeling that they were not "living up to society's work ethic" (Nilsson, 1995, p 41). Certainly it was Berglind's view that the unemployed came to be labelled as "work-shy and incapable" by their more successful peers (Berglind, 1972, p 111).

Other studies have commented on the consequences of long-term unemployment in more specific ways. In a study of young unemployed people Hammarström (1995) concluded that poor health and substance misuse were the result of unemployment.

> Unemployment is the worst threat to public health. (Hammarström, 1995, p 30)

Gustafsson (1994), in a review of different studies of mass unemployment, suggested that the most common and pressing worry among redundant workers was how to make ends meet. Economic worries in their turn produced psycho-social symptoms "such as sleep problems, headaches and impotence" (Gustafsson, 1994, p 20). There was, in her view, also the danger of increased crime and ethnic conflict, although only studies over a longer period could confirm this, she insisted.

A more recent consideration of the concept of marginality has led one Swedish researcher to conclude that an appropriate way to analyse the experience of unemployment was to relate it to a dynamic continuum ranging from a feeling of *rootedness* to that of *exclusion* (Svedberg, 1995, p 44). The mid-point on this continuum is *marginality*. This is a useful construct because it enables us to consider that many unemployed people may, for a variety of reasons, be considered marginal. Social exclusion may follow, but not necessarily. Those who have strong social support and networks find it easier to adapt to their situation than those who do not (Nilsson, 1995, p 41). Gustafsson made a similar point when she commented on the differential impact of stress on those who were able to compensate for unemployment through other activities. The *active* were less stressed and the *passive* more stressed. While *social exclusion* for some might be a consequence of long-term unemployment, for some it meant only that they were *marginal* while others might retain a sense of belonging to or *rootedness* in society. As will be seen in Chapter Nine, the long-term unemployed people interviewed in Sweden could be said to range across this continuum.

Obstacles and opportunities

Obstacles facing the long-term unemployed can come from either complex interactions between employers, the employed and the long-term unemployed, that is, the employment system or from the social security system.

Employment system

A 1991 report from the Department of Employment put forward three explanations for the position of the long-term unemployed: *duration*, *selection* and *insider/outsider* (Ds, 1991:52, pp 65-8). *Duration* of unemployment implied that the longer people are unemployed the more likely they are to lose their employability – the skills, knowledge, attitudes necessary to help them find and keep a job. *Selection* emphasises the likelihood that employers will select those applicants from the labour market who have stronger competitive qualities. In the third explanation the employed are seen to be in an advantageous position to protect their jobs by adapting to the needs of the employer. Employers will depend on the experienced *insider* more than on the inexperienced *outsider*.

Gustafsson has cited Norwegian research which asked employers the question: "How long can someone be unemployed before they become less attractive to employ?" (Gustafsson, 1994, p 14). The percentages answering one to five months were quite small. The big difference came at six months to which 34% of employers responded; 43% said 12 months. Gustafsson also points out that in a recession – should extra work need doing – employers are more likely to offer overtime to existing employees than create extra jobs (Gustafsson, 1994, p 22). Employers try to reduce the risk of taking on too many workers. Similarly, the employed are more likely to protect themselves against the possibility of unemployment by endorsing rights and rules which make their position more secure. In doing so, however, according to Schück, a financial journalist, the majority of workers who are 'insiders' have greater influence than 'outsiders' (*Dagens Nyheter*, 1995f). Schück clearly believes that this is more true for Sweden than it is for other countries.

Diderichsen, writing about disability pensions, has argued that as the duration of unemployment for the individual increases, so the likelihood of the person affected becoming physically and/or mentally ill also grows. As the person becomes less employable so the chances of being pensioned off increase (Diderichsen, 1994) and the motivation to seek work decreases. Agell, in interviews with the unemployed, has shown that one third of them have given up hope of finding a job (*Dagens Nyheter*, 1995g).

Social security system

Some have argued that unemployed people are happier playing the benefit/labour market measures system so that they do not have to experience the rigours of *real* employment while others have suggested that the high level of benefits and allowances for the unemployed and those on government schemes act as a disincentive to those who might otherwise seek work. The two are, in a sense, sides of the same coin with the emphasis in one being placed on the individual claimant and on the other, the system.

Calmfors and Herin (1993:52) have argued that the high levels of a-kassa are in part to blame for the worsening opportunities of the unemployed. Arbetslinjen may have worked in a time of full employment when it was reasonable to insist that people seek work, but in a time of unemployment it was unrealistic. There was no incentive for those on high benefits to seek work when the pay they were offered was lower than their benefit. There was also no restraint on union negotiators to moderate their pay claims, since those made unemployed still enjoyed a similar standard of living to those in work. The legal right to relief work when a-kassa ran out, according to Calmfors and Herin, might prevent the long-term unemployed from becoming passive but since payment for relief work was higher than a-kassa and since those who completed their relief work again became entitled to a-kassa, the incentive to find employment was substantially reduced (Calmfors and Herin, 1993:52, p 13).

Calmfors, in an article in *Dagens Nyheter* (1995c) claimed that:

> The biggest problem from the point of view of incentives are the opportunities of an 'eternal merry-go-round' between unemployment benefit and AMS measures. (*Dagens Nyheter*, 1995c)

Other economists have concluded that because of this system "people collect unemployment benefits several years in a row". (Agell et al, 1995, p 124). She writes that between 1991-94:

> ... exits to programmes accounted for one third of all exits out of unemployment whereas about half went to a job in the regular labour market. Further, within one year, over 80% of those who left for a programme had another spell of unemployment. The corresponding number for those who exited from unemployment was about 60%. (Agell et al, 1995, p 125)

The authors realised that a disproportionate number of those on the roundabout were non-Nordic citizens, people with disabilities and those with low qualifications. Nonetheless they clearly believed that the proposal, that people should be entitled to a maximum of two 60-week spells of unemployment benefit with one period on a labour market programme, enacted by the centre-right coalition in July 1994 but abolished by the incoming Social Democratic government, should be reintroduced. This 120-week limit would help avoid long-term unemployment "by a change in behaviour" (Agell et al, 1995, p 126): the unemployed would seek work, such as temporary jobs, something the present system discourages them from doing.

Korpi (1995, p 119), on the other hand, has argued strongly that there is substantial evidence to show that high benefits do not in themselves create unemployment. Why, he asks, in the years between 1950 and 1990, when benefits were rising and opportunities to go on labour market measures plentiful, was unemployment low? Why in the 1990s when benefits have been reduced has unemployment risen? The obstacle to employment opportunities lay not in the benefit system but in the lack of demand for labour. If Korpi is right then much of the publicity given to high benefits, the merry-go-round of benefits and labour market measures and the lack of incentives for and pressure on claimants is little more than a scapegoating of the long-term unemployed.

Alternative policies

There is clearly a conviction among some (although for different reasons) that Sweden's labour market policy might have dealt well with the circumstances of the past but that it is not adapting rapidly enough to the needs of the present. A *Dagens Nyheter* editorial expressed this recently when it was said that:

> The volume [of measures] is too high, not too low. It is a failure not a success. It is not efficient but desperate. In the absence of means that give results, billions are being spent to show good will. Symbols and potentiality have become more important than employment and cogency. (*Dagens Nyheter*, 1995h)

In the view of the editor, growth and jobs would be created by flexible pay, labour mobility and lower interest rates (*Dagens Nyheter*, 1995i).

Similar doubts about labour market policy have been expressed to the Labour Market Committee by Gunnar Wetterburg, the Director of the Association of Communes, who warned against using old methods to tackle new problems. If labour market measures were not used in a more discriminating way, economic growth would be damaged. In spite of the fact that recent AMS reports predicted that unemployment would fall, Wetterburg thought it was more likely that the country would become locked into mass unemployment (*Dagens Nyheter*, 1995g).

It is one thing to criticise existing policies and institutions but another to suggest viable alternatives. It is not surprising that right-wing economists and commentators have put the emphasis on reducing wages generally and young workers' pay in particular. Some criticised employment rights while others such as Isaakson criticised the whole concept of a right to employment (*Dagens Nyheter*, 1994c). He claimed that in order to get elected politicians promised what they could not deliver. Subsequently, they finished up creating "opportunities" for the unemployed, who in return for high benefits, had to be forced on to various labour market schemes and submit themselves to the ineffective social engineering of counsellors, career advisors, therapists and rehabilitators. In his view, it would be better to recognise that the epoch of the welfare state was over and to establish a system in which the state provided a basic security and then allowed individuals to choose for themselves what they would do.

Others, also looking for a solution which might solve the problem at a stroke, were putting their faith in a redistribution of work itself. The arguments for a shorter working day or week were being considered by an investigating committee appointed to consider Swedish law in the light of an EU directive (*Riksdag och Departement*, 1994, p 17). This was the third time that this issue had been investigated since 1989, which suggested that it had some political support. Various individuals and groups, including the powerful metal workers union, had spoken up for the idea. However, opposition was strong and included the then Minister for Health and Social Affairs, Anna Hedborg.

The Christian Democratic Union (CDU) has suggested a different way of redistributing work. Temporary employment could be created if middle-aged workers were encouraged to take sabbaticals (*Riksdag och Departement*, 1995d, p 9). A similar idea was much discussed in the UK in the early 1980s but came to nothing. Such a measure is possible in Sweden where adult education is more popular and educational leave for adults has been a legal right since 1975 (Gould, 1983). However, it tended to be the Left and Environment parties which made the strongest case for some form of worksharing. The Left Party saw unemployment as a distributive issue. Many workers were working long hours and others were doing overtime, when there were thousands without work. In these circumstances a six-hour day would make a lot of sense, the party argued (*Motion till Riksdagen*, 1994/95a, pp 11-12). Employers who agreed to participate in an experiment to measure the social economic benefits of fewer working hours could be compensated with lower social security contributions. A similar proposal had been made by the Environment Party. It had stated that the government was guilty of driving up unemployment so long as it did nothing about Sweden's 40-hour week – one of the longest in Europe, the party claimed. It should introduce a 35-hour week immediately with a view to creating a 30-hour week (six-hour day) by the year 2,000 (*Motion till Riksdagen*, 1994/95b, p 3). The Environment Party has also argued for sabbaticals along Danish lines with the exception that it would have to be unemployed workers who replaced those on leave (*Motion till Riksdagen*, 1994/95b, p 4). While it is possible to imagine that Sweden might well take such proposals seriously in the future, it must be remembered that the same proposals were made in the UK in the 1980s and got nowhere.

A recent conference held by the Nordic Council on unemployment considered the arguments for and against another proposal which has had a significant airing in Britain but without any practical outcome – that of a *citizen's income* (Nord, 1994, pp 22-5). While no decision was reached, it will be interesting to see the reaction of Swedish authorities in the future if traditional methods for dealing with unemployment show little sign of success.

Conclusions

The defenders of Sweden's active labour market policy would argue that it is better that the unemployed do something useful for themselves and society, rather than simply live on benefits. They would also argue that it is better to have high benefits and a plentiful supply of high quality labour market measures since these prevent the type of poverty, degradation and social exclusion that has characterised long-term unemployment in the rest of Europe. The critics of the system maintain that it is itself responsible for creating long spells of unemployment through a combination of high benefits and the merry-go-round of benefits and measures. These concerns were reflected in the policy interviews reported on in the next chapter.

FOUR

Policy interviews in Sweden

Interviews

The interviews with members of Sweden's policy community were carried out in September 1995. As it turned out, this was a particularly apposite time for such work. The country had experienced a number of years of growing unemployment; public debate had begun to focus on the emergence of a two thirds/one third society and, as has been seen in Chapter Three, labour market policies and AMS were increasingly coming under scrutiny, if not outright attack. The centre-right coalition had reduced a number of welfare benefits including unemployment benefit and had tried to limit the time claimants could spend on 'the merry-go-round'. The Social Democratic government elected in 1994 had begun to revise some of its predecessor's reforms but soon found itself having to admit the need for major revisions in labour market policy.

Altogether 26 individuals were interviewed (see Table 6 for the breakdown). People were asked about their perception of the problem of long-term unemployment and its consequences, their thoughts on existing measures for dealing with the problem and, lastly, what they saw as the major obstacles to improving the present situation and their suggestions as to creating opportunities and incentives for those affected in the future.

The national politicians among the interviewees were all members of the parliamentary standing committee on employment: the chair, representing the ruling Social Democratic Party, the Liberal vice-chair, and ordinary members from the Conservative, Centre and Left (old Communist) parties. The civil servants included the secretaries to the parliamentary standing committee and the Labour Market Committee (set up by the government to examine the way in which labour market policy was working). The national administrators came from AMS and Tryggetsråd (Employment Security Council), a body which gives advice and assistance to unemployed white-collar workers. The local authority

Table 6: Policy actors interviewed in Sweden

National politicians	5
Civil servants	4
Administrators (national)	2
Administrator (local)	1
Trade union federations	2
Local authority federation	1
Local politicians (Örebro)	2
Local projects (Örebro)	2
Local project (Umeå)	1
Researchers (university)	4
Researchers (trade union)	1
Researcher (institute)	1
Total	26

representative worked for the Association of Swedish Communes. The local politicians, local administrator and local project leaders came from Örebro and Umeå. The trade union federation representatives were from the manual worker union federation LO and the white-collar worker federation TCO. Researchers came from Stockholm, Örebro and Umeå Universities, the Trade Union Research Institute and the Institute for Research into Working Life. Although the Swedish Employers Federation (SAF) was approached, its representatives declined to be interviewed. Of the 26 people interviewed, five were women.

Assessment of the situation

Most respondents considered that that high unemployment levels were going to be a characteristic of the Swedish economy for many years to come. However, there were those who thought that although hopes for the present generation of long-term unemployed were not high, it should be possible, in the future, to reduce the percentage of the unemployed out of work for more than six months. While some felt that long-term unemployment remained a fairly small problem in Sweden, others pointed out that the official figures rather understated the problem since they excluded many workers who were in between labour market measures. The growth of unemployment and long-term unemployment had been a shock to a country which had prided itself on being able to maintain full employment. As one of the civil servants put it:

> "Mass unemployment is humiliating for us since we've prided ourselves on our active labour market policy."

Most respondents regarded the problem as a serious one with some fearing that it threatened the future stability of Swedish society.

When describing the categories of those worst affected by long-term unemployment, there was something of a consensus but also a good deal of variation. Young and older workers, immigrants and women service workers with poor education and training were mentioned frequently. The construction industry was singled out as an area where a disproportionate number of employees were experiencing long spells of unemployment, while the effect of current and future cuts to local authority services were expected to affect women very badly. One view was that the situation in the construction industry had a high profile and received extra government support in consequence whereas female office workers remained largely invisible in terms of special measures. A trade union official summed up these views:

> "[Women office workers] did not shout and protest like male industrial and construction workers. This is a silent group of women who are about 50 years old, who want the sort of work they have become used to, but find that there is little society is prepared to do for them."

Causes and incidence of long-term unemployment

The causes of long-term unemployment were seen by many to be related to the recession and the growth in unemployment generally. Others talked about the restructuring of the economy or the structural shift in the economy from an industrial society to a knowledge society. While the attitudes of employers were also seen as responsible for keeping many long-term unemployed workers unemployed, this was largely considered to be understandable and rational given the availability of employees with greater skills and more recent employment experience. A related factor in long-term unemployment was the loss of the individual worker's human capital and motivation. Clear political differences emerged between those who blamed the high taxation and social contributions levied on employers and those who blamed employers for lacking responsibility and successive governments for abandoning a policy of full employment.

It was felt by some that the devaluation of the Krona in 1982 had been a disaster since neither the government nor employers had exploited the opportunity to its best advantage. Instead, devaluation had merely served to postpone Sweden's economic crisis.

Present policies and programmes

Overall situation

In spite of a current debate about the effectiveness of AMS measures based on the work of some economists such as Agell, the vast majority of respondents did not wish to see the board abolished. The active labour market policy adopted by the AMS with its emphasis on arbetslinjen was seen as absolutely necessary. It was strongly believed that having something to do such as training, a place on a job creation scheme or work experience was of the utmost importance for individuals, society and the economy. If AMS measures were cut back then the cost of unemployment would simply fall on local municipalities, the social insurance board and the education system. However, there were criticisms.

There was general agreement on the declining quality of AMS measures. For some of the interviewees this was largely explained by the growth in unemployment which had not been matched by a commensurate increase in resources for AMS. It was pointed out more than once that AMS had never been intended to provide for more than 3% of the workforce yet it was being expected to provide for 5%. Two critics complained about the displacement effect of many AMS measures. In their view, the complicated contribution/grant system was a waste of time since employers would have done many of the things they were being induced to do anyway. They said:

> "If AMS did not exist, we would have more open unemployment. However, it is silly for employers to pay high employment contributions to get allowances in return for tasks that they would have done anyway." (local Conservative politician)

> "AMS has become too monolithic. It is responsible for too much. No one knows how effective it is. Grants are thrown at a large number of measures that might have been provided by employers anyway." (civil servant)

Better, they thought, to leave decisions to employers in the first place. Others claimed that AMS was out of touch with the needs of employers in the private sector and thought that it ought to play a more supervisory role, leaving provision to a multiplicity of agencies. AMS was seen as too bureaucratic, being obsessed with general rules and procedures, and failing to tailor measures to the requirements of individual applicants.

One respondent felt that AMS should not prioritise the long-term unemployed but should ensure that they received fair treatment and were not neglected. However, another argued that many unemployed people did not need AMS measures but took up the automatic offer of placements anyway. They could and would find employment if left to their own devices. The Public Employment Service, in this interviewee's view, should identify those who were, or were likely to become, long-term unemployed and provide them with opportunities. The long-term unemployed needed placements in the private sector where there would be job vacancies in the future – not in the public sector where jobs were in decline. A related point was made by other respondents who felt that the automatic offer of measures to the unemployed generally acted as a disincentive to seek a proper job.

It was suggested that Sweden could learn from countries such as Germany, Denmark and Norway where the quality of placements was much more closely monitored than in Sweden. A related worry concerned the possibility that real jobs had been reduced in number only for AMS to finance the same work. It was felt that it would be difficult for the reverse process to take place – for AMS jobs to become real jobs again.

However, AMS had its defenders. They claimed it was the least bureaucratic and one of the most flexible of state agencies. They also claimed that AMS measures, which prevented people becoming socially excluded, were what distinguished Sweden from the rest of Europe.

> "AMS is the most flexible and least remote of Swedish bureaucracies. Local offices have a great deal of autonomy." (institute researcher)

They refuted criticism, associated with the work of Agell (see Chapter Three), that AMS failed to create employment and should be abolished. It was not possible for, nor was it an aim of, AMS to create real jobs. Many of those on AMS measures were the least employable, and the scheme should not be judged by whether those people found jobs.

> "Labour market measures are effective at increasing skills, preventing despair and enabling people to maintain social contacts." (university researcher)

Specific policies and programmes

Views on particular measures varied much more than views on the desirability of AMS generally. A broad range of respondents thought that there should be a limit on the maximum time an unemployed person could requalify for benefit after spending time on different programmes. There was a tendency for AMS and the unemployed only to raise the question of participation in programmes when entitlement to benefit was running out. The longer entitlement lasted the more danger of an unemployment culture developing. The principal job creation scheme, ALU, was seen by many as a useful way of keeping people in touch with the world of work but of little intrinsic value. The volume of places had been allowed to rise but the quality was often poor. One respondent blamed the lack of trade union involvement for the decline in quality, claiming that when the bourgeois government had proposed that 70,000 places a month be created, TCO had suggested less than half this figure was appropriate to maintain quality. Another criticism of ALU was that it was too automatic. Too little research had been carried to know how effective specific measures were.

A range of respondents thought that the training programme (AMU) had been excellent in the past but that it too had declined in quality, that there was no longer any certainty about what type of training the unemployed needed and that AMU was too craft-oriented, too specific. The 'temporary replacement' scheme was well spoken of, although here too there was a feeling that employers might have implemented such ideas themselves without the intervention of government policy.

Some respondents felt that work experience worked well for the young while others claimed it was abused by employers as a form of cheap labour. Job creation schemes and wage subsidies were considered to be more suitable for older workers. RAS (the recently-introduced direct recruitment support for employers who took on unemployed people) was criticised as inadequate and ineffective in its present form but it was suggested that it would be a more appropriate measure for the long-term unemployed.

It was also argued that it was not so much the quality of the intervention that was important but its timing: the unemployed should be offered something before they began to lose their self-confidence.

Consequences of long-term unemployment

Among the consequences of long-term unemployment mentioned for the individual were poverty, apathy, illness, depression, divorce, loss of sleep, declining self-confidence and drug misuse. However, many respondents were more concerned about the problems for society in general. The economic costs of benefits, labour market measures and the costs of dealing with social problems were mentioned by a number of respondents. Long-term unemployment was seen as a threat to democracy and tolerance. There were worries about the emergence of "dark forces" encouraging Swedes to blame immigrants for taking their jobs. One respondent said it was extremely important to reduce unemployment generally and long-term unemployment in particular:

> "If high levels of structural unemployment are accepted now they will be higher in the next recession." (national administrator)

However, there were dangers in unemployment becoming too low. Demands for wage increases needed to be kept low or inflation would rise, the currency would lose value, interest rates would rise, investment would decline and unemployment would rise even further.

When asked about social exclusion the majority of respondents said that it existed in Sweden and agreed that long-term unemployment was an important factor in bringing it about. Others were unsure whether long-term unemployment caused social exclusion or vice versa. While there were those who insisted that social exclusion was nothing like as bad as in the rest of Europe, largely because the active labour market policy had prevented it, others saw the problem as a growing one. Concern was expressed about the increasing segregation of immigrant communities, begging on the streets, the growing visibility of homelessness and the increasing demand on Salvation Army hostels:

> "Social exclusion is on the increase. There are those who are homeless, who stand outside society and the labour market. It is visible." (national Centre Party politician)

> "Social exclusion does exist. We are producing a whole generation of unemployed youngsters many of whom will finish up abusing drugs." (national Social Democratic politician)

> "You can't keep getting refused jobs, lose your social life, stop meeting people, become isolated and get a drink problem and not be described as socially excluded." (local project worker)

Some thought that in a society such as Sweden with a strong work ethic social exclusion could be a consequence of long-term unemployment. There was some speculation as to whether there might be a greater tendency for unemployed Swedes to become socially isolated compared with workers from more tightly-knit ethnic minority communities and as to whether social exclusion might be worse for those unemployed in the north compared with the south and for older men compared with older women.

In connection with a different question, one respondent expressed a concern that by reducing benefits and making the conditions for benefit tougher, the unemployed would be forced to seek demeaning work, such as being household servants:

> "Do we want to force such low pay on people that they become servants, such low benefits that they become an underclass?" (university researcher)

Obstacles, opportunities and incentives

There was some overlap here between what interviewees saw as the causes of long-term unemployment and what they saw as obstacles to the unemployed obtaining work. Many respondents mentioned the reluctance of employers to take on people who had been unemployed for a long time. Sometimes this was stated as a fact, other times as understandable and by others as regrettable. There was the suggestion that employment rights be relaxed to encourage employers to take on more labour. However, it was also argued that the reluctance to take on unemployed immigrants was more a matter of discrimination by employers than immigrants' language skills and poor education. While it was argued that the long-term unemployed could still help their cause by improving their interview and presentation skills, employers were criticised by one of the university researchers for demanding "experience of applicants which they cannot possibly have and which the job does not require".

The decline in motivation that besets people the longer they are unemployed was also regarded as an obstacle to getting work. However, one researcher was of the opinion that the personal qualities of the long-term unemployed should not be regarded as a major hindrance. In this person's view, it was the lack of jobs and cuts in the public sector which had created the severe unemployment problem which Sweden now faced.

Poor educational qualifications were mentioned by a number of respondents and this was seen as a problem for older workers in particular. A related obstacle was the difficulty unemployed people found in receiving finance to improve their education. The grant loan system for higher education meant that it was difficult for the authorities to provide the unemployed with finance when others were having to incur substantial debts to receive an education.

Another area frequently commented on was the possible combined adverse effects of high benefits and the duration of benefits and labour market measures. Many were concerned that the 'merry-go-round' of benefits and measures induced passivity among the unemployed and locked people into long-term unemployment. The general guarantee of labour market measures for the unemployed was also criticised and it was feared that an 'AMS culture' would develop among unemployed people.

The interviewees gave a much wider range of responses when asked what in their view needed to be done to provide opportunities and incentives for the long-term unemployed. While improvements to education and the limitation of the 'merry-go-round' duration were mentioned by several respondents, the maximum number of times the same proposal was made was four. Related responses have been grouped together below. It is interesting not only that there should be such a wide variety but also that respondents gave much longer answers to the question on opportunities and incentives than to any other.

Labour market measures

A few thought that the recruitment allowance (RAS) introduced for the unemployed in general would have been better directed at the long-term unemployed, a measure also apparently advocated by the director of AMS. Others thought that the long-term unemployed should receive extra help, additional subsidies, and earlier intervention.

There was fairly widespread support for reducing the a-kassa from 75% of income to a lower percentage over time. It was also felt by many that the merry-go-round of benefits and labour market schemes should be limited in duration. The automatic offer and even guarantee of labour market measures was criticised with the rider that measures should be tailored for individuals, in particular, the long-term unemployed. Employment service officials were criticised by one of the university researchers for concentrating on the easy-to-place rather than using their professional skills and judgement to help the most vulnerable:

> "In my own training courses for such officials I encourage them to tell jobseekers that the employment office is a dream factory in which [the unemployed] should allow their career aspirations free rein."

Another respondent felt that it was wasteful to send jobseekers for hundreds of jobs which they could not possibly get rather than a limited number for which they stood a reasonable chance. One interviewee suggested that the unemployed be encouraged to advertise their skills (with the financial support of AMS) in the same way that employers advertise vacancies.

While the importance of retaining an active labour market policy was stressed by some, the balance between active and passive measures was felt to have swung too much towards the latter. It was thought that AMS could be more effective if measures were more streamlined and timed to match the stages of the economic cycle.

Cross-party support existed for making more demands upon the unemployed. However, whereas those politicians on the right and centre of Swedish politics were concerned that the unemployed should be given the chance through training vouchers to decide which schemes they wished to participate in, those on the left expressed anxiety about the way in which employers used labour market schemes for cheap labour.

A number of respondents thought that employment rights, unemployment benefit and labour market policy could and should be coordinated more effectively in the future.

Increased cooperation

The corollary of many respondents' criticisms of AMS was that they wanted to see the agency cooperate more with local communes, trade unions and the private sector. This was a view shared by a wide range of respondents. Those operating at a local level were agreed that the communes could play an effective role in dealing with the long-term unemployed. AMS was seen as a bureaucratic and remote organisation. Even at the national level it was suggested that AMS activities should be spread among a number of agencies, leaving AMS with just a coordinating role.

Activity centres

More cooperation with the government and AMS was pressed for by trade union representatives. In particular, the trade unions felt that the agreement reached with AMS over the organisation of activity centres was of great importance in dealing with the problem of long-term unemployment. Activity centres were described by the TCO representative as being places where the unemployed could go to and meet other unemployed people; do something together; receive vocational training, take part in seminars and study visits; receive computer training; have access to labour market information; and improve their jobsearch skills.

An agreement had been reached on 'increased cooperation' between the three main trade union federations and the Labour Market Board in May 1995 (Swedish National Labour Market Board, 1995). Activity centres formed part of that agreement which allowed for outreach workers to make contact with unemployed people and for the staffing of the centres to be financed by 'employing' people under the ALU scheme. The financing of equipment and premises was undertaken jointly by the local labour market board, the local authority (which often provided the premises) and trade union (using its educational funds). While activity centres had existed for some time, the agreement between the three parties, plus the adoption of a proactive stance by TCO in particular, meant that more long-term unemployed people would be reached by such centres in the future.

Education

There was considerable support for the idea that better education could provide a solution to long-term unemployment in the long run. The alternative to a low wage economy was that *competence development* be encouraged through gymnasia, higher and adult education. Some respondents saw this as a task for the education system itself while others felt that employers and AMS should be doing more in this area. This was clearly an area which the government, SAF and employers were already addressing. It was felt that the demand for people who were computer literate already existed and would increase in the future. Unless people could be motivated to take up educational opportunities they would become locked into long-term unemployment. With the decline in routine white-collar employment, computer literacy and language skills would become of greater importance.

Employers

On the role employers could play in reducing unemployment, there was a clear political division. Centre-right politicians were more likely to say that taxes and contributions made by employers should be reduced and employment protection should be weakened. Such measures, they argued, would provide employers with an incentive to employ more people. Trade unions and those on the left were more likely to argue that employers should not be able to sack employees at will. They should act more responsibly before they threw vulnerable workers on to the labour market. In particular, one national Left Party politician argued that:

> "... collective agreements should exist to ensure that employers train young workers, develop the competence of older workers and rehabilitate sick employees. Those that do so should have their taxes and social security contributions reduced."

The economy

As one politician put it, left and right seem to be meeting in Sweden where it concerns economic policy. It was widely accepted, he claimed, that business needed a better climate in which to thrive and that the public sector needed to be reduced. Beyond these proposals a variety of suggestions were made as to how improvements in the economy or changes to economic policy could influence levels of long-term unemployment. Some suggested that the wages of young people be reduced and a greater emphasis be placed on developing the regions and the infrastructure (education, motorways and telecommunications). Some wanted to see lower wage claims, lower inflation, lower interest rates and a reduced public sector deficit. While one respondent was optimistic that unemployment could be reduced to less than 10%, another expressed the fear that any future increase in unemployment would leave Sweden with nothing in reserve to cope with the problem. A few respondents wanted to see a renewed Keynesian emphasis on economic policy: revival of demand, full employment restored as a policy goal and the stimulation of *real jobs*. One researcher wanted Sweden to leave the EU, while another wanted to see a coordinated macro/industrial policy. The latter argued that the public sector deficit was almost entirely due to the 1990 tax reform and the increase in unemployment. It was a mistake to blame public expenditure and a folly to lay off public sector workers. There was, he claimed, a short-sighted view among employers in the private and public sectors that it was essential to reduce costs by making redundancies. This was irresponsible since the public sector picked up the tab in terms of the costs of maintaining the unemployed and in dealing with the consequent social problems.

Worksharing

There was some support on the left for a reduction in working hours in the hope that it would help to create jobs for the unemployed.

> "TCO's aim is that the working week should be reduced to 37.5 hours during the 1990s, 35 hours by the year 2000 and 30 early on in the century." (union official)

One respondent said that an investigation into reduced working hours was already underway and could be linked to an idea whereby employers who participate should be allowed reduced contributions. Another suggested that:

> "... an overtime ban will create 45,000 jobs and reduce unemployment by 1%." (national Liberal politician)

Early retirement was suggested as a way of redistributing work as were sabbaticals:

> "The right of all workers to a sabbatical every 10 years would ease the unemployment situation – releasing the employed from work, while the unemployed take their place." (local administrator)

More attention should be paid to developing people's lives outside work, argued one respondent, while another suggested that there needed to be a shift away from lives based on the work ethic. However, there were those who were dubious that any form of worksharing could reduce unemployment. One respondent claimed that an 'alliance' between employers and some trade unions made it difficult to promote the idea of worksharing through reducing working hours as employers put their existing employees first and trade unions did the same for their working members.

Good practice

One respondent felt that Sweden could learn a lot from Denmark (where the unemployed create an individual plan for their own development) and Germany when it came to dealing with the long-term unemployed. He also suggested that some communes were much better than others at coping with the problem and that good practice needed to be shared. Another researcher spoke highly of the practice in Germany and Norway of providing high quality placements for the long-term unemployed. In Norway, she said, engineers were given engineering placements, not expected to "serve in a hamburger bar".

Conclusions

The interviews with policy makers in Sweden demonstrate:

- an acceptance that there have been economic mistakes and that only by placing public finances on a sounder footing can employment prospects be improved;
- a reluctance to accept that mass unemployment and long-term unemployment are here to stay.

While there were many criticisms of AMS, the idea of an active labour market policy pursuing the 'work line' (arbetslinjen), has taken a strong hold on the Swedish political imagination. The role of AMS may have to change; it may have to play a more coordinating role among a number of players, especially the local authorities. However, its existence would not appear to be under threat.

Although there was evidence of a faith in old ideas and institutions, there seemed little in the way of new ideas for dealing with the long-term unemployed. The activity centres offer some hope. They resemble what in Britain are called job clubs. A principle difference is that in Sweden they are run under the auspices of the trade unions rather than public employment services agencies. It will be interesting to see the extent of their impact in the future. However, it is difficult to imagine that they can make a substantial difference to the situation of the long-term unemployed.

The proposal for better education, which many stressed as a solution to the problem of long-term unemployment, seems likely to suffer either from a lack of the necessary resources or from contradictions endemic in the Swedish loan grant system.

There was a realisation that social exclusion is on the increase and that this was a threat to the whole nature of the Swedish model. Little in the interviews gave any hope that the Swedes had come up with policy innovations which could transform the lot of the long-term unemployed either in Sweden or in other countries.

Recent developments in employment policy – concerning unemployment insurance, employment rights, shorter working hours and labour market programmes – suggest that a stormy time lies ahead for a

Social Democratic government committed to reducing unemployment and public expenditure. The Labour Market Committee produced a report in 1996 which recommended that:

- the scope of AMS goals and measures be limited;
- measures be more individually-oriented;
- unemployment benefits be reduced;
- the duration of the merry-go-round be limited.

However, the government has been forced by the trade unions to reverse the decision to reduce a-kassa from 80% of income to 75%; employers and unions have resisted proposed changes to employment rights – although for different reasons; while the women's section of the Social Democratic Party persuaded the Party Congress to commit itself to a shorter working week in the face of opposition from ministers.

The organised interests of Swedish society inside and outside the labour movement are not prepared to take the political consequences of globalisation and deregulation lying down.

FIVE

British context

Introduction

During the last two decades in Britain, levels of unemployment, the composition of the labour force and the structure of the labour market have changed radically. From conditions of near full employment throughout the 1960s and most of the 1970s, the story subsequently was very different. Unemployment in all western nations rose during the 1980s; in Britain the rise was particularly steep, with rates higher than most other OECD countries (Convery, 1997a). Unemployment rose again in 1989 and did not start to fall until 1993.

However, comparisons of rates over time are difficult because there have been some 30 changes to the calculation and presentation of the unemployment count in Britain since 1979 (A. Walker, 1997). In 1997, unemployment counts may be based on the 'claimant count' – that is, those who are claiming unemployment-related benefit – or on the International Labour Organisation (ILO) measure. The Unemployment Unit (1995) argues that the claimant count "significantly under-counts the totals out of work" because it omits certain groups. These include people who are unemployed but not claiming benefit, for example, because they cannot fulfil the availability or other conditions for entitlement and people who are partly or wholly labour market active and receiving Income Support without having to meet those conditions, for example, lone parents or men aged above 60.

More recently, the Department for Education and Employment (DfEE) (the Departments of Education and of Employment were merged in July 1995) has also used the Labour Force Survey to calculate unemployment rates. This enables international comparisons. The ILO criteria for unemployment are that the person:

- is undertaking no paid work;
- wants work;

- is available to start work within two weeks;
- has looked for work during the previous four weeks.

However, the ILO measure omits some people, such as those who have not looked for work within the last four weeks because of caring responsibilities or sickness. Consequently, the Unemployment Unit proposes that this condition be relaxed (1994; 1995).

Long-term unemployment in Britain (unemployed for at least a year) grew along with unemployment, from 25% of all unemployed people in the mid-1970s to more than 40% by the end of the 1980s. Although the numbers have since fallen, in early 1996, 39% of all unemployed, or 900,000 people, had been out of work for at least one year, and almost 17% for at least three years (ONS, 1996). Perversely, the increases in unemployment occurred during a macroeconomic 'boom'. The explanation lies in the changing structure of employment and labour market conditions (White and Lakey, 1992). Britain's manufacturing industry contracted severely during the 1980s (the number of jobs fell by 36%) while jobs in service industries expanded by 15% (Walker, 1994). In general, full-time, secure work paying reasonable wages was lost, while jobs which mostly were part-time, temporary or casual/insecure were created (Gregg and Wadsworth, 1995). Men lost opportunities for employment and women gained them (Shaw and Walker, 1996).

The outlook is not promising. Economists believe that economic growth sufficient to restore full employment and a return to earlier patterns of employment is unlikely. Long-term unemployment threatens to become a permanent feature.

Social security

Unemployment-related benefits

Until October 1996, unemployed people could claim Unemployment Benefit and/or Income Support. They could also be credited with their National Insurance contributions (an uninterrupted record was needed to maintain pension rights). A new benefit, Jobseeker's Allowance (JSA), was introduced in October 1996. Different rules governed each benefit and imposed different eligibility criteria and penalties.

Unemployment Benefit was an insurance-based benefit, with eligibility dependent on the person's National Insurance record; in consequence, people with a history of irregular or temporary work were often excluded.

It could be claimed for a period of 12 months. It was always paid to the minority of unemployed people and during the last 15 years, fewer and fewer have been eligible. In 1978, 41% of unemployed people received this benefit; this fell to 32% in 1983 and to 23% in 1993 (Walker et al, 1995). The qualifying criteria for contribution-based JSA will reduce coverage still further; in addition, it will be paid for only six months.

The link between the levels of Unemployment Benefit and Income Support and earnings was severed in 1980; now benefits are linked to the cost of living index. In the late 1980s, Britain had the lowest rate for insurance-based Unemployment Benefit claimants in the EU: on average, 23% of previous earnings compared with the EU average of 61% (I. Murray, 1994). Britain is the only EU country where expenditure on Unemployment Benefit has fallen since 1980 (Commission, 1994). Income Support was paid to people not eligible for Unemployment Benefit. It was the main benefit for unemployed people prior to JSA. It is now received by people whose claim is not based on unemployment, such as lone parents. Income Support is a means-tested benefit; the amount of any award depends on family circumstances, including the number and age of dependent household members, and their overall income and savings. In principle, it is paid out indefinitely. Income Support recipients qualify for 'passported' benefits such as Housing Benefit and Council Tax Benefit, free prescriptions, spectacles and school meals.

During the last 15 years, the value of both Unemployment Benefit and Income Support has fallen against earnings. The protection offered by the state now stands at a lower proportion of current earnings than at any time since the Second World War (Bradshaw and Lynes, 1995). Research shows that people find it very difficult to manage on Income Support alone (Shaw et al, 1996; White, 1991). Claimants' entitlement to unemployment-related benefit depended on their fulfilling two main labour market conditions: they had to be available for employment (that is, willing and able to take up any employment immediately) and actively seeking work. People who failed to satisfy either of these conditions lost their entitlement and were disallowed. Other breaches of the rules such as refusing a job or leaving a job voluntarily could result in benefit being reduced. Donnelly (1997) showed that the 'available-for-work' rules denied unemployed people opportunities for education and training. They could be pressured into leaving courses "either with the offer of a low skill, low wage vacancy or without the offer of a job because of the strict, contradictory and target-led Employment Service rules".

Jobseeker's Allowance

Jobseeker's Allowance, which replaced Unemployment Benefit and Income Support for unemployed people, was fully implemented in October 1996. The new scheme has two components: contribution-based JSA replaces Unemployment Benefit and means-tested, income-based JSA replaces Income Support for unemployed claimants. The need to comply with basic eligibility criteria to receive benefit has been retained, and new ones have been added (Bottomley et al, 1997): claimants undertake a 'Jobseeker's Agreement' and the rules relating to disqualification and disallowance have been strengthened and simplified. Changes to the administration should ensure that claimants only need to visit one office, an Employment Service Jobcentre, in connection with their benefit claim and their jobsearch (HMSO, 1994).

Overall cost of benefits

The benefit system has become increasingly expensive. The cost of unemployment to the Exchequer in 1995/96 has been estimated to be £23.4 billion – equivalent to 4.6% of gross domestic product (Convery, 1997b). This cost includes direct central government expenditure on benefits to unemployed people, lost revenue from taxes and National Insurance contributions, as well as indirect taxes.

During the 1980s, the Conservative government introduced measures intended to reduce social security costs (Howard, 1997). These included increased targeting and means-testing and reduced benefit levels. Even so, projected figures for 1996/97 suggest that spending on social security will account for 29% of all planned public spending, with unemployment-related benefits accounting for around a half of the total. Consequently, the Major government, towards the end of its term, turned its attention to administrative costs, and introduced a target to reduce them by 25% over three years (DSS, 1996).

Labour market policy

Two main government departments are involved in delivering benefits and schemes to unemployed people. Each has its own executive agency which provides services through networks of local offices (Finn et al, 1996). The Department of Social Security (DSS) is responsible for Income Support and other means-tested benefits; services are delivered through the Benefits Agency. The DfEE is responsible for education and training policies and programmes. The delivery of most services for unemployed people is undertaken by the Employment Service, the Executive Agency of the DfEE. The Employment Service has a network of more than 1,000 local offices (Jobcentres) and 42,000 staff.

Each year the Employment Service agrees a three-year business plan, an agency performance agreement and an annual operational plan. The Employment Service is given targets of the number of claimants to be helped into jobs or schemes (Finn et al, 1996). Targets have been criticised for encouraging staff to get claimants off the register by pushing them into inappropriate jobs and schemes. 'Positive outcomes' are counted only when a claimant signs off JSA or has a penalty imposed. Donnelly (1997) argues that voluntary work or part-time education or training do not count, but should, because they improve long-term employment prospects, and that a benefit penalty should not count because it is not a positive step towards employment.

Training programmes are mainly delivered by a national network of private sector Training and Enterprise Councils (TECs) – known as Local Enterprise Companies (LECs) in Scotland – established in 1991. At least two thirds of the directors of a TEC, including the chair, must be senior executives from the private sector; the others are drawn from local authorities, the voluntary sector and trades unions (Finn et al, 1996). Each TEC is an independent company which enters into a contract with the government. They are responsible for developing training strategies based on local skill needs and for delivering programmes. They mainly subcontract their programmes to other providers and are responsible for maintaining standards. The requirement to design schemes to meet local needs and achieve better value for money brings diversity in local programmes (CRG, 1996), although all TECs are still subject to national rules (Finn et al, 1996).

Macro policy

The Conservative governments of the 1980s and 1990s viewed unemployment as a supply-side issue, with a consequent focus on the need for a deregulated, flexible labour market. Chancellors stressed the need to remove unnecessary rigidities and argued that high labour costs could squeeze British firms out of international markets (Walker et al, 1995). The position was exemplified by Eric Forth, Employment Minister:

> This government believes that employers and businesses, not governments, create jobs – and that it is the role of government to create a framework within which business can flourish. (DfEE, 1996)

Economists and other social analysts took opposing views of the government's approach. Some believed that a flexible labour market and government deregulation were key to economic success. Negative economic indicators were interpreted as evidence that the policy had been pursued half-heartedly. Others did not deny the importance of supply-side policies, and of improved quality and effectiveness, but also pressed for active job creation and local regeneration policies. For example, White (1991) suggested a large-scale job creation scheme, funded centrally but let by competitive tender locally, with quotas for the employment of disadvantaged workers under temporary contracts. He offered the example of an environmental scheme. Layard and Philpott (1991) proposed offering anyone who had been unemployed for more than a year the chance to prove him or herself through a public sector job in a regular workplace. Such proposals were not adopted.

Active labour market policies

The White Paper *Competitiveness, forging ahead* (HMSO, 1995) set out the government's strategy to improve labour market performance. In line with its broad policy, the focus was on helping individuals with their jobsearch and attachment to the labour market. The proportion of claimants directed to take specific forms of action increased with their time on benefit. The increase in take-up beyond the 12 months threshold was marked: whereas only 13% of claimants who had been on benefit between nine and 12 months had been directed to a training course and 15% to a government programme, the corresponding proportions jumped to 32% and 42% for people who had been claiming for one to two years (Bottomley et al, 1997).

However, compulsory programmes were judged "wholly ineffective" in helping long-term unemployed people back into work (Murray, 1996). Only 4% of participants in the two largest mandatory programmes, Jobplan workshops and Restart courses, found a job. Just over one quarter of participants on Restart courses and less than one third of those attending Jobplan workshops achieved a positive outcome. Most of the outcomes consisted of a move to another scheme.

Restart

Restart began in 1986 as a pilot scheme and was soon extended nationally. The central feature of the scheme is an interview between a Restart counsellor (or 'claimant adviser') and registered unemployed person every six months. The aim is to re-establish the individual in the labour market. The adviser also ensures the claimant is 'actively seeking work'. At the first six-month interview, claimants are offered a place on a scheme such as Jobclub, Job Interview Guarantee (JIG) or Training for Work (TfW), which make up what is called the Restart 'menu' (Finn et al, 1996). Other schemes are introduced later on. As mentioned above, failure to comply brings cuts to benefit.

An evaluation of the Restart programme (White and Lakey, 1992) concluded that Restart does make a difference: time unemployed was reduced and people who had undertaken Restart were more likely to be in employment or on a training scheme than those who had not. White and Lakey suggest that Restart derives its effect from 'adding value' to a range of programmes, services and follow-up actions, often with the direct assistance of the counsellor (adviser). However, they found little evidence to suggest that Restart stimulates a higher amount of jobsearch activity.

Training for Work

Training for Work is the major programme available for long-term unemployed adults. Claimants are eligible after six months unemployment, but cannot undertake more than one training course every six months. The trainee receives benefit plus a small cash inducement and is offered job specific training, the opportunity to study for a National Vocational Qualification (NVQ) or temporary work experience. TfW is operated by the local TEC. TECs and their training providers are paid 'by results', with most of their funding dependent on the success of participants in getting jobs or vocational qualifications. A consequence is that providers are under pressure to be selective about recruitment and to aim for quick results (Finn et al, 1996). The TUC's 1995 budget submission (TUC, 1995) cited a Department of Employment study that one third of the people who left TfW in August 1994 had failed to complete their course; 48% were unemployed, and 56% had gained no qualification or even a credit towards one.

Jobclubs

Jobclubs are also available after six months unemployment to help people with jobsearch activities. Set up in the mid-1980s Jobclubs offer advice and guidance on jobhunting techniques and various facilities. In return, Jobclub members usually agree to attend for four half-day sessions each week and to pursue up to 10 'job leads' every day. The number of Jobclub opportunities was cut by 16% (from 243,000 to 204,000) in 1996/97 (Unemployment Unit, 1996). Outcome statistics for Jobclub leavers, for April to September 1995, show that 40% got jobs, 10% achieved another 'positive outcome', usually a training scheme, and half left without a job or other 'positive outcome' (Finn et al, 1996).

Job Interview Guarantee and Work Trials

Job Interview Guarantee and Work Trials provide a linked programme designed to "break down employer reluctance to consider long-term unemployed people for their vacancies" (JIG, 1995). Under the JIG scheme, an employer guarantees to interview job applicants sent by the Employment Service in return for receiving an enhanced recruitment service in which claimants are matched and screened against employer requirements, or given a period of job preparation or customised training. Matching and screening has proved to be the most popular and successful option (JIG, 1995). Participation was voluntary until the introduction of JSA; subsequently, a referral became compulsory and carries the threat of a benefit sanction. The initial assessment includes a check on the unemployed person's suitability for a Work Trial. Work Trials enable employers to try out claimants in a particular job for up to three weeks while they remain on benefit. The government estimated that half of all participants end up in employment as a result (Finn et al, 1996).

Bridging the move from benefits into work

Eight 'work incentives' were brought into the benefits system during 1995 and 1996. The changes were to assist the move from benefit to paid employment by bridging the gaps between benefits and wages and to encourage employers to take on long-term unemployed people. The eight changes, which added to an already complex system, were as follows:

- the extension of Housing Benefit and Council Tax Benefit, at the level paid under Income Support, for four weeks into a period of employment, and a fast-track scheme for payment of renewed claims;

- faster payment of Family Credit (Family Credit is a means-tested, in-work benefit for people with children);
- reduction in National Insurance contributions made by employers who take on long-term unemployed people;
- a premium for Family Credit and Disability Working Allowance claimants working 30 hours or more;
- employers' National Insurance contributions 'holiday';
- pilot of Earnings Top-Up (a means-tested, in-work benefit for people without children);
- Child Maintenance Bonus;
- Back to Work Bonus, to reward those who take part-time work while receiving JSA; although cash benefit continues to be reduced pound for pound for part-time earnings above £10 (£15 for single parents), half the retained benefit is allocated to the bonus – when the person moves into full-time work, they receive up to £1,000 of the bonus as a grant.

None of these initiatives have been in operation long enough to be evaluated and the results published, although some are currently being studied.

Consequences of long-term unemployment

High levels of unemployment and long-term unemployment have consequences for society and individuals. Society suffers from increased public expenditure and taxation, lost production and wasted skills, crime, social unrest and possibly social exclusion (Philpott, 1993a; Walsh, 1987).

In Britain, long-term unemployment has particular effects on individuals. Jahoda's pioneering study (1982) stressed the importance of employment on people's well-being: it confers social status and identity, gives a routine and time structure, and provides social contacts. People suffer particular negative effects from long-term unemployment. Studies show that the longer people are unemployed, the more likely they are to leave the effective labour supply through loss of skills, demotivation, falling ill or reaching retirement age (Dawes, 1993; Fryer, 1992; White, 1991; Warr and Jackson, 1985; 1987).

Research highlights the link between joblessness, deprivation, family breakdown, psychological stress and poor health (Warr and Jackson, 1985; Gallie and Vogler, 1994a). Engaging in activities while unemployed does not give people the self-esteem, status and social contact provided by employment itself. Families where there is long-term unemployed often suffer severe financial consequences because most people who become unemployed do not receive large redundancy payments or have personal savings – half have no savings at all (Morgan, 1994). In consequence, they have no buffer against the hard times. Dawes (1993) showed that savings are rapidly depleted during periods of unemployment, to be replaced by debts.

As the disparity between rich and poor, working and unemployed households grows, concern has been expressed about the possible emergence of groups excluded from the expected rights of citizenship (McRae, 1987). Dyson (1989) refers to a "lost generation" of people who have been unemployed for five years or longer. He contrasts the 'insiders', with secure jobs in the formal economy and increasing earnings, with the 'outsiders' who are unemployed or have insecure, low-paid jobs. Similarly, Walker and Walker (1997) refer to "Britain divided". They and their contributors examined the record of the Conservative governments since 1979 and concluded that poverty and social exclusion had "increased remorselessly" as the gap between the richest and the poorest widened. Walker and Walker took the Conservative government's repeated re-election to indicate British society's apparent acceptance of "widespread impoverishment" and "sometimes grotesque inequalities". They argued that while surveys showed a rising preference for increased taxation and more spending on health, education and social benefits, electors seemed to favour economic policy over social policy and self-interest over community interest.

Inequalities have a spatial dimension. The recessions of the 1980s hit the manufacturing areas in the North particularly hard, exacerbating the traditional North/South divide. Dyson (1989) maintained that "long-term unemployment within the UK is closely linked to the decay of distinctive regional economies." However, the severe impact of the early 1990s recession on the South East brought a decline in the relative fortunes of London and an upturn in those of Scotland (Green, 1994). Green found that the traditional North/South divide had been eroded, as regional unemployment rates converged. Intraregional differences became more important, in particular unemployment and non-employment in large urban areas. There also appears to be an association between youth, unemployment and homelessness in inner cities (Ginsburg, 1997).

However, Martin (1994) argued that while the divide in employment and unemployment between the North and the South may have been (temporarily) closed, the income gap between the North and South that widened in the 1980s lingered on. The factors contributing to this included persistent high unemployment, divergent rates of earnings growth among the employed, the shift of employment away from full-time jobs towards part-time work, the expansion in self-employment, the increase in the retired population, the move to a more restrictive and discriminatory social benefit system, and changes to personal and indirect taxation (Goodman and Webb, 1994; Jenkins, 1994).

Long-term unemployment, poverty and social exclusion

The association between long-term unemployment, the receipt of benefits and poverty is widely, although not universally, accepted. Britain's Conservative government had long promoted the view that the level of benefits in Britain was sufficiently high to make the word poverty redundant and to encourage large numbers of people to live on benefits who did not need them. Ideological support for this view was given considerable publicity in 1989 when the *Sunday Times* published a series of articles by the American commentator, Charles Murray, on Britain's "emerging underclass". In a subsequent publication, Murray argued that the growth of crime, the rise in one-parent families and youth unemployment could not be blamed upon either Thatcherism or structural factors associated with the 1980s (Murray, 1990). These phenomena had been on the increase since the early 1950s. In his view they were the consequence of permissiveness and the refusal by society to disapprove sufficiently strongly of deviant behaviour. These criminals, lone parents and long-term unemployed people had become so detached from the values of mainstream society that they constituted an underclass.

This analysis was rejected by a number of commentators. Frank Field had already used the term underclass but had squarely laid the blame at the door of growing inequalities, the increase in unemployment, the reduction in state benefit levels and a hardening of public attitudes towards the poor which had occurred throughout the 1980s (Field, 1989). Others had also sought to define the underclass in structural terms as those excluded from the labour market. Lister argued that those who used the term underclass had a tendency to present its members as "powerless victims" underestimating the degree to which they "struggled to gain control over their own lives" (Lister, 1996, p 12). Murray's methodology, his evidence, arguments and policy prescriptions may have been soundly criticised, but the very existence of the debate illustrated a recurring tendency in Britain's policy history for the authorities to blame the poor, the unemployed and the dependent for their own, so called, feckless behaviour.

Debate has also centred on the relationship between poverty and social exclusion. Room (1995) argued that the notion of poverty concerns distributional issues and the lack of resources, while social exclusion refers to relational issues to do with social participation, integration and power. British research into poverty focuses on the resources a person can command and the problems that occur when their resources are inadequate. By contrast, the issue of social exclusion arises from a model of society as collectivities, bound by mutual rights and obligations within a broad moral order. Social exclusion is the process of becoming detached from that moral order.

Attempts have been made to synthesise the two conceptual traditions, root their analysis in exclusion from the social rights of citizenship and examine patterns and processes of generalised disadvantage in terms of education, training, employment, housing, financial resources and so on. The investigation is couched in relational and distributional terms:

> To evaluate, on the one hand, the extent to which some groups of the population are denied access to the principal social and occupational milieux and to the welfare institutions that embody modern notions of citizenship; to examine, on the other hand, the patterns of multidimensional disadvantage to which these groups are then vulnerable, especially insofar as these persist over time. (Room, 1995)

Duffy's (1997) review of the meaning of the term social exclusion argued that there is no common and agreed use of the term and that the relationship between poverty and social exclusion has not been fully clarified. Measures of social exclusion tend to refer to relative poverty and deprivation indices, and thus to resource inequalities. However, she says of social exclusion:

> ... the term is increasingly used, and found increasingly useful, as a way of describing a variety of phenomena which relate to exclusion from networks, institutions and markets, and detachment from dominant norms and values. There is concern that together, these phenomena point to an increasing problem of the integrative and absorptive capacities of modern societies.... (Duffy, 1997, p 4)

An important development in the conceptualisation of poverty and social exclusion emphasises the dynamics of social processes:

> Simple but important insights into the relationship between poverty and social exclusion result from making time explicit in the conceptualisation, definition and measurement of the two concepts". (Walker, 1995, p 103)

Walker (1995; 1997a) notes that cross-sectional measures of poverty considerably underestimate: the number who move in and out of poverty over a period of time; the interaction between the duration of spells of poverty, their severity and social exclusion; and that poverty may be both a pre-cursor of social exclusion and a consequence of it. Walker (1997b) shows that unemployment is a major factor precipitating poverty, while obtaining employment or increasing hours of work is the main route out of poverty.

Duffy's analysis indicates that governments are concerned about any association between long-term unemployment, poverty and social exclusion. For national governments, the main point is that poverty and social exclusion present different threats:

> Social exclusion (rupture of the social tie) is primarily perceived as a threat to cohesion (fear of crime and ghettos) in addition to the threat to state budgets (high cost of supporting the unemployed and pensioners) posed by poverty (low material resources). (Duffy, 1997, p 9)

Escaping long-term unemployment: obstacles and opportunities

The metaphor of a queue has been used to describe the experience of long-term unemployment. Unemployed people are imagined as queuing up to find work, but the queue is not orderly. People who possess certain skills and qualifications generally go to the front. This means that those at the back, who have already been unemployed for some time, take even longer to find jobs. They are the last to benefit from a fall in unemployment (Budd et al, 1987; OECD, 1988). A number of explanations have been offered for this phenomenon.

The change in the structure of employment presented many people with obstacles to finding a job. Walker et al (1995) showed that unemployment is heavily concentrated on particular groups of people. The recession of the early 1980s created many redundancies in traditional industries. The people who were affected tended to be male, older workers who were either unskilled or whose skills had become outdated. They found it difficult to take advantage of the jobs being created which were typically in the service sector, part time, and requiring higher or different skills (OECD, 1988).

Overall, the main risks of unemployment fall disproportionately on those who are poorly qualified and unskilled, those who are young and inexperienced, older people in the 10 or 15 years before statutory pension age, workers with poor health or who have a disability and people from ethnic minorities (Convery, 1997a). Analysis of the British Household Panel Study suggests that long-term unemployed people are most likely to be single males with no qualifications, either young or at the end of their working lives (Walker and Ashworth, 1998). Long-term unemployment itself becomes a barrier as it erodes skills, and self-confidence and motivation may be undermined by unsuccessful jobsearch and rejection (Shaw et al, 1996).

Discrimination by employers presents a further obstacle. Studies show that the stigma of long-term unemployment itself can act as a deterrent for employers (Budd et al, 1987; Meadows et al, 1988; Dawes, 1993). The British labour market can increasingly be seen as having primary and secondary sectors. Full-time jobs tend to go to people already in employment, while the secondary sector is characterised by higher labour turnover in lower-paid, part-time or temporary work (Gregg and Wadsworth, 1995).

Just as importantly, long-term unemployed people can face serious financial disincentives to finding employment. Most people are keen to stop living on Income Support and to find work (Hedges, 1993; Dobson et al, 1994; Gallie and Vogler, 1994b; Kempson and Bryson, 1994; Shaw et al, 1996). However, they can find themselves in an 'unemployment trap' in which employment would provide them with very little extra income or even make them worse off. In part, this effect derives from the prospect of low pay. The evidence suggests that unemployed people do not set high 'reservation wages' (Shaw et al, 1996). Dawes' (1993) study of long-term unemployed people suggests that many look diligently for work and are willing to lower their reservation wage. The non-financial incentives to work – such as improved social status and self-esteem, reduced incidence of ill health and domestic stress – lead to significant numbers working for benefit-level incomes, with some people actually working for less income than they would receive from out-of-work social security benefits (McKay and Marsh, 1994).

Means-testing for benefits applies to the family unit as a whole. One consequence is that the male partner's unemployment can significantly affect the female partner's employment. The analysis by Davies et al (1994) found a modest but significant effect: after a year, at the point at which insurance-based benefit is replaced by means-tested benefit, the female partners were inclined to give up work.

The calculation as to whether the person can be better off in work is complicated by the potential loss of 'passported' benefits such as free school meals and prescriptions, and the costs of travel, clothes and tools or equipment entailed by the job. Home purchasers who are unemployed face particular disincentives to taking up work which is not well paid and secure. Mortgage repayments, unlike rent, are not eligible for Housing Benefit so the break-even point for work to be financially viable for mortgagepayers is increased. Also, under JSA mortgage interest is not paid for the first six months of any period of unemployment.

The administrative and practical difficulties encountered when moving on and off benefit further discourage people from taking insecure employment which generates an irregular income. As we have seen, a number of changes have been put in train to tackle these problems. However, the need for secure employment and a reliable income may be paramount, in particular for parents and mortgagepayers. Claimants point out that the greatest problem is the lack of 'proper jobs' (Vincent and Dobson, 1997).

Lone parents face extra difficulties and particularly complex 'better-off' calculations (Shaw et al, 1996). Their needs for information and advice about benefits, which they require to make informed decisions about a return to work or education or training, are not always met (Hedges, 1993;Vincent et al, 1995). Maintenance by the absent parent is currently treated in full as income for the purposes of Income Support (JSA), but earned income up to £15 is disregarded in the calculation. In addition to the usual expenses entailed by working, lone parents have to consider the availability and cost of childcare. A proportion of those costs is disregarded in the Family Credit calculation. Consequently, lone parents, whose standard of living is on average lower than any other sociodemographic group, have little financial incentive to enter paid employment.

Conclusions

Britain suffered unemployment and long-term unemployment earlier than elsewhere in Europe and at higher rates. Britain's unemployment-related benefits are more or less universal, but insurance-based benefits are giving way to selective, means-tested benefits. Benefit levels are lower than in Germany and Sweden and are falling in relation to average wages; the rules of eligibility and the conditionality of benefit are becoming stronger and an element of compulsion is more evident in JSA; and savings are to be made on administration to bring down the overall costs.

Aspects of the rules and administration of benefits, allied with the availability of largely part-time and insecure work, make the move from benefit receipt into paid employment problematic. Recently, changes were introduced to help bridge the move from benefit to earned income and to encourage employers to take on long-term unemployed people. Service delivery for unemployed people has been relatively distanced from government through changes to the machinery of government and the development of private and quasi-private provision. Control is exerted through targets and contracts.

Elected local authorities have no role in the delivery of services specifically for unemployed people but they do undertake economic development. Authorities which were eligible on the grounds of deprivation, which included unemployment rates, could apply for certain government schemes or to the European Social Fund. Such local economic development was not intended specifically to alleviate the circumstances of long-term unemployed people.

In line with neo-liberal orthodoxy, British Conservative government policy was to deregulate the labour market, increase labour 'flexibility' and to focus on 'supply-side' measures. Labour market interventions were aimed at individuals, with the aim of helping them with their jobsearch and training in order to make them more employable. Critical evaluation of these policies differed across a spectrum: on the one hand they were seen as the only means to successful regeneration and 'real' jobs; on the other, they were seen as partial, failing to consider labour demand which should be tackled through job creation schemes. At worst, they were interpreted as a strategy of inequality, to provide incentives at the top and the bottom of society.

However, commentators agree that the consequences of long-term unemployment for individuals, communities and society are dire. The consequences may be seen in terms of unequal access to resources or of social dislocation and exclusion.

SIX

Policy interviews in Britain

Interviews

This chapter presents the results of the policy interviews into the ways in which the problem of long-term unemployment is conceptualised as a policy issue in Britain. The interviews took place in the summer of 1995, during the last years of the Conservative government, with 20 'policy actors', who were prominent representatives of government departments, pressure groups, parliamentary select committees, and local policy settings (see Table 7 for a breakdown). All could be said to have an influence on policy development and/or implementation from a national or local perspective. Care was taken to ensure that they represented the range of interests and political positions. They can be broadly categorised into the following four groups:

- civil servants from the DfEE, the DSS and the Employment Service (the agency of the DfEE);
- pressure group representatives from the Unemployment Unit, Confederation of British Industry (CBI), Trades Union Congress (TUC) and Association of Metropolitan Authorities (AMA);
- Members of Parliament (MPs) on relevant parliamentary select committees;
- seven local policy actors from the city in which the interviews with long-term unemployed people took place, two TEC representatives, two pressure group representatives and three from local government.

Assessment of situation

According to the interviewees, 'long-term' unemployment in Britain may be defined as a spell of six months or of one year. Those who used one year as the benchmark did so because of the very large numbers of people who left the unemployment figures within nine months. Others

Table 7: Policy actors interviewed in Britain

Civil servants	5*
Pressure groups	4
Members of Parliament	4
Local actors	7
Total	20

Note: * Four individual interviews and one group discussion

chose six months because most unemployed people then become eligible for government programmes such as TfW and Restart. This lack of clarity is reflected in government publications. For the purposes of this chapter, long-term unemployment refers to one year or more – which was also the defining period for our interviews with long-term unemployed people.

Respondents also disagreed about the measurement of unemployment. In Britain, two definitions are used: those claiming unemployment-related benefit, and those meeting the ILO criteria. The representative from the Unemployment Unit and both Labour MPs believed that the claimant count significantly undercounted the totals out of work. They also referred to "hidden" long-term unemployment, believing that the data fails to take account of people who work only intermittently, accumulating many spells of unemployment, none of which may be as long as one year. People who have short periods of employment or training, and seasonal work in agriculture were given as examples.

In contrast, a local respondent argued that long-term unemployment could be exaggerated by the claimant count if people are working in the informal economy and are not "really" unemployed. The significance of flows into and out of unemployment was also raised: a civil servant suggested that the misrepresentation of the data collection and presentation was not all in one direction:

> "To look at counts suggests they're a relatively homogeneous mass, whereas in fact there's quite a lot of movement off the count even once you're more than a year unemployed."

Long-term unemployment as a policy issue

None of our respondents believed that unemployment or long-term unemployment was top of the policy agenda for either the Conservative or Labour parties. As a Labour MP pointed out, until the 1979 election unemployment was an important policy issue, but its salience had declined since, despite the higher rates. Two types of explanation were offered: on the one hand, respondents said that Britain was no longer in recession, unemployment was falling and it was of less importance; on the other, these reasons were given: trade unions had less power and they tended to concentrate on defending people in work; the Labour Party no longer campaigned for full employment; the public had come almost to expect job insecurity and the possibility of unemployment; and the widespread belief that many unemployed people 'work on the side' anyway.

A Labour MP and some local policy actors thought high levels of unemployment had almost become accepted, and that there was less "moral outrage" than during the 1980s. The Conservative government had then been re-elected even though it had made no commitment to full employment and that had "taken a lot of heat out" of the issue. Recent demonstrations against unemployment in France were referred to which, it was felt, would never happen in Britain. A Labour MP said British people accepted blame individually:

> "If you're unemployed it doesn't necessarily follow that you feel collective about your unemployment."

Some felt that reorganisation of the machinery of government had lowered the salience of long-term unemployment as an issue of public concern. The Departments of Education and Employment were merged in July 1995 (to form the DfEE) and the Select Committee for Employment was abolished. A Labour MP argued that both were deliberate moves by the then government to diffuse concern and lessen debate on unemployment. He suggested that the practical effect of the abolition of the select committee would certainly be to reduce the number of questions on employment matters in the House of Commons. A civil servant thought that while unemployment had been top of the agenda for the Department of Employment before the merger, now it was top of the agenda for just one of the directorates of the DfEE. Despite this, the civil servants thought there had been more focus on long-term unemployment during the last five or six years, illustrated by the increased targets for placing long-term unemployed people in work and various changes to benefits designed as work incentives.

Although long-term unemployment was not seen as the overriding priority of the day, no one denied its importance. A Conservative MP said:

> "So I don't think it's totally neglected. I think it's just a change in the shades, a change in the colours, but it's still the same issue, and it's still of significance."

Similarly, the CBI had recently completed a study of long-term unemployment (CBI, undated) and the TUC made it an important theme in its Budget Submission to the Chancellor (TUC, 1995). Neither gave it top priority because pressure groups tend to be reactive to current policy rather than proactive in setting the policy agenda. Inevitably, this was the local position as well, because local initiatives depend on funding decisions at national level. The AMA representative said a recent report of the organisation showed that local authorities "shifted their priorities in line with what they can get funding for".

Each group of policy actors tended to define the importance of long-term unemployment in terms of its consequences for the groups they represent. The TUC and Unemployment Unit representatives focused on the economic and social costs, and the AMA representative stressed the effects on individuals and local economies. However, the CBI representative referred to its assumption that unemployment would decrease with economic growth, and focused on the causes of inefficiencies in the labour market and government action on that problem:

> "Our basic economic strategy is one of economic growth being the necessary part of making sure that unemployment per se is reduced.... But from then you have a core problem of structural, long-term unemployment, and it was that that was causing the biggest inefficiencies in the labour market and was the biggest problem that had to be tackled...."

Civil servants stressed the importance of long-term unemployment according to the remit of their departments: the effect on benefit expenditure (DSS), and economic development and the labour supply (DfEE). However, several saw beyond their narrow departmental focus and acknowledged that long-term unemployment can also cause social problems.

Local policy actors saw long-term unemployment as one of a range of interconnected issues that need to be addressed in attempting to regenerate the city's economy. For example, a local respondent described economic well-being as the underlying theme in local policy, through which ran a "big circle" of long-term unemployment, less disposable income, business doing badly, rent arrears and homelessness.

Causes and incidence of long-term unemployment

The policy actors interviewed offered a variety of interpretations of the causes of long-term unemployment at the macro level and in terms of individual barriers to re-entering paid work.

A popular element in current debate on the causes of unemployment is the combined influences of technological change and the globalisation of the world economy. The argument suggests that human labour in industrial economies is being replaced by technological innovations and by cheaper labour in other parts of the world. Most respondents who expressed an opinion dismissed this line of reasoning. A civil servant pointed to the fact that the UK now has a relatively low share of long-term unemployment compared to the rest of Europe, and the TUC representative mentioned that only 5% of European GDP is dependent on non-EU trade. However, some acknowledged that Britain is operating in a world market. They were concerned about the ability of the then government to pursue independent policies within the constraints of capital flows and world financial markets.

Most respondents distinguished between the recessions of the 1980s and the 1990s. The earlier one affected traditional industries and male older workers who were unskilled or whose skills had become outdated, leaving them prone to long-term unemployment. A change had taken place in the structure of employment with a downward trend in manufacturing and a growth in the service sector. This led to more part-time jobs, which were seen as suited to women. Local policy actors were particularly concerned because many jobs with the city's traditional employers had been lost.

The recession of the early 1990s was seen, as a pressure group representative put it, as a more "democratic recession" in that it had hit people in all spheres of the economy. The representative from the Unemployment Unit argued that, in consequence, being unemployed or on the edge of the labour market affected all types:

> "... [they] are not a homogeneous group in any way at all, and in fact have recently become exceptionally heterogeneous, although things are shifting back a little bit."

However, the idea that long-term unemployment was primarily a structural problem was dismissed, although the TUC representative suggested that there might be some male structural unemployment because of the shrinking bastions of traditional manual employment which the new opportunities in the service sector could not meet. A common theme was the effect of the rapid pace of change, in which "you have to run like hell to stand still", which itself caused unemployment at higher levels than formerly.

At an individual level, a common theme was that people without skills or vocational qualifications, or whose skills were obsolete, were at risk. Most pressure group respondents, MPs and local actors identified young and older people as being particularly affected by long-term unemployment because they lacked relevant skills.

Present policies and programmes

Although respondents raised concerns about current and planned policies and programmes, they generally suggested alterations to the present system rather than radical change. The main themes which emerged were macroeconomic policy, active labour market policies and the benefits system.

Benefits system

Britain has the lowest benefit rate for unemployment-related claimants in the EU and is the only EU country to cut overall expenditure. All respondents had strong but differing opinions about the benefits system as a whole. However, the interview questions tended to concentrate on two aspects: the 'unemployment trap' and in-work benefits. People become 'trapped' on unemployment-related benefit when they are unable to earn enough to provide more than they would receive on benefit. Several respondents thought this caused long-term unemployment. They pointed in particular to high marginal tax rates, the transitional costs of obtaining work, the pound-for-pound clawback of benefit as wages rise, and the loss of passported benefits.

Family Credit, a means-tested in-work benefit paid to low-earning families with children, was described by a Conservative MP as the "great unsung success story". However, this view was far from unanimous. Although all the respondents believed that Family Credit helped families, there were two main areas of concern: that it perpetuates people's dependency on benefit, and that it provides a subsidy to employers to pay low wages. Continuing dependency on benefit was a concern for the majority of respondents. A pressure group representative believed that Family Credit, because of its high marginal withdrawal rates, "locks people into poverty", although the civil servants suggested adjustments to Family Credit rules would enable it to alleviate rather than perpetuate benefit dependency. Representatives from the Unemployment Unit and the TUC were particularly concerned about the "wage subsidy" implications of Family Credit. One of them did not see why taxpayers should subsidise the "stingy elements" of British industry. However, the CBI representative disagreed, and said that research suggested that there is no significant tendency for employers to use Family Credit to keep wages low.

Opinion was sharply divided on the issue of a minimum wage. Several respondents, including Labour MPs, pressure group representatives and a civil servant, believed that the introduction of a minimum wage would solve the problems raised by Family Credit. They argued that it would prevent abuse by employers and that any in-work benefits system without a minimum wage could too easily create "in-work poverty". Steps should also be taken to ensure in-work benefits complement earnings rather than subsidise them. In contrast, a Conservative MP and the CBI representative were convinced that a national minimum wage would raise unemployment and put many firms out of business.

Civil servants emphasised the various policy initiatives available to facilitate the transition from benefit to work and to encourage employers to take on long-term unemployed people. They thought everything possible was being tried or had been tried.

Macroeconomic policy

All the civil servants stressed the Conservative government's belief that only economic growth and a flexible labour market can reduce unemployment. A Conservative MP argued vehemently that the government had been successful in its management of the economy, pointing out that unemployment had never reached five million as predicted in the report *Faith in the city* (Commission on Urban Priority Areas, 1985). Deregulation of the labour market was central to the approach. The civil servants confirmed this and also explained how government policy concentrated on increasing the effective labour supply within public expenditure constraints. As a Conservative MP said:

> "Job flexibility is more and more the key thing, and flexibility is the new buzz word."

The CBI representative agreed with this policy prescription which he believed made for a growth in "real" jobs. This in turn made supply-side measures necessary:

> "That will afford greater chance for [employers] to create new jobs as opposed to something that might be more prescriptive and not allow them to respond to business needs as they want ... building up employment growth in a way which means people are doing real jobs, and are doing jobs which are adding value to companies and the economy generally, and we have a labour market and a supply of labour which is able to take advantage of those new jobs...."

Several of the civil servants drew attention to the way in which employment policy had changed since the 1980s:

> "Labour supply reduction in the early 1980s – things like the job release scheme – were almost an admission of failure: we're never going to get jobs for young people, therefore if the old people wish to leave and be replaced by young people, then everybody's better off."

Not surprisingly, Labour MPs, the representatives from the Unemployment Unit and the TUC, and some local commentators were markedly unenthusiastic about current policy and the concentration on supply-side issues. All these respondents shared the view that the lack of jobs should be addressed: what one MP described as "the rather large gap on the demand side". The same MP was very worried that current policies put the responsibility of getting into the situation of being unemployed people on to the individual rather than on the lack of jobs:

> "... [they imply that] there are enough jobs if only people would look hard enough. I mean, we know that's not the case. And it's trying to blame the individual for the situation they've found themselves in."

A pressure group representative said that the system maintained a "reserve army of labour" of long-term unemployed people for whom there was no work. This group of respondents did not deny the need for effective programmes to improve unemployed people's skills, but said other measures were also needed. Deregulation was not a positive policy and the resulting job insecurity was deplorable. As an alternative they suggested public investment: the TUC wanted £1 billion public investment in public housing, matched by £0.5 billion of private funds, to generate 30,000 jobs, and the Unemployment Unit called for public expenditure, coordinated with Europe, to stimulate demand.

Several respondents took up the theme of job creation and local regeneration. A Labour MP mentioned Labour's proposals for an environmental task force which would tackle youth unemployment. However, the idea was most positively endorsed by a Conservative MP who believed that there was scope for the creation of many jobs in the caring and environment sectors:

> "There's limitless work which could be done, which would cheer us all up, make us feel proud of ourselves and revitalise society."

Local respondents viewed job creation in terms of inward investment. The city council had devoted much effort and resources to economic development, but they had to be seen to be providing for the general good rather than just the most disadvantaged, otherwise, "It causes resentment and reinforces this issue of social exclusion."

When the study was carried out, most national and European support for local economic development came as grants for specific schemes. The AMA representative wanted this changed from "property-led development" to more emphasis on people so that jobs went to unemployed people in the locality; AMA was understood to be pressing this with the Labour Party (then in opposition). The organisation wanted more freedom for local authorities to determine their own needs and ways forward, to:

> "... get away from the standard approaches to regeneration, economic development and anti-poverty stuff given by government schemes."

Several local actors felt the restrictions imposed on local government were a further obstacle to effective schemes and job creation. They felt that while some schemes might physically improve deprived areas, endemic unemployment was not tackled: appearances and subjective feelings might improve, but no corresponding improvement was made to root problems.

The same respondents criticised the low level of government funding for local schemes. The AMA representative gave the example of budget cuts of 15% to economic development programmes, though these remained a crucial source of support; a local councillor emphasised how vital it was for the city to be successful in its bidding for grants. A local joint-agency trust had been established expressly to improve knowledge of bidding systems.

Active labour market policies

The then Conservative government had promised to improve labour market performance, including programmes to keep people who had been unemployed for longer than six months in contact with the market. One civil servant said the current philosophy underlying policy development was that to help individuals with their jobsearch and attachment to the market was a better avenue than mass training. This was reflected in government policies. Respondents discussed several of the programmes described in the previous chapter. They gave most attention to Restart, TfW and JSA (which came fully into effect in October 1996). Many commented on the way TECs and the Employment Service operated.

Restart

A civil servant explained that the government was increasingly persuaded of the effectiveness of providing advice and guidance, rather than training, for long-term unemployed people. The Restart scheme had been developed because training measures were felt to be having no effect on the count of unemployed people. The philosophy was to improve the supply of labour by:

> "... reacquainting people who are most disadvantaged and most marginalised from the labour market with the labour market."

Many respondents felt that interventions such as Restart were effective in keeping up people's jobsearch skills, motivation, contact with the labour market and social skills. However, the Unemployment Unit representative felt that, at the moment, Restart interviews can be used to penalise a person who is judged to be not actively seeking work.

Training for Work

Despite the government's rejection of mass training programmes, almost all the respondents thought training was a very important aspect of employment policy:

> "The lesson that we've got to learn from Singapore is that you can create jobs by moving a country forward in a high technology, highly educated, highly trained environment, although it's more difficult in a democracy where people have the right not to train themselves, not to skill themselves up to a level that's needed and that causes one

> to have a lot of low employers and low employment in terms of salary, opportunities." (Conservative MP)

> "Now I happen to believe that training is a really important issue. It's not just about getting people off the register for the short term. It's actually getting these people to think more about training and retraining." (local TEC)

> "Arguably people have to learn, retrain and train right throughout their working lives now, because [of the] technical innovation, different working practices and so on required." (pressure group representative)

Despite their concern for training, the national representatives appeared unenthusiastic about TfW. They said:

- the reasons for its "relatively poor performance" could be that not enough attention was paid to who participated or to providing subsequent support;
- its only real effect was to reduce the unemployment figures;
- its poor results made unemployed people cynical.

They felt that priority should be given to improving the quality of the courses, with more vocational skills training and higher level NVQs, rather than increasing the number of places. However, local actors were more positive about TfW and regretted recent cuts in funding for the scheme. The local TEC's remit was described as providing jobs with training, not training for jobs. One of the TEC representatives stressed the value of work-based training, and said the TEC had set its own target of placing half of its TfW candidates into work. He said:

> "If you take people on, into a room, and give them training, and then as a result of that training expect them to get jobs, forget it."

TECs

Most of the discussion about TECs was with local policy actors, pressure group representatives and MPs. They focused on the themes of partnership and local accountability.

Several respondents believed the effectiveness of TECs was "patchy" and "ad hoc" and differed by area. They saw poor relationships with other local agencies as a major cause of low effectiveness. However, the local representatives thought the TEC in their area was developing effective partnerships with agencies such as the local authority and the Chamber of Commerce and admired it for its innovation and initiative. The council and the TEC were jointly funding an urban regeneration officer, which they believed was unusual. They thought that partnership would bring more efficient and better thought out schemes. Most of the respondents were concerned about TECs' lack of local accountability. Many wanted wider representation on TEC boards and abolition of their private company status. However, a representative from the TEC in the focus city for this study believed that it was accountable, not least because funding depended on performance. He also thought elected board members who did not have relevant knowledge would be counterproductive.

Responsibility for training

The main proposals for change centred around the question of who should take responsibility for training: individuals, employers or the government. The employer representative said responsibility lay with all three, "a sort of triangle of responsibilities if you like."

Members of all policy groups felt it was vital for individuals to be motivated to undertake training. A Conservative MP wanted training vouchers to which people could add from their own savings, but a pressure group representative thought individuals would best be motivated if training schemes were tied to a wage formula. Also, some thought that because the "voluntarism" of encouraging employers to provide more and better training had not worked, a statutory "carrot and stick" system in which provision was funded by taxation of employers should be put in place.

Opinions regarding the extent of governmental responsibility for training varied. On the one hand, a Conservative MP felt their duty was limited to basic skills: he argued that state training schemes were ineffective, illustrating this with reference to engineers trained to a high standard at Rolls Royce. On the other hand, a Labour MP believed it was necessary to bring training schemes into the public ambit because the quality and wider relevance of employer training could not be guaranteed. The need for training to be relevant and focused on future needs was also taken up by the CBI representative.

Employment Service

The Employment Service is the agency of the DfEE. Some differences in approach and emphasis were apparent among the respondents from the DfEE and the Employment Service. DfEE civil servants expressed some concern that the agency as a whole did not fully understand the Department's objectives, but felt this problem was generally overcome because the DfEE set the agency's targets which made it strongly "outcome orientated". However, this led in turn to other worries. One of these was that an element of "creaming" might occur, in which people who were more likely to succeed were selected for programmes rather than those most in need of help. A civil servant said:

> "If you or I were in the Employment Service, we'd sell the beans too if they cleared faster than the sweetcorn."

One civil servant suggested the agency concentrated on outcomes to the detriment of presentation, so people were not well enough informed of the various schemes on offer. A local respondent criticised the Employment Service for poor staff training and internal organisation.

Consequences of long-term unemployment

Perceived consequences for individuals

It is significant that policy actors tended to think of long-term unemployment in terms of its impact upon the interest groups they represent because the way in which they perceive consequences has implications for their policy prescriptions. However, all of the respondents were also concerned with the effects of long-term unemployment on people generally. They pointed to possible damaging consequences for labour market skills, health and well-being.

All felt that prolonged absence from the labour market damaged work skills, jobsearch skills and work ethic. A civil servant referred to the deterioration of human capital, while a Conservative MP thought individuals would:

> "... develop anti-social behaviour in some form or another and make themselves unsuitable for employment...."

Many respondents thought people would lose the motivation to work, through a combination of diminished hope and the loss of any work habit.

Almost all the respondents shared a belief in the importance of work for a person's identity. In consequence, they linked unemployment to stress and trauma, with serious implications for an individual's self-esteem. In the long term this was thought to lead to psychological problems and family breakdown. Some respondents on the left of the political spectrum highlighted the link between joblessness, deprivation and poor health.

A further theme was the link between unemployment and crime. Two perspectives were apparent: a civil servant mentioned only fraud, but most local policy actors, MPs from both parties and almost all the representatives of pressure groups suggested a relationship between unemployment and some criminal activities. They felt that in the long term, unemployment brought boredom, loss of values and low levels of income and, in some circumstances, could contribute to drug use, vandalism, theft and burglary.

Consequences for communities and society

Several respondents referred to the effects of geographical concentrations of people who have been unemployed for long periods. Some areas, often council housing estates, were identified as having high concentrations of long-term unemployed people. Respondents shared the view that this could lead to further problems: the TUC representative termed this a "cycle of decline" in which areas become deprived in terms of income, housing and education resources, and have high levels of crime. The local policy actors all named the particular estates in their city which suffered in this way. Concern was also raised about possible generational effects of living in such communities, where children might grow up with little ambition of hope. A further cyclical effect came from employers who would not employ residents of particular estates because they thought they had lost their work ethic. It also became difficult to attract inward investment to the area.

Many respondents were worried about the effects on society as a whole. The CBI representative described his members' understanding that "business had an obligation, duty, an interest in this problem being addressed." We have seen that respondents thought long-term unemployment inclined people to criminal activities. Many also felt that society was increasingly divided between the 'haves' and the 'have nots' and that there was a real danger of the division leading to social unrest, as it had historically. A Labour MP thought that young long-term unemployed people were getting angrier and angrier and would force the issue on to the political agenda.

Economic consequences

The most visible consequence of long-term unemployment is perhaps its cost in public expenditure terms. These costs were not overlooked by our respondents. A Conservative MP estimated the costs to be between £9-£23 billion, and believed "those are the bills of failure".

A less observable economic consequence is the informal economy: none of the respondents denied its existence, although one civil servant stressed that the government's economic strategy had limited its development by promoting enterprise through deregulation and low taxation. The informal economy was seen as costly in terms of unnecessary benefit expenditure and the displacement effects of legitimate businesses losing work to cheaper competition. A few respondents thought the existence of an informal economy was not entirely negative because it "oils the wheels" and usually works its way into the 'formal' economy and GDP. The city council and the TEC provided supported premises so that firms would be encouraged to become part of the formal economy, without the constraint of overheads.

Social exclusion

When pressed to see if they thought that the results of long-term unemployment might be seen as 'social exclusion', no respondent used the term without prompting, although they did refer to "marginalisation", "alienation" and linked "cycles of deprivation". Several considered the term to be "Euro speak", used in bids for funding. Civil servants felt it was not an accepted governmental definition, but was "one of those odd concepts that seminars are held on". Many concluded that 'social exclusion' is not prevalent in Britain. A civil servant said it could not exist because "the welfare state includes them in society". A local policy actor said that "so-called" socially excluded groups may not think of themselves in those terms at all:

> "... they're not socially excluded from their own community, their family and friends. It depends what you mean. Whether they're excluded from what society's perception is of where they should be is a different matter. They may never be able to attain what society thinks they should attain...."

However, on reflection most could see that certain groups might become excluded from society, such as 16- and 17-year-olds who were ineligible for benefits. Two themes emerged: a link with long-term unemployment and with geographical concentration.

All of the respondents made the link between social exclusion, as they understood it, and long-term unemployment. Most saw social exclusion as comprising a number of factors, usually the combination of individual and community consequences of long-term unemployment. These were believed to lead to material and social divisions. A local policy actor referred to a "whole complex of disadvantage and alienation", created in the first instance by unemployment. The material divide was felt to be exacerbated by the media and advertising, which stigmatised people and served to remind them how badly off they were in relation to others.

Most respondents tended to associate social exclusion with particular localities, especially inner-city housing estates plagued by high levels of long-term unemployment. The general view was that the communities themselves became excluded. A Conservative MP saw the cause as "particular problems that are personal to them and their group". The local policy actors agreed on the specific estates that were socially excluded within their city.

Obstacles, opportunities and incentives

We have seen that respondents agreed that long-term unemployment was not at the top of the policy agenda, which limited the action taken to counteract it. They acknowledged the difficulties experienced as claimants moved from benefit receipt into work, and the ways in which the system itself could be said to encourage 'benefit dependency'.

Nor were all respondents confident that current 'supply-side' measures, focused on claimants, would be successful in helping them back to work. Many thought that substantial job generation programmes were needed. They also discussed the role of employers, and expressed concern that discrimination by employers increased people's difficulties when they were trying to re-enter the labour market after a lengthy period of unemployment. Most of the policy actors thought that employers discriminate against long-term unemployed people because they expect them to have lost their skills and their motivation to work. Some of the respondents thought that particular groups were more at risk of employer discrimination. They felt that in an extremely competitive labour market there was more scope for discrimination against people on the grounds of race (which is illegal), disability and age.

The timing of interventions and programmes was criticised on the grounds that they should be provided when they could best prevent long-term unemployment. Civil servants pointed out that most programmes do not begin until people have been out of work for at least six months because long-term unemployment cannot be predicted. One said that his department's philosophy rested on the uniqueness of each individual case. Civil servants emphasised the 'dead weight' aspect of programmes: they said that interventions are costly and, since more than 60% of unemployment clears itself within six months, earlier intervention would be a waste of resources. However, several other respondents disagreed. They felt that unemployed people should be eligible for programmes sooner, a view summarised by one local policy actor:

> "The help that's offered to long-term unemployed people doesn't come soon enough. People are long-term unemployed because they don't get the help they need quickly enough."

Conclusions

The positions taken by the policy interviewees reflected the political division between those who supported the neo-liberal views of the Conservative administration and those who opposed them. This was illustrated by the different positions taken on the then government's 'supply-side' measures to combat unemployment and long-term unemployment. On the one hand were respondents who thought such measures were appropriate and would be successful; on the other were those who thought that lack of jobs was equally a problem and advocated interventions to increase job availability. Similarly, some respondents endorsed a 'hands-off' approach, in which there was little role for the state and much for the private sector; in the absence of private sector provision then the government should create quasi-private organisations run on commercial lines. However, other respondents opposed such developments, seeing them as unaccountable, and bringing an inappropriate ethos to public provision.

Respondents were more inclined to agree about the shortcomings of the benefits system, although even there they were divided on such aspects as the effects of in-work benefit and a minimum wage. Again, they were more united in their qualified approval of Restart and other active labour market policies, although some thought that increased local accountability would improve the quality of TEC provision.

The evidence suggests that the relationship between the DfEE and the Employment Service may be problematic: the DfEE appears to control the activities of the service through imposed targets, but criticises the consequences when routes are taken to meet the targets. Other central-local differences emerged in discussions of the competition for central government funding and schemes.

While the respondents could not agree on the causes of long-term unemployment and what should be done about it, they were more in accord on the consequences of long-term unemployment for individuals and their families, for communities, and for the economy. Also, although they generally rejected the use of the term social exclusion they accepted that long-term unemployment could bring individual and community effects which led to material and social divisions. They associated disadvantaged groups with particular localities which could themselves reinforce the cycle of decline.

SEVEN

Conclusion

Introduction

Chapters One to Six have focused on literature reviews and interviews with policy communities in the three countries under consideration. This chapter will:

- summarise some of the main conclusions from a comparative perspective with the aim of identifying commonalties and contrasts between the three countries;
- discuss how far responses from national policy communities correspond with the notion of distinct national welfare, or better, unemployment support, regimes as outlined in the introductory chapter;
- reflect on the debate about long-term unemployment and 'social exclusion'.

Long-term unemployment in a cross-national perspective

Part One has shown that while there is a link between the level of unemployment and long-term unemployment, this link is not inevitable. The example of Sweden – where high unemployment does not coincide with high levels of long-term unemployment – demonstrates this. However, Swedish unemployment has risen since the early 1990s and the number of people out of work for longer periods has increased as well. As far as causes for long-term unemployment are concerned, respondents from all three countries referred to a lack of labour demand and 'jobless growth' generally and to structural changes such as the globalisation of national economies, the deregulation of financial markets, the decline of traditional industries and the consequent loss of 'male' manual jobs in particular.

Yet the relevance of global economic restructuring appears to be perceived differently in the three countries. British respondents referred to wider changes but emphasised the particular nature of the British economy and the effect of the more advanced process of deindustrialisation and rapid transformation towards a low-waged service economy compared with other European nations. In Sweden, high unemployment levels were linked by respondents to entry to the EU and, more generally, to a shift from an industrial-based to a knowledge-based society. German interviewees were most worried about the effects of the increasing internationalisation of markets. At the time of the interviews, the debate about the *Standort Deutschland* (Germany as a location for investment) was rife, that is, there was a widespread fear that due to high direct and indirect labour costs, economic globalisation threatened Germany as a location for investment. This is remarkable, and demonstrates the volatility of public discourses, given that interviews with a similar group of policy actors only a few years earlier indicated no such concerns but rather displayed broad confidence in the future of the German social market economy (Taylor-Gooby, 1996; Bonoli et al, 1996).

Cross-national differences in the incidence of long-term unemployment are important both for an understanding of national debates about the conceptualisation of the problem and for propagating solutions. Certain social groups are disproportionately affected in all three countries, such as those with no or few qualifications, older workers and those with some form of medical impairment. However, much more so than in the other two countries, in the old Länder of Germany long-term unemployment is predominantly a problem for older people, while younger groups are less affected than in Sweden or Britain. The latter might indicate the continuing effectiveness of the 'dual system' of education and vocational training in Germany (Wallace, 1994) while the former reflects a predominant response to high and persistent unemployment, that is, the promotion of different forms of early labour market exit which was characteristic for continental welfare states in the 1980s and early 1990s (Esping-Andersen, 1996). This, in addition to a merely sluggish expansion in public or private service sector employment, has increasingly created a situation of labour market insiders and outsiders.

Many respondents underlined this by pointing to processes of social closure and segmentation in the German labour market which provided secure positions for insiders but obstacles for unemployed outsiders, and in particular those who are older. There was a general consensus that unemployed people above the age of 45, compared with 55 some years ago, have a much reduced chance of finding gainful employment. Some interviewees suggested that this was partly due to personal motivations, arguing that the figures for long-term unemployment were inflated by older workers who in effect saw themselves as 'retired' rather than 'unemployed'. However, more common was the notion that 'retirement' is enforced at 45 years.

In Sweden, long-term unemployment is still much less prevalent than in most other European countries. This can be explained in the light of policies which, since the late 1960s, have pursued an expansion of service sector employment and the creation of dual breadwinner families, thus favouring labour market inclusion and entry rather than exit (Stephens, 1996). The welfare state acted as an "employer of first resort" (Leibfried, 1993) and as a "virtual employment machine" (Esping-Andersen, 1990, p 149), providing jobs for those groups who in other countries were either made redundant or managed to remain in the labour market at the cost of reduced real wages. However, since the early 1990s unemployment has risen dramatically in Sweden and interviews with the Swedish policy community conveyed the impression that those with few qualifications were the most vulnerable to long-term unemployment and that within this group, middle-aged female clerical workers had considerable problems finding work.

British data suggests that long-term unemployment is correlated with a lack of qualifications and limited recent work experience. What is more, those out of the labour market for longer periods of time tend to have unstable employment histories, with often frequent spells of unemployment. This is distinctively different to Sweden but also Germany where many long-term unemployed are out of work for the first time after what has often been a long working life with a strong labour market attachment. These differences correspond with the longer history of relatively higher levels of unemployment in Britain as well as a more deregulated labour market and less employment protection compared with the other two countries (Adnett, 1996). An indicator of these differences is the comparatively shorter average job tenure in the UK (OECD, 1994).

Obstacles, opportunities and incentives

Removing whatever is regarded as an obstacle to employment will create employment opportunities for long-term unemployed people. Some respondents identified structural changes in the economy and labour markets, the overall lack of labour demand and other factors, such as ineffective policies, as major types of barriers to paid work. Others saw long-term unemployed people themselves as partly to blame for their problem. As discussed, this has been related to personal characteristics as well as to assumed counterproductive functions of benefits and policies. Despite the lack of consensus as to the relevance of these factors, there were some obstacles as well as opportunities commonly identified within and across countries.

For example, respondents in all three countries widely accepted that employers preferred applicants who are qualified and experienced and are reluctant to take on young people with low educational qualifications, older workers whose skills they deemed obsolete, applicants with physical or mental health problems or caring responsibilities or those who had been unemployed for a long time. To some extent, interviewees in all countries saw this as a rational and understandable response to a situation characterised by a plentiful supply of applications. However, and perhaps reflecting the more developed notion of social partnership in the two continental countries compared with the higher degree and more entrenched notion of liberalism in Britain, employers' refusal to take on 'problem groups' was much more criticised in Germany and Sweden as an evasion of social responsibility. Some Swedish respondents in particular argued that employers should be made to act more responsibly towards particular sections of long-term unemployed people. They should train young workers, improve the competence of older workers and help with the rehabilitation of those who had suffered accidents and sickness.

The need to tailor measures more to individual needs was the one recommendation made most frequently by respondents in all three countries. This echoes recent EU initiatives (ERGO, 1996) which have advocated a multidimensional approach with specific policy programmes for different groups of long-term unemployed people, including 'support chains' for those with a combination of disadvantages. The need for different types, and sometimes combinations, of support programmes to increase the chance to find a way back to employment was pointed out in all countries, albeit perhaps most frequently by German respondents who stressed the heterogeneous nature of long-term unemployment. While useful for some, training, for example, does not improve the job chances of many who were already relatively highly qualified.

Another common theme was that all three countries called for a much greater involvement of private sector companies in labour market programmes with this being more targeted than hitherto. All three stressed the need for more coordinated response from central and local policy actors. This required specific national improvements, such as increasing the accountability and effectiveness of TECs and LECs in Britain and restructuring principal labour market agencies in Sweden and Germany to allow a more decentralised organisation of national labour market programmes and better cooperation between local employment offices, local authorities and the voluntary sector. Another common theme was the need to link policies directed at improving labour supply with macroeconomic policies able to stimulate labour demand and economic regeneration in particular regions (Gaß et al, 1997; Webster, 1997).

Within a broader policy framework, other options were mentioned such as partial retirement for older workers in Germany or the issue of worksharing in Sweden, where interest is also being shown in the Danish idea of a worker's sabbatical. Proposals for a shorter working week have been popular among some of those on the left in Sweden, particularly women, and seemed to be more intensively discussed there than in either Germany or Britain, which is perhaps an indication of the longer history of mass unemployment in the latter two countries.

All of these ideas can be linked with the stress made in all countries on preventing long-term unemployment. For example, in Britain it was suggested that help should be provided before six months had elapsed to prevent problems setting in and employers from discriminating against applicants. Intervention for those likely to become unemployed for a long time needed to be provided much sooner. However, the difficulty of predicting who will suffer long-term unemployment has been indicated by respondents.

The issue of job placement, often overlooked in the debate on long-term unemployment, deserves to be mentioned. As illustrated in Chapter One, the German special 'placement initiative' in 1995 was remarkable both for the lack of public discussion compared with other programmes and also its relative success. Local employment offices were ordered to target their efforts on long-term unemployed people and to approach local employers directly, irrespective of whether vacancies had been notified or not. While adopting policies across countries is often difficult, similar initiatives could be explored in Britain and Sweden. If implemented, they would represent another sign of a tentative trend towards policy convergence which can be identified across all three countries.

Labour market policies – signs of convergence?

Both Germany and Sweden have shown a greater commitment to employment regulation and public spending on labour market matters.

Sweden has traditionally devoted more resources to active measures than either Germany or Britain, although in the wake of unification, Germany's expenditure was narrowing the gap with Sweden (Adnett, 1996, p 38). National differences in the financial effort and policy direction of labour market programmes have remained largely intact. However, both the review of the literature and interviews with policy community representatives revealed some degree of cross-national convergence in two directions: in Britain, some of the ideas behind recent and traditional German and Swedish labour market programmes seem to have become more acceptable while the two continental countries have moved towards Britain in other respects.

Interviews with respondents in both Sweden and Germany revealed criticism of traditional labour market programmes. These were regarded as insufficiently targeted at the long-term unemployed, although this problem has recently been addressed in both countries (Gaß et al, 1997). What is more, there was no consensus as to the effectiveness of specific programmes. Yet there is still broad support in favour of maintaining the array of labour market measures in Sweden, such as training, work experience for young workers, work relief for older workers and recruitment grants. The same is true for Germany where the government recently started a new round of wage subsidies for employers taking on long-term unemployed people on a non-fixed-term basis. This was welcomed by respondents from across the political spectrum, despite some expected dead-weight losses and substitution effects. Another initiative, compensating employers for some types of non-wage labour costs incurred when taking on long-term unemployed applicants, demonstrates that this approach towards tackling the problem is becoming well established.

In Britain, governments of the 1980s and early 1990s would have staunchly rejected such initiatives as counterproductive since unemployment was largely regarded as a supply-side issue, with a consequent focus on the need for a flexible labour market. Their policies deregulated the labour market and aimed to remove rigidities. The emphasis was on helping individuals with their jobsearch activities and to achieve attachment to the labour market. Accordingly, long-term unemployed people were believed to be primarily in need of guidance and advice, which is the rationale for schemes such as Restart. An evaluation of Restart towards the end of the 1980s concluded that the scheme reduces the length of unemployment by acting as a gateway to a wide range of programmes, services and follow-up actions. While respondents criticised the programme for not significantly improving the situation for women and older workers and also for failing to provide sufficient guidance, it was felt that Restart was effective in keeping up people's jobsearch skills, motivation and contact with the labour market.

Even before the election of New Labour, the preoccupation with exclusively labour-supply policies seemed to have changed. For example, the idea to introduce a limited number of job creation schemes with quotas for disadvantaged workers and long-term unemployed people was endorsed by respondents from both the Labour and the Conservative parties, as well as members of local policy communities, while civil servants considered such schemes expensive and inefficient, bringing substitution and displacement effects. Similar arguments could be made against targeted subsidies for employers which have not played a significant role in the UK, but have now become part of New Labour's attempt to tackle long-term unemployment among younger claimants and those out of the labour market for more than two years (see Finn, 1997).

At the same time as the debate in Britain was shifting, there were signs of growing unease with traditional forms of labour market programmes in Germany and Sweden, especially with regard to their quality and scope of job creation programmes. This was reflected in the interviews undertaken for this study. The main Swedish scheme (ALU) was seen by many respondents as a useful programme, keeping people in touch with the world of work, although many projects were thought to be poor quality, having little intrinsic value. In Germany, respondents feared that many job creation and job placement schemes did not represent a 'bridge' back into employment but merely a temporary interruption of unemployment. Left and environmentalist groups believed temporary job creation and other types of so-called secondary labour market schemes to be the only remaining opportunity for many long-term unemployed to keep in touch with the labour market. However, while they wanted these schemes expanded, German employers and many centre-right politicians feared that a substantial expansion of subsidised labour would crowd out regular types of employment. Echoing demands made by Swedish respondents of similar persuasion, the latter group's preferred solution was a weakening of employment rights, a higher degree of labour flexibility and the payment of lower 'entry wages' for 'disadvantaged jobseekers' such as the long-term unemployed which, they said, would encourage employers to take on more labour. Perhaps indicating some degree of cross-national convergence, both Swedish and German governments and parliamentary commissions have increasingly considered these options.

Labour market policy regimes and patterns of support

British labour market programmes are much more centrally controlled by government ministries and executive agencies compared with the ones in Sweden and Germany. In these countries labour market policies are the responsibility of national semi-autonomous corporatist organisations or boards with regional and local employment offices. A crucial difference between the AMS in Sweden and the FLO in Germany is that the latter is also in charge of unemployment insurance benefits and both labour market programmes and benefits are jointly funded out of earmarked, earnings-related contributions by employees and employers.

These, and other, institutional differences are represented in particular programmes. They provide the framework with which to conceptualise both national policy problems and proposals for solutions. For example, 'Training for Work', a potentially relevant scheme for the long-term unemployed in the UK, can be regarded as a 'residual' type of labour market support. This is because it provides participants with a small addition to their benefits only and, according to interviewees, does not for many participants lead to acquiring qualifications. By contrast, the 'selectivity' of German labour market policy is manifested in the fragmentation of support mechanisms both in terms of types and generosity of maintenance grants for participants as well as administrative separation of responsibilities. While the FLO is, in principle, responsible for all registered unemployed in Germany, there is a bias towards favouring recipients of unemployment insurance benefits. A clear distinction seems to be made between them and those on social assistance and schemes (Leibfried and Tennstedt, 1985).

In both Sweden and Germany local authorities administer and finance social assistance benefits and have acquired a growing role in active labour market programmes due to the rising number of long-term unemployed without any or with insufficient entitlement to insurance benefits. The difference is that in Germany this role has been resented by local authorities which reluctantly, and only as a consequence of financial pressure, began to provide work or placement contracts for some of their unemployed social assistance claimants. This institutional separation of responsibility for long-term unemployed people has been identified as counterproductive. Even FLO employees claimed that federal programmes were too much concentrated on 'their clientele' and that those in need of additional programmes, such as counselling, debt advice, psychological help or help with drug and alcohol addictions, are often left to local authorities or projects in the voluntary sector which might provide work experience, training, advice or job creation places for disadvantaged unemployed people but whose funding base can be precarious. While there is some cooperation between these sectors and local authorities might be subsidised by the FLO or a particular Land, the ad hoc and 'goodwill' basis of this cooperation was widely criticised.

In Sweden, participants in training schemes organised by the AMS receive maintenance grants which, albeit related to previous earnings as in Germany, are on average more generous. Unlike in Germany, unemployed people also have a right to some form of 'active' labour market support and communes are obliged to provide the long-term unemployed with temporary employment. This is perhaps the reason for the apparently less entrenched demarcation between 'better' nationally-run programmes and 'inferior' schemes organised by local authorities. In this respect the Swedish system seems to be more comprehensive, although Swedish respondents called for even closer cooperation between local authorities, AMS, trade unions and the private sector.

Regimes of unemployment compensation

Even more than national labour market programmes, unemployment compensation systems can be conceptualised as representing different welfare regimes (Ploug and Kvist, 1996), as 'residual', 'selective' or 'comprehensive' (as discussed in the introductory chapter). In Sweden and Germany most unemployed people receive either earnings-related unemployment insurance or unemployment assistance benefits, leaving a small, albeit growing, proportion of unemployed claiming social assistance. As discussed in Chapters One and Three, even for long-term unemployed people insurance benefits represent an important form of financial support in both countries since the standard benefit duration can be extended for certain claimant groups, depending on age and contribution record (Germany), or, indicating a somewhat easier access, on age or participation in a labour market programme (Sweden).

This contrasts markedly with the situation in Britain where only a small minority of unemployed people receive insurance benefits. It is also one of the few European countries without a particular form of unemployment assistance benefit (Reissert, 1994). Both German and Swedish unemployment benefit and unemployment assistance rates exceed the flat-rate unemployment insurance benefit in the UK, although the means-tested top-ups from Income Support and Housing and Council

Tax benefits could raise the net replacement ratios for low paid workers to a level comparable to Germany and Sweden.

These differences in benefit levels and principles became evident in interviews with the national policy players through their perceptions of the obstacles and barriers to combating long-term unemployment. For example, the 'residual egalitarian' character of unemployment compensation is manifest in the widespread use of means-testing which implies that individuals as well as families dependent on Income Support, including all long-term unemployed in receipt of social security transfers, can stand to lose much in means-tested and passported benefits if they take a low-paid job. This background helps to give an understanding of the comparatively extensive academic and political debate about the problem of the unemployment and poverty traps (Walker, 1994; Shaw et al, 1996) reflected in the relative importance British respondents devoted to the topic of work incentives.

In Germany, the vast majority of the unemployed were regarded as keen to move off benefit and into paid work, not least since employment continued to be seen as 'socially desirable' and conferring an 'identity' in German society. More importantly, and reflecting the more differential or 'selective' character of social support for the unemployed compared with Britain, this was particularly true for those receiving unemployment insurance benefits. This indicates a broad agreement with traditional welfare principles, such as the notion of 'deserved' benefits as deferred wages based on contributions (Clasen, 1994a). Concerns about benefit abuse or their potentially adverse impact on work incentives were not entirely absent but directed mainly at a minority of unemployed, those in receipt of means-tested social assistance.

In accordance with the higher degree of 'universality' within the Swedish welfare state and its more 'comprehensive' unemployment compensation system, a higher proportion of unemployed people receive generally higher insurance-based benefits than is the case in Germany. As in Germany, there was no moral panic about the effect of benefits on work incentives. However, unlike in Germany traditional welfare principles in particular, and the notion of encompassing and continuing support on a high level were criticised. For example, there was some support for the idea of reducing benefits to a lower percentage over time. There was also suspicion among some that the combination of benefit level, duration and labour market measures would lock some people into long-term unemployment. However, this was not consensual since many respondents pointed to structural labour market problems which had to be blamed for the level of long-term unemployment rather than a combination of welfare support and behavioural factors.

Focusing on the relationship between the welfare state, paid and unpaid labour, Sweden has been characterised as a 'weak male breadwinner' country (Lewis, 1992) due to the extensive availability of subsidised public childcare arrangements and parental leave arrangements (Esping-Andersen, 1990; Esping-Andersen et al, 1993). This makes it more feasible to combine paid employment with raising children than in 'strong male breadwinner' countries such as Germany and Britain. Although different in many factors affecting patterns of gender division of paid and unpaid work (such as tax and transfer systems), in neither Germany nor the UK is public provision of care for children as readily available as in Nordic countries. These national differences were in accordance with respondents' perceptions which pointed to the difficulties lone parents face in finding work in Britain and Germany.

Long-term unemployment and social exclusion

Not only has the term social exclusion been applied to groups other than the long-term unemployed – the low paid and ethnic minorities may be socially excluded yet remain in employment (Silver, 1994/95; Engbergsen and Timmer, 1993) – but it may not always be applicable to this group. In Germany, Kronauer (1993) emphasised the way in which exclusion might be resisted by long-term unemployed people through relying on their own resources. In Sweden, Svedberg (1995) saw the long-term unemployed as marginal rather than excluded since many of them subsequently re-entered the labour market. Similarly, in Britain, Walker (1995) has pointed out that poverty and social exclusion are something which people experience for a period of time. This means that more people suffer poverty than is implied by a snapshot picture taken at one point in time. It also means that those for whom poverty is brought about by long-term unemployment, may be reabsorbed into the labour market – although in many cases remaining on its margins.

The link between long-term unemployment and poverty was emphasised more in Britain than in the other two countries. What is more, there was a tendency in the British literature, and also among respondents from that country, to point to a spatial dimension in the problem of long-term unemployment. Deindustrialisation had left large areas lacking jobs. The social problems which subsequently arose acted as a disincentive to private investors. Local authorities were restricted by central government from taking action. While many long-term unemployed people might continue to enjoy social and familial relationships, it was thought that the complex of disadvantages faced in deprived areas were such as to leave people excluded and powerless. It is surely no coincidence that only in Britain had there been a debate about the existence of an underclass.

The respondents in all three countries recognised that the longer unemployment continues and the higher the percentage of the population affected, the more severe the consequences for individuals, communities and society as a whole. The literature confirmed that many long-term unemployed people can lose their motivation to work and suffer psychologically and physically, that the families of long-term unemployed people are more prone to break up and that the temptation to cope by resorting to drink, drugs and/or crime is greater. It was widely accepted that many long-term unemployed people suffered from social isolation, depression and insecurity.

The prospect of riots and social unrest were real fears expressed by those interviewed in Britain. In Germany, the risk of political radicalisation as one possible outcome of persistent long-term unemployment was mentioned. Swedish respondents commented on a range of social and economic costs and some were worried about the threat from 'darker forces' within society which tended to blame immigrants for the unemployment experienced by 'native' Swedes.

While respondents recognised that long-term unemployment could mean a substantial reduction in living standards, German, and also Swedish, interviewees were confident that it would not necessarily lead to poverty and marginalisation because of the provision of vocational training and comparatively generous social security benefits. A principal argument for active labour market policies was precisely that they prevented people from becoming cut off from the rest of society. Reflecting the widely-held notion of a relatively closed labour market in Germany, 'labour market exclusion' rather than 'social exclusion' was regarded as the more immediate problem for many German long-term unemployed. It was thought that the emphasis placed on the work ethic in Sweden and Germany made the stigma of labour market exclusion that much harder to bear. However, overall German respondents felt that their welfare and labour market measures prevented the type of social exclusion that could be found elsewhere such as in Britain and in the US. Swedish respondents made the same point but still saw themselves as distinct from the rest of Europe.

Conclusions

Part One has shown that similarities between welfare regimes and responses to unemployment in Sweden and Germany appear to be greater than those between Britain and either of the other two countries. This goes beyond having more regulated labour markets and involving social partners in labour market policies. Concerns about possible disincentive effects of unemployment benefits and labour market schemes, for example, seem to be much more extensive in Britain. The form of unemployment compensation (insurance rather than means-tested benefits) appears to be of importance in this respect. Similarly, despite possible displacement effects and a sometimes small impact on the overall level of unemployment, there was a broad agreement in both Sweden and Germany that such labour market policies as job creation and wage subsidy programmes have a role to play, even if only to keep long-term unemployed people in touch with labour markets and prevent processes of social marginalisation. A preliminary conclusion for Germany and Sweden seems to be that while labour market policies might not create or even lead to 'real' jobs, they play an important role in maintaining employability, morale and motivation. In Britain, the lack of faith in state intervention, which has characterised the dominant New Right thinking, has led to a residual role for such schemes and a stronger focus on the actions and responsibilities of unemployed individuals.

However, a closer look revealed not only cross-national similarities but also a trend of convergence in policy directions in labour market programmes. Britain has tentatively shifted towards ideas such as targeted wage subsidies for employers who take on long-term unemployed while Germany and Sweden have become more willing to listen to suggestions made by employers and others in favour of reducing labour laws and introducing lower 'entry wages' for certain groups of jobseekers, such as the long-term unemployed. However, so far policy implementation allowing for greater flexibility in Germany and Sweden does not point to the adoption of a deregulated low wage economy as in Britain.

In Germany and Sweden there was concern about growing evidence of social exclusion and society becoming more divided in the future. However, there was a preference for using terms such as labour market exclusion or marginalisation in the belief that their social programmes prevented the extreme manifestations of social exclusion which characterised countries such as Britain. In Britain, the debates on the underclass and social exclusion concentrated more on how such phenomena were to be explained rather on whether they existed.

With regard to institutional structures, types and principles of both labour market policies and, perhaps even more so, national systems of social security support, a distinction was made between 'residual', 'selective' and 'comprehensive' characters of British, German and Swedish support mechanisms for the long-term unemployed. Despite cross-national similarities, it became evident in interviews with policy respondents that such a categorisation provided frames of reference for conceptualising problems and solutions to these. In this respect, there seems to be some justification for conceptualising distinct unemployment support regimes not only from above or 'without' (Reissert, 1994; Ploug and Kvist, 1996) but also from 'within'. Bringing in the views of long-term unemployed people themselves, Part Two will put this claim to the test.

Part Two

Interviews with long-term unemployed people

EIGHT

Long-term unemployed people in Germany

Introduction

Interviews with long-term unemployed people were conducted in Hildesheim in the Land of Lower Saxony, situated about 30 kilometres south of Hanover. Services and retailing are important areas in this city, which has a population of 110,000. Yet in 1994, more than one third of the labour force was employed in manufacturing and there were 13 companies with more than 500 employees. In the same year the unemployment rate was somewhat higher than the average for Germany (old Länder) and slightly higher than the average for Lower Saxony. The rate for long-term unemployment was about the same as for Germany.

As indicated in the introduction to this book, access to the interviewees came from two sources: a training agency which provides different types of programmes for those out of work for longer periods and the local social assistance office, which agreed to allow access mainly (but not exclusively) to claimants who were, or were about to start, a so-called 'help-to-work' programme (see Chapter One). Correspondingly, respondents can be divided into those who received social assistance solely or additionally (seven respondents) and those who received a maintenance grant for the duration of a training period. The latter can be paid either by the respective pension or accident insurance scheme for recipients who undergo some type of work rehabilitation programme after a previous work-related illness or accident, or by the unemployment insurance office. This office can 'invite' claimants of unemployment benefit, and especially unemployment assistance, to take part in a 'suitable' training or retraining scheme. The maintenance grant is related to former earnings but is usually higher than unemployment compensation, thus acting as an incentive to accept a training 'offer'.

Table 8: Household types of the German unemployed respondents

Single	7
Lone parent	5
Couple	4
Couple with children	8
Total	24

In total, 24 long-term unemployed people (18 male, 6 female) were interviewed plus four partners. Four of the six females were lone parents and two were living with a partner and children. The household types are outlined in Table 8.

The majority of the respondents were German. Two of them had moved from the former GDR to the western part of the country after unification in 1990. Two interviewees were ethnic Germans from Kasachstan who settled in Germany in the early 1990s. Two others came from Yugoslavia and Poland and another from Turkey, the latter having moved to Germany in 1970. Typically for Germany (see Kleinman, 1994) the vast majority of respondents lived in privately-rented accommodation, often supported by either housing benefit or social assistance which covers the rent.

Education and employment histories

Despite some degree of flexibility between the levels, the German school system remains three-tiered (Wallace, 1994). To successfully complete the Hauptschule pupils are required to have undergone nine years of schooling and achieved the necessary grades. The intermediary Realschule is intellectually more demanding and requires 10 years of schooling. Successful completion of Gymnasium education enables pupils to attend university after at least 13 years of schooling. The majority of the respondents in our sample (14) attended the Hauptschule and most of them (10) completed their education successfully. Six respondents attended the Realschule and two acquired the necessary qualifications for university education.

Only three respondents started work directly after school or did not complete their post-school training. By comparison, 18 respondents started and successfully completed apprenticeships, which were accompanied by state-provided topic-related education and usually lasted three years. The most frequently mentioned occupations were bakery (4), car mechanics (4), bricklaying and roofing (2) and plumbing and gas fitting (2). However, many of those respondents subsequently worked in other areas and often underwent further training or retraining. A typical path involved working in the chosen area for some time after completing an apprenticeship, a break because of national service, followed by a move into less skilled but better paid work in one of the bigger companies in the region (such as Bosch, Blaupunkt or Volkswagen), to work away on some type of construction job or to retrain in a more skilled area (electronics, telecommunications).

The vast majority of respondents had been unemployed between one and three years following a working life which, although in different companies and different types of jobs, had nevertheless consisted of relatively continuous employment since leaving training. Most respondents considered the current period of unemployment as their first 'serious' one compared with previous spells which had generally lasted not more than 'a few weeks', and which were sometimes caused by leaving voluntarily due to the knowledge or certainty of another job 'round the corner' or training programme to go to. A work-related illness or injury was for almost half of the respondents the cause for 'real' absence from regular work and the beginning of long-term unemployment.

The major exception to this pattern was the group of respondents who were lone parents. Three out of these five respondents had been out of gainful employment for more than 10 years and one even for more than 20 years, although having an odd job on the side was common. These long absences from standard types of employment were either the result of a conscious decision not to seek full-time employment while their children were young, or because it proved impossible to combine bringing up children with the requirements of continuing previous employment (due to lack of childcare facilities, school hours and so on).

> "This changing shift-work system made it impossible for me to look after my son. Thus, since his birth I have done only odd jobs, generally on a temporary basis." (male lone parent)

Long-term unemployment and its impacts

Attitudes towards unemployment

There were two typical reactions concerning initial attitudes to unemployment. Some respondents referred to the experience of being off work involuntarily as a "shock" or even "catastrophe" and remembered feelings of "worthlessness", "uselessness" and "inferiority" after what had often been decades of continuous work. Others, especially those who suffered a work-related accident or illness, were initially more relaxed, hoping that the interruption from work would only be brief. However, when the period of recuperation or rehabilitation was over and not succeeded by a return to the previous company but redundancy, feelings of "boredom of being at home all day" or even "resignation" set in.

Adverse effects of the lack of paid work on respondents' self-esteem became more dominant the longer unemployment lasted. Feelings of "inferiority" and "degradation" and loss of "self-worth" were associated with unemployment. The importance of regular work also became obvious in other respects. Many missed the social contact with colleagues and being able to tell partners and friends about "what happened at work". A few respondents pursued activities such as voluntary work in the community or in sports clubs or attended adult education courses. These were not considered as equivalent to the way in which regular work structured daily life.

> "As unemployed you are quickly in a certain routine, every day is the same. Sunday is no different from Monday...." (single male)

Irrespective of age or family status, many respondents considered themselves to be "active" people who were experiencing serious difficulties coping with "sitting at home all day". A male single person expressed what was claimed by many:

> "I am not the type who can sit around, putting my hands in my lap, switching on the TV at 9am in the morning and simply waiting to see what will happen."

Some respondents claimed to know of people who "didn't mind" being out of work but steadfastly distanced themselves from them.

Impact on family and social life

Five respondents claimed that long-term unemployment had put a strain on the relationship with their partner and family due to the increased tension or frustration it caused. One relationship had actually broken down because of unemployment and one respondent had difficulties with the idea that he was unemployed while his wife was earning the family's wage. Nevertheless, a majority emphasised the positive aspect of having somebody to talk to about their situation.

Perhaps surprisingly, many respondents denied that their long-term unemployment had adverse social consequences for their children and even pointed to positive aspects, such as having more time for them and being able to supervise homework. Compared with their friends, missing out on holiday trips was one negative aspect mentioned. However, lone parents in particular made use of the social welfare office which pays for school trips and welfare organisations such as Caritas (see Lorenz, 1994) which can cover the costs of summer holiday trips for children of social assistance recipients.

Welcoming these options, respondents criticised the lack of information about them. While some social assistance recipients chose not to inform themselves about their rights or were reluctant to claim these and other school-related expenses, some (and in particular lone parents) made a conscious use of them. Discrimination against pupils whose parents are unemployed was not regarded as a problem. However, two lone parents receiving social assistance appeared to be aware of such a potential problem and emphasised the need to dress both themselves and their children so that they would not appear to be any different from other parents and school children. As one of them put it:

> "My son attends the Gymnasium where they, how can I say this, put an emphasis on clothes. I don't want him to be disadvantaged in this respect or having to listen to ... 'ha, ha they are social assistance recipients'. I would not like that." (female lone parent)

However, parents pointed out that brandname trainers or the latest fashion jeans, which were most desired by teenage children, were beyond their financial scope. Lone parents in particular (with longer periods of unemployment) claimed that their children coped with this restriction relatively well since they were used to the situation and had learned to save up pocket money for such expenditure. A female lone parent said:

> "It doesn't matter what he sees in town. When I tell him, look I would like to buy this for you now but it is impossible at the moment then he understands. He does not moan or grumble ... he knows that next time when I have some money spare he might get it."

Others have more problems coping with the lack of money as far as their children are concerned:

> "I was ashamed. I couldn't buy them anything. We couldn't go to the cinema or to MacDonalds. It wasn't easy for me to look the children in the eye." (male partner of a couple with children)

As coping strategies, parents most frequently stated that they would buy clothes from second-hand shops and also relied on family and friends who gave their children some money at Christmas and birthdays and sometimes contributed to the purchase of more expensive items such as computers, TVs or hi-fis.

As far as the participation in other spheres of life is concerned, there were some signs that respondents had retreated from activities previously considered to be normal such as going out with partners or friends for a drink or a meal, strolling through the town to windowshop, going bowling or to see a football match. Almost all respondents had cut back the frequency of these leisure activities, mainly due to less spending power which made it more difficult to pay for a round of drinks, for example. However, three respondents (two of whom were on social assistance) mentioned that they had made a conscious decision to go out with friends for a meal, the pub or the cinema at least once a month "in order to get out and about" and mix with people. While some respondents said they had retreated from friendships and had fewer friends than before, the majority claimed that unemployment had made no difference and that their friendships had not suffered.

> "I cannot claim that friends disappeared just because of my unemployment. On the contrary, they support us from time to time, inviting us for a meal so that we get out of the house now and again." (male partner of a couple with children)

Family members, especially those of lone parents, were generally portrayed as sympathetic and supportive, relating the fact of being off work with the need to look after children. Hardly any respondent felt accused or blamed for their situation by friends or relatives. One comment about former colleagues who would now "avoid contact" was exceptional. More typical were two indirect consequences of unemployment on friendships: feelings of awkwardness at not being able to contribute to conversations which were often about "what happened at work" and embarrassment when invited for a meal by well-meaning friends or relatives.

Respondents believed that less sympathetic and more prejudiced views towards unemployed people came from society as a whole:

> "There are these stupid comments, ... he is unemployed, is that really necessary? etc. But nobody wants to know about the circumstances, ... why somebody is unemployed." (male partner of a couple with children)

A number of respondents stressed the fact that it is much easier to talk about being on a training programme than introducing oneself as being unemployed:

> "... long-term unemployment is often seen as a blemish. People say, actually he does not really want to work." (female partner of a couple with children)

Others try not to make their status too obvious in public:

> "It starts already when you want to go to the zoo for example. For a reduced ticket you have to present your unemployment certificate which I don't like to do publicly. At some point you feel a bit strange being unemployed." (single male)

Material impact

The financial situation unemployed people in Germany find themselves in varies enormously depending on the types of benefit payments they are receiving. These vary from earnings-related unemployment insurance, unemployment assistance, maintenance grants for people participating in training courses, or means-tested social assistance (see Chapter One).

Many respondents regarded their previous in-work income as at least "normal" or for some "really good".

> "We had no reason to complain." (male partner of a couple with children)

> "My earnings were pretty good, I would say, I was able to afford everything, two holidays a year, car, motorcycle. Really good." (single male)

The reduction of disposable income due to unemployment felt like "a jump into cold water" according to a male partner of a couple with children. Even those in receipt of unemployment benefit commented on difficulties in adjusting and the need to stick to a household plan, to look out for bargains and to monitor expenditure much more carefully in order to be able to manage. (The level of unemployment benefit can represent less than half of previous net earnings since certain payments such as overtime or bonuses are disregarded in the calculation of benefit levels.) A female lone parent claiming social assistance argued that:

> "... there are always problems. It is never enough. The situation overall is difficult."

Criticisms about the inadequate level or frequency of payments within the social assistance system which are meant to cover costs for items such as washing machines, cookers or redecorating were more frequent.

The single most frequently mentioned item foregone due to unemployment was a holiday trip. One respondent resorted to visiting relatives, another one made use of a friend's place in the Alps and a third stopped going abroad. The rest had not been away on holiday for the duration of their unemployment. Other restrictions included not being able to eat out, to go to the theatre or to keep a car. For many, unemployment also meant being forced to look out for bargains and going shopping in special discount shops. Some respondents mentioned that banks refused overdrafts and that they had to return credit cards.

> "When I go to a new bank and can prove that I have a certain amount of monthly earnings, I will be treated differently from somebody on half the amount as unemployment benefit. Of course the bank knows that after one year the income will go down." (single male)

However, even some social assistance claimants said that they could manage relatively well with the financial implications of unemployment. Lone parents in particular stressed that they had learned to live with the little money available.

> "Apart from luxuries we have got everything. OK we cannot go away on holidays and we haven't got a car. But I think we don't really need one either." (female lone parent)

Others also appeared to manage because they received a training allowance which was higher than previous social security benefits.

> "OK there are financial restrictions, let us say, but for a normal life there is enough. Definitely." (female partner of a couple with children)

Debts are a frequent problem, albeit in varying degrees. Apart from overdrafts, not one of the single people among the respondents (none of whom was on social assistance) appeared to have had any debts and some stressed the importance of not getting into debt because that would "only be the start of real problems" (single male). Some couples with children had similar attitudes and were anxious to remain debt-free. However, more than half of this group were in debt for amounts between around DM1,000 and DM10,000 (£400 and £4,000). One respondent owed DM50,000 to the bank which translated into a monthly repayment of DM750 (£300). However, most respondents did not associate debts with unemployment since they acquired them when they had been in work. This was different for lone parents for whom the long periods spent out of the labour market were generally accompanied with being in debt. Four out of five of them owed money to relatives but also to banks, mail order companies and even social security offices who had overpaid them in the past. Often repayments were relatively small and debts old, up to 15 years, for household goods such as TVs. Many of the debtors claimed that because of repayment problems they were now blacklisted and therefore ineligible, for example, to open a bank account. Some had been visited by the bailiffs.

Attitudes to benefits and other sources of income

As mentioned in the introduction to the book, the two main types of income for most of the long-term unemployed Germans (or immigrants to Germany) involved in this study were either a training allowance or social assistance. Only a few received unemployment assistance or benefit. Attitudes towards social security benefits differ strongly by the benefit type. Receipt of means-tested and locally provided social assistance was accompanied by feelings of shame and stigma.

> "I mean there is a difference. If somebody asked me: What do you do? I don't do anything at the moment. I see, you are with the employment office.... Which is bad enough to admit. But I live off social assistance, which I do not mention. I am always just unemployed,

> which is not the full truth.... The fact that I live off social assistance, nobody needs to know." (male lone parent)

Another respondent had problems admitting to her children that she received social assistance:

> "My children have known about it only for a short while. I always used to say I have got to go the office. It could as well have been the employment office. I never said welfare office." (female lone parent)

The stigma associated with social assistance was also reflected in comments made by respondents not actually receiving this type of benefit:

> "I would not like to apply for social assistance. Definitely not. That is really bad." (male partner of a couple with children)

> "Yes, those on social assistance, or alcoholics, or something like that, you fall deeper and deeper." (male partner of a couple with children)

Applying for social assistance for the first time was described by many as being associated with "bad feelings" and difficulties to "bring oneself" to go to the office (single male). However, a small number of mainly younger recipients experienced fewer problems. A lone parent was grateful for having been told by social assistance staff that she was allowed the time to "look after my child – I did not have to look for work". Another interviewee complained that he had to give up his car in order to be eligible for social assistance but generally thought it was "great that something like it exists" (male partner of a couple with children). Another did not feel discriminated against since "where we live there are many others also on social assistance" (male partner of a couple without children).

Attitudes towards staff administering social assistance varied. Some had no complaints and spoke of friendly encounters and helpful personnel. Others complained about the lack of knowledge officers had about the system and their failure to inform about the ability to claim, for example, subsidies towards TV licences, telephone line rentals, insurance premiums and holidays for children. One respondent said she would not have claimed those things if it had not been for friends who pointed out her rights. Another frequent criticism was the constant need to apply for these subsidies and, at times, being turned down for such things as washing machines or replacement of wardrobes which was described as cumbersome and associated with feelings of embarrassment.

> "I don't feel that great always having to go there in order to claim for something I need.... I know it is my right but I feel a little embarrassed, I don't know, I cannot cope with it." (female lone parent)

Overall, there was a clear intention to move off social assistance or never to have to reapply.

> "I would never want to be a social assistance recipient again." (female lone parent)

> "I'd prefer to work for it [an income] myself ... if I am in regular work and receive an income then I know what it is for." (female lone parent)

> "You are dependent on social assistance but what you want is to work for yourself, .. .in order to have some control.... To have your own money, that is best." (male partner of a couple without children)

Feelings about receiving insurance-based unemployment benefits were different. Although some respondents considered benefit levels as "mean" or too low, others thought them to be adequate: "You cannot grumble", said one single male. The principle of equivalence between earnings-related contributions and benefits was generally accepted as a fair one.

> "I think it is OK to receive unemployment benefit when out of work because you have paid in. As for higher benefits, if I would say I'd like more money, that would also mean I would have to contribute more once being back in work in order for others to get higher benefits." (single male)

Respondents receiving unemployment assistance were comparatively less content. Many complained about the insufficient level of the benefit and one person about the fact that it was not based on his previous earnings but, after a work-related accident, on likely future earnings in a different occupation. Some former recipients felt they were forced to accept an offer to participate in a training scheme in order not to be suspended from benefit receipt (see also below).

Those most satisfied with their financial situation were respondents currently on a training scheme and receiving an earnings-related training allowance equal to, and sometimes even higher than, unemployment benefit. One respondent was able to repay outstanding debts and another claimed he was "able to live well off the allowance – I'll be happy if I received the same amount when in work" (single male). Nevertheless, even unemployment benefits and training allowances were generally regarded as second to earnings:

> "Although I know I have paid in, I only take this money because I have to. But nice it isn't.... I want to earn my own money." (male partner of a couple with children)

Other sources of income were mainly from family and from work on the side. Family members were much more likely to lend small sums of interest-free money rather than give out regular or irregular payments which did not have to be paid back. Even relatively well-off siblings were either not asked for, or unwilling to give, money to respondents which was not a loan. The children of one lone parent were an exception since they had been generously and frequently supported by relatives.

Six respondents, three of them single, managed to make small but regular monthly savings. One respondent even had some money invested in property and longer-term investment plans. Despite being on social assistance, one lone parent managed to save small amounts due to her job on the side, as the first DM200 earnings per month were disregarded from benefit calculations. Six other respondents relied on some small earnings from regular or irregular, but declared, jobs. Monthly earnings of between DM100 and DM600 for cleaning work for up to 12 hours a week was not uncommon. Other casual types of work included gardening, caretaking, but also software programming. Two respondents claimed that they would have liked to do some work on the side but were unable to find adequate work or suitable working hours. With respect to his medical condition, one unemployed man pointed out:

> "When I was still in employment I had more opportunity to work in the black economy. Those times have gone." (single male)

Escaping unemployment

One of the most striking features of the interviews was that no respondent can be said to have made a conscious decision in favour of what sometimes might be considered as a hedonistic lifestyle beyond waged work. All of them had a clear intention to return to regular employment, if at all possible. Unemployment was not considered to be a viable alternative by any interviewee, partly because of a reduced standard of living but also for a number of other factors such as boredom at home, the lack of daily structures and a feeling of being left out when friends talk about work. Contacts with colleagues was another important aspect.

> "It is simply a different thing if you have a job and you get on well with colleagues and talk about things. It really gives you a buzz." (female partner of a couple)

> "The main thing is to be among people ... if you are always at home, the friends at work, I mean I want to work mainly because of the money, but also so that I am among people and to get out of the house." (single male)

A greater sense of independence due to a higher income was an important motive, albeit not merely in order to have a higher living standard. A "secure", "steady and reliable income" as well as having "your own money in your pocket rather than being dependent on somebody else, such as the welfare office" were two other typical comments. Some respondents emphasised the need to work in order to feel better. For example, one male partner of a couple with children said:

> "I really would like to work, also because it has become a need somehow. You are away for the day and in the evening much more balanced, also within the family. I have noticed that, when I was ill and unemployed afterwards, I was more irritated."

Perhaps indicative of the German insurance-based social security system, the prospect of a public retirement pension proved to be another important work incentive, even for younger respondents:

> "I just think, one day I would like to receive a retirement pension which I would not be entitled to if I lived permanently on social assistance." (male partner of a couple without children)

To be in paid employment for a male lone parent meant that:

> "... my contributions to health insurance and pension insurance would be normal once again, rather than [being] the minimum compulsory contributions paid by the welfare office."

Attitudes towards training and work programmes

As explained earlier, a number of respondents in the sample were currently on training or work rehabilitation courses, often, but not exclusively, after a time out of work due to illness or accident. Others, who were receiving social assistance benefits, were participating in, or about to start, a 'help-to-work' programme under the auspices of the local authority. Many of those in the latter group were lone parents who had not been in regular employment for long periods of time.

The 'help-to-work' programmes generally started with a period of four hours work per day for three months during which participants received a small addition to their social assistance benefit. This was followed by a work contract with regular remuneration for a normal eight-hour working day for a period of usually one year. There were two typical responses to the prospect of such a programme being offered. Some welcomed it as an opportunity:

> "It was superb. I really wanted to work again. I was fed up with being at home. Also, my son is old enough now. He's got his own interests." (female lone parent)

The temporary nature of the employment was not a deterrent:

> "Maybe I will be lucky and my contract will be extended. If not, I can apply for other jobs. With one year's work experience I should have a better chance. If not, I can go to the employment office and be trained further." (female lone parent)

Others were more critical. Another, older, lone parent was not happy about the level of payment she would receive and the prospect of losing a 'secure job' on the side and, she added:

> "... the small amount of unemployment benefit I can expect afterwards means I will have to reapply for social assistance anyway again." (female lone parent)

The same criticism was made by another female lone parent who felt she was pressurised into "compulsory work" by the welfare office which was only interested in saving expenditure and passing on costs to the employment office.

A total of 15 respondents were taking part in rehabilitation or retraining programmes in areas as diverse as electronics, computer programming and forklift-truck driving. Of these, 12 were happy to receive a higher income (training allowance) or to have prevented a drop in benefit level. They believed the programme might improve their job chances, not least because of a three months guaranteed trial work period, which was to follow the actual retraining itself, paid for by the employment office or the pension fund:

> "I consider the work trial period as my only remaining chance to get back into employment." (single male)

Other positive aspects of the training related to feelings of personal well-being and the social status conferred:

> "After having been here the whole day I come home and feel calmer, more balanced. It gives you something to do." (male partner of a couple with children)

> "You can proudly claim: I am back at college again. Of course, people know it is subsidised by the employment office but you will find that it is easier to say you are a student than to admit you are unemployed." (single male)

However, of the 15 taking part in these programmes three were more critical. They felt the training was irrelevant, did not take account of individual circumstances and was unlikely to improve their job chances. They believed that the programme's rationale was merely to manipulate the unemployment statistics and that the trainers lacked motivation. Most participants were believed to take part only so that they received a higher benefit or to prevent a benefit suspension. Many were leaving frustrated before the end of the course. One respondent, a single male, commented:

> "The way in which the employment office is mindlessly wasting money is really shocking."

Seeking work

Respondents generally pursued a variety of jobseeking strategies. Most important for almost all of them was responding to job offers advertised in newspapers: "I check the paper each Saturday for jobs", said a male partner of a couple without children. 'Word of mouth' appeared to be particularly relevant for six respondents who explicitly emphasised the support and information they received from friends and family about potential jobs. Speculative letters, phone calls or visits to potential employers were also common. "I'd rather go directly to the company and ask in their office", said one single male. By contrast, private job agencies were hardly used, mainly because the jobs available were generally of a temporary nature, often for a few weeks only or were below the earnings threshold for social insurance:

> "You receive DM580 and later in life you don't get a pension. That is also important." (female partner of a couple without children)

Support for jobsearch

All respondents were registered with the public employment office. Some had given up any attempt to find work with the help of the office but most were still in regular contact, hoping to be offered suitable vacancies. However, complaints about the lack of advice and information were common:

> "In my opinion the advice given was deficient. What I needed to know I read in brochures." (single male)

Some respondents claimed to have been given outdated information:

> "Twice they have told me about vacancies which had already been filled weeks before. It is incredible." (male lone parent)

Other criticisms concerned the lack of effort made to place claimants in work or to refuse retraining courses to those aged above 40:

> "He said to me:You are 45 years old. What do you expect? He said that quite frankly." (male partner of a couple with children)

A 41-year-old former plumber who, after a work-related accident, was looking for work which was physically less strenuous claimed:

> "The employment office told me: it is impossible to place you ... the deciding factor was my age."

Taking part in a rehabilitation programme, the same person explained:

> "For a retraining course I was considered to be too old. This here is a reintegration programme. Just to check what I am still capable of doing."

The couple from Kasachstan was an exception: "Everybody was very polite and we were treated in a nice and pleasant way". More common were descriptions of staff as condescending and impolite and treating jobseekers in an anonymous and insensitive way, "just like a number", said one female lone parent. Some who have had contacts with both the social assistance office and the employment office, stressed the better and more personal service provided by the former.

Respondents did not feel particularly that they were being checked up on by the employment office.

> "Just to go there once in two months. Why not? Nothing else to do. You just go, wait for two hours, get your stamp and go home again." (male partner of a couple with children)

Unemployed social assistance recipients felt even less controlled:

> "I checked up on them more than they did on me." (female lone parent)

> "I feel a little abandoned by the employment office. They send me a piece of paper once a year. Are you still interested in finding work? If I didn't respond they would take me out of their computer. If that's all, I don't know." (male lone parent)

Obstacles to employment

Unrealistic wage expectations do not seem to be an obstacle in the attempt to get back into work. Only one highly-qualified respondent was hoping for earnings higher than his previous in-work income because of additional training he had undergone since then. The majority emphasised a readiness to accept wages much lower than previous earnings:

> "I cannot ask for a plumber's hourly wage of say DM22, which would be normal nowadays. I cannot expect anything like that. Not after having been out of that business for 15 years." (male lone parent)

Hourly wages as low as DM12 for working as a night watchman were regarded as "acceptable" and one respondent was even willing to accept DM10. The main criterion for wage expectations was to increase the overall household income to a level which should allow for a "normal life", to cover essential expenditure, including bills, and, for many, to save a little for holidays. Expectations of earnings at or below half average earnings were typical. At most, respondents were hoping for 20% above their current benefit level and at least for as much as their current income:

> "I would say yes to a job if I knew that I would be able to keep it and it was at the same level as my unemployment benefit." (male partner of a couple with children)

Recipients of social assistance hoped to find regular work with an income so that, in the words of one male lone parent:

> "I don't need any addition form social assistance, housing benefit or anything like that."

Respondents' restrictions and limits regarding working hours and the type of work they were seeking were also nothing out of the ordinary. Some were willing to accept any working time. "I do early and late shifts, weekend work. I don't mind", said one female lone parent. Others were less flexible as far as working hours or time to travel to work were concerned:

> "My marriage broke up not least because I was away from home so much. I used to travel 120 miles each day." (male partner of a couple with children)

Only a few respondents explicitly hoped to be able to find work which was "interesting" or "qualified". One respondent, a single male, commented:

> "The idea of still having to do monotonous work at my age would be hard to accept. I would run away if I was on an assembly line."

Some respondents set limits to the type of job they were seeking and many acknowledged that it was impossible to return to their former type of job as a consequence of a work-related accident or injury. Former bricklayers and bakers in their early 40s were now seeking work as caretakers, porters or watchmen, either on a full- or a part-time basis.

The most frequently mentioned obstacles to finding employment were caring responsibilities, disabilities and age levels. Lone parents pointed out that bringing up children and pursuing regular employment proved difficult due to lack of childcare facilities, school hours and school holidays or employment which required shift work or a lengthy journey to and from work. One male lone parent said:

> "It is always the crucial question, it always starts with lone parenthood."

Generally, lone parents only started to seek more regular or full-time employment once children were older (the ages of 10 and 13 were mentioned) and were more independent and also pursued regular afternoon activities (such as sports clubs, school help, visiting friends in the neighbourhood). However, even then there were still difficulties in having work:

> "Children can become ill. If he has chickenpox, for example, I cannot ask just anybody to look after him. I would have to do that myself. Well, if I mention that at the interview they will say: 'You will hear from us'." (male lone parent)

A total of 11 respondents suffered from work-related accidents or injuries. Typical were slipped discs and other chronic back problems. They had to restrict themselves to certain types of work which, for example, would allow them to sit down periodically or be exempt from lifting heavy goods. One male partner of a couple with children commented:

> "This is a major obstacle. I am not allowed to lift more than 10 kilograms. Bending down is not that healthy either."

Depending on their size, German companies are obliged to employ a certain number of workers with disabilities. However, while that might improve the chances for some jobseekers, it also creates uncertainty. A female partner of a couple with children said:

> "With one company you hope they want to fill their disability quota and with the other having some sort of physical restriction is an immediate blemish. You just don't know whether to mention it in your application or not."

In general, employers were portrayed as "not interested" as soon as applicants mentioned that they were not fully fit.

Respondents older than 40 were very pessimistic about being able to find a job:

> "Since last year I have intensively tried but I have received nothing but rejections.... I saw a few ads in the paper which said: 'we are pleased to consider older candidates'. But when I phoned they said, 'well not that old'. First the health restriction and then your age ..., although the physical restriction is less detrimental than my age." (41-year-old single male)

The employment office also appeared unambiguous about an age barrier, even for those without physical restrictions due to disabilities:

> "They have told me openly, at 45 there is no hope of being placed into a job." (male partner of a couple with children)

Retraining courses were claimed to have been refused also because of the respondent's age:

> "I have enquired about retraining. This was quickly rejected because of my age. They told me, once you have finished your course, nobody will want to take you on." (44-year-old male partner of a couple with children)

Another obstacle was debt. Partly out of experience, respondents expected their wages to be seized at source by creditors once they found employment:

> "That implies additional bureaucracy for the employer who might accept it once or twice but then he has had enough. He will say, you are too expensive for me. It is not worth it." (male partner of a couple with children)

Some immigrant respondents experienced prejudice:

> "If you want to phone somewhere about a flat or a job or whatever, you always think, oh God, I am a foreigner, I receive social assistance, is my German OK?" (female partner of a couple without children)

However, a Polish respondent, seeking work as a lorry driver, did not think his job chances were diminished simply because he was an immigrant. Ethnic Germans from Kasachstan believed that their lack of

German was making it difficult for them to find work. "Now we are waiting to start an intensive language class", said the male partner of this couple without children. Other personal obstacles were perceived to be a lack of academic qualifications, length of time spent out of work and lacking a driving licence.

> "When you go to job placement they always ask:'have you got a driving licence?' If not, that is that. It doesn't matter where you go for an interview, they all want you to have a driving licence." (single male)

Irrespective of objective restrictions and prejudices on the side of employers, respondents were fairly pessimistic about the labour market situation generally and the local labour market in particular. The number of job applications made ranged from between 10-20 to about 90 for one respondent who had been out of work for three years. Only very few responses had been positive. "Out of the 90, four led to interviews", said this respondent, a male partner of a couple with children. The labour market was described by another male partner of a couple with children as, "totally in ruins here in our area. Another two big companies have recently closed down. It does not look good."

Replying to a part-time secretarial job at the local newspaper, a respondent was told "we already have 300 applications" (female lone parent). Part-time work was especially sought after by lone parents but openings were few.

> "Many women would like to leave social assistance. And for many of them a part-time job would be sufficient since they receive alimony payments and child and housing benefit. They would be able to cope. But nothing is available." (female lone parent)

The majority of respondents would prefer to find work within their local region, often because of the lack of a car. Relying on local transport would make it difficult to seek work further away, unless it was in a larger town with a good connection to Hildesheim. Nevertheless, a number of respondents were prepared to travel for up to 50 km to work (one claimed 100 km), or one hour, daily. A few would accept a move to bigger cities such as Berlin, Hamburg or Stuttgart and one emphasised his willingness to go abroad, provided there was a prospect of a good and steady job. However, others were reluctant because of family, in particular having children of school age, because of local contacts, the uncertainty of finding accommodation and the costs involved in setting up a new home. This was different for the relatively recently arrived ethnic Germans from Kasachstan, who said: "Work is most important. Where I find work, there I would want to live".

Policy improvements

There were only a few suggestions for improvements to policy. As far as employment office staff were concerned, respondents acknowledged that their position was difficult because of the lack of jobs overall. However, a better staff/claimant ratio and a more sensitive service, especially for those with specific medical problems, was believed to be an improvement to the situation. To increase the job prospects for the long-term unemployed, increased wage subsidies were proposed which would compensate employers for the reduced productivity of especially those with health restrictions. Retraining courses would be valued more highly, it was believed, if they would end with a test and a certificate for those who passed. Social companies (see Chapter One) were regarded as another positive attempt to find work for some long-term unemployed. However, hardly any of the respondents had been in contact with such an organisation or were clear about what they were.

Conclusions

The majority of the long-term unemployed in this study were either social assistance claimants who had been offered a 'help-to-work' programme or receivers of a training allowance who were taking part in a retraining or rehabilitation programme. While typical of long-term unemployed people, the respondents cannot be claimed to be representative of the group as a whole. For Germany, any attempt to capture the experience of long-term unemployment more comprehensively would have to include those not in receipt of any social security benefits and perhaps also those not registered as unemployed. It would also have to take account of those who are officially counted as unemployed, and might receive benefits, but who tend not to be considered for training or work programmes because of additional personal problems such as drug or alcohol addictions or psychological problems. While this study does not claim to be representative, it does hope at least to explore and illustrate the experiences of people affected by long-term unemployment in individual countries and, in a second step, to compare these experiences with those encountered in other countries (see Chapter Eleven).

The vast majority of German respondents had acquired vocational qualifications. Confirming earlier indications of the social structure of long-term unemployment in Germany, employment histories were generally not characterised by recurrent or continuous unemployment, except for lone parents, who were beginning to seek more regular employment after a period mainly devoted to childrearing. It was clearly established that unemployment has had an adverse effect on the living standard of all respondents. However, for many the consequence was not necessarily a life in poverty. Instead, despite some restrictions, many interviewees, even some in receipt of social assistance, claimed to have learned to live with having less disposable income and to manage on a smaller budget, hoping to return to a better level of income after a return to employment.

Overall, there was little sign of respondents feeling 'cut off' from society or social networks. A few interviewees, who were asked directly, claimed not to feel marginalised by either society as a whole or the local community. Others denied that being unemployed had made a difference to the number or groups of friends with whom they socialised. There was no 'ghettoisation' in terms of accommodation, for example. Rather than concentrated in particular estates, respondents' homes were spread across the town and surrounding villages and most of them lived in private-rented accommodation, which is the most common form of dwelling in Germany.

Nevertheless, some societal effects of unemployment were observable. Because of the lack of work, many respondents felt embarrassed or awkward in communications with others since they felt unable to contribute to conversations which often revolved around employment. The dominance that work has on daily life also became obvious in comments about the unanimous intention to get back into employment. A number of the motives for this were intrinsic to work (social contacts, identity) and some were negative, associated with unemployment (boredom, worthlessness, lack of daily structure). In this sense, being cut off from employment in a society which continues to be dominated by, and revolves around, work, does signify a type of marginalisation, even for those who do not fall into poverty because of unemployment.

Gainful employment is linked to inclusion in the social insurance system. This connection seems to function as a type of work incentive according to interviewees, who stressed the importance of getting back into work to secure entitlement to a public pension and other social insurance-based benefits. The tiered structure of social security provision in Germany does not only merely signify different standards of living but also underlines the importance of paid work in relation to social status. By incorporating different principles, it appears to reinforce different attitudes towards being unemployed, depending on the type of benefit received. The receipt of a contributory-based training allowance, for example, lends recipients a social status which respondents regarded as higher than simply being unemployed. Claimants of unemployment benefit justified the receipt of state support with reference to reciprocity and restitution dominant in insurance-based social security provision. Respondents who received either of these two types of support expressed worries of having to rely on social assistance at some time, a scheme which in the eyes of many interviewees, including current recipients, continues to be associated with poverty, destitution and social stigma. Social assistance receipt, rather than long-term unemployment as such, can be regarded as a threat to causing social marginalisation in Germany. However, this was less true for some respondents. Lone parents especially had a more instrumental attitude towards social assistance, making use of it for long periods to have the financial security which allowed them to look after their children. Nevertheless, even those claimants who were less ashamed to receive social assistance, were keen to overcome the need to depend on it as soon as possible.

Other aspects in relation to living standards, motivation to work, jobsearch strategies and obstacles to work have been illustrated in this chapter. Subsequent chapters will examine whether these are specific to Germany or whether, and to what extent, the perception and experiences of long-term unemployed people in Sweden and Britain are similar.

NINE

Long-term unemployed people in Sweden

Introduction

The interviews with the Swedish long-term unemployed were carried out in Örebro, a medium-sized city half way between Stockholm and Gothenburg, consisting of 120,000 inhabitants. While it has some industry it is very much an administrative centre. In 1995 and 1996 its open unemployment rate was similar to that of the country as a whole. In the early 1980s, as unemployment among young people had begun to increase, the Örebro model ensured that young people were guaranteed employment. Subsequently, the city set up its own labour market office, Arbetsmarknadskontoret (AMK), which for some years has had the task of providing measures for the hard to employ, particularly through placements in the services run by the local city council (the commune), its autonomous districts and the county council. The most recent initiative undertaken was Project 2000 which aimed to provide 1,000 work experience places for young unemployed people by the end of the century (AMK, 1996). It was hoped, that in the longer term, most of these would become permanent jobs. Early in 1996, shortly after the interviews for this study took place, Örebro Commune was providing half of all 3,400 labour market measures financed by AMS in the city.

The sample of long-term unemployed people and their unemployed partners was drawn up by AMK and social services departments in two commune districts. Most of those interviewed lived in flats on one of two of the city's housing estates administered by the Örebro Bostäder Organisation (ÖBO), a quasi-autonomous local government housing organisation.

The distribution of the 31 interviewees between the four main household categories is shown in Table 9. The majority of those

Table 9: Household types of the Swedish unemployed respondents

	Male (and female partner)	Female (and) male partner)	Total
Single	7	3	10
Lone parent	1	4	5
Couple (partner)	3 (3)	-	3 (3)
Couple with children (partner)	3 (3)	2 (2)	5 (5)
Total	14 (6)	9 (2)	23 (8)

interviewed (22) were Swedish by birth. Four were from the Nordic region, there were three refugees from Eritrea, one from Somalia and a Kurd from Iraq. Most of the Swedes had lived the best part of their lives in the region of Örebro, some had left Örebro and returned or had moved in from other parts of Sweden.

As already indicated, the selection criteria for those interviewed were couched in terms of age, whether they had partners and/or children living with them and the length of time they had been unemployed. The respondents had little else in common and their experiences of long-term unemployment and their attitudes towards it were very individual. Even the occupational backgrounds of the interviewees' parents were diverse. One respondent's father was a minister of the church; the parents of another were both teachers, and two of the non-Nordic immigrants had fathers who were accountants. Four respondents' parents owned their own small businesses. Another was a craftsman who became an instructor for AMU, the labour market training agency, one was a nurse and another was an artist who sought employment when times were hard. Among the manual worker parents were builders, cleaners, electricians, a forestry worker, an agricultural worker, factory workers and a plumber.

Childhood for many of the respondents was relatively secure and by some accounts idyllic. Not surprisingly, most parents had had secure employment in postwar Sweden. A minority of respondents came from homes where the parents had divorced. The most traumatic life was that of a single man whose hated stepfather killed himself and whose loved partner died in the *Estonia* disaster. While two of the respondents came from obviously poor backgrounds, only one, a man (living with his partner and their children) seemingly content with life, came from a 'deprived' background characterised by crime, drugs and alcohol. The sample did not seem to have had the stereotypical backgrounds often associated with the long-term unemployed.

Education and employment histories

All Swedish children spend nine years at grundskola from 7-16 and in the last 20 years most young people have stayed on to spend a further two or three years in the gymnasium. Two-year gymnasium programmes – roughly speaking – prepare you for manual trades and routine white-collar jobs while three-year programmes are preparations for professional work and academic study at university. Table 10 shows that half of the sample did not stay on at school after 16 and five left before 16. Not one of the respondents went straight from school to university. One single man later did a successful preparatory course for university but did not take up a place. Two other men had started university courses as a mature students but neither completed the course (they hated the group work).

Most of those who stayed on to gymnasium level attended two-year programmes aimed at trades (painting, carpentry, mechanic electrician) or the service sector (retail and distribution, clerical and commercial).

However, the educational history of the sample does not end with initial schooling. The Swedish system is one which has always encouraged adult education and since the mid-1970s many have had the opportunity to have education grants for adults (KOMVUX) to make up for their lack of basic education and the level of education attained during their gymnasium years. Others had the opportunity to attend folk high schools (FHS). A total of 11 respondents received KOMVUX grants at some time and/or attended FHS in order to complement or complete their school education. Four did not complete their courses. Ultimately, 19 of the sample achieved a gymnasium level of education. All of the five non-Scandinavian refugees benefited from free courses in Swedish (from which, judging from the interviews, four had gained a high level of competence). A Somalian man had also completed an electrical course but had failed the written part.

Table 10: Highest initial school level reached by the Swedish unemployed respondents

Incomplete grundskola	5
Grundskola	11
Incomplete gymnasium	1
Gymnasium	14
Total	31

The sample, as a whole, cannot be said to be poorly educated. Most had either attended gymnasium or had achieved gymnasium levels of education. However, a number of respondents, especially those who left school early, were clearly unhappy at school, describing their experiences as follows:

> "awful, awful"; "a plague"; "hated it"; "terrible, I was bullied because I was born a Finn"; "tired of it"; "played truant"; "no desire to go back ... the very thought gives me a pain in my stomach."

Another deterrent to pursuing education further came from two of the men's partners. They could not get grants to continue with their studies and were not prepared to take out loans to do so.

While some were motivated to continue with or take up education in the future, a sizeable minority had been put off by the experience from going further. This hardly bodes well for the hope expressed by the policy interviewees in Chapter Four that education would provide the answer to the problem of long-term unemployment.

It is difficult to provide a comprehensive summary of the employment/unemployment histories of these individuals. Not only did they each start their working lives doing very different jobs, but most of them went on to do such a variety of jobs that is not possible to describe them as having an 'occupation' or a 'career'. Perhaps this is not surprising. Not one of the respondents was fantastically well-qualified and in the Sweden of the 1970s it was quite easy to get another job if you lost one or gave one up. As one respondent said, changing your job was as easy as changing a shirt.

First jobs consisted of factory work, being a shop assistant, nurse, childminder, electrician, mechanic, hospital assistant or sailor or working in a bakery or park. Subsequently, people went on to clean windows, do office, construction or forestry work, military service, hairdressing, work in kitchens and restaurants, driving cars and lorries. Most of those who stayed in related lines of work were single. One man took on a variety of jobs in construction and forestry in between travelling abroad to Australia and South America but even he subsequently worked in a nudist commune and as a club bouncer; one of the women, when young, travelled around the world but eventually settled in Stockholm and worked in the same printing firm for 15 years. One man worked for many years as a window cleaner and in a cardboard box factory; another worked in a variety of factories but did sports training on the side; the jobs of another were mostly in hospitals where he was qualified to act as an assistant or orderly in a number of departments. One couple worked together for many years in the same bakery. A male respondent who went off the rails while still at school, had spent most of his working life on labour market programmes, as had a partially-sighted single woman. For many of the women, there were extensive periods spent out of work caring for their children.

Illness and injury – caused by or aggravated by work – had plagued many of the respondents. The list below provides a good picture of the problem:

- spinal damage through lifting;
- neck, arm and shoulder pains;
- tennis elbow, leg tumour, knee, thigh and back problems;
- eczema;
- vibration damage to hands;
- asthma;
- back problems.

A few talked about other problems they had had. A single man had a drink problem for a while and was taken into compulsory care under Swedish law, while another experienced a mental breakdown following the sinking of the ferry *Estonia*. Another broke down and suffered from paranoia when his partner left him.

Long-term unemployment and its impacts

Attitudes towards unemployment

All of these problems, incidents and conditions resulted in broken work patterns which were bound subsequently to influence the chances of that person securing a job in a difficult employment climate. Unemployment had been experienced by many of the sample prior to Sweden's sudden experience of mass unemployment in the 1990s. A common reaction to unemployment, perhaps because of the stress and monotony of a lot of jobs, was, as two men said, one of relief. One couple watched a lot of TV together and rang in to all the game shows.

> "I experienced it as something positive. You wouldn't want to be unemployed for the rest of your life but ... it was a rest, a break, something I thought of as positive. It felt great. When you got up you had time to clean and fix everything. When I fetched my son I was bright and cheerful. When you work eight hours a day, you get home stressed and

> have to do some shopping and cook the meal. You could be a mother and a wife." (female partner of a couple with children)

She got up early to see the kids off and went to see friends. "[Unemployment for me] is not like it is for an 18-year-old," she said. "Not the same thing at all." One single woman was also relieved to have time to do a lot of things including looking after elderly parents.

One respondent "went up the wall" at first because he'd been used to shiftwork and overtime shaping his life. He couldn't cope with the sudden break. One man watched too much TV and stayed in bed all day. Another got angry and depressed and felt worthless. "It is like a sickness", he said, "It is a sickness". One male respondent also felt degraded and useless. Another had had mixed feelings on becoming unemployed:

> "I have experienced great relief. Sometimes it has been great to have a rest. At other times I've felt empty as though something were missing. There was this hole. Work provides a routine. But the first reaction is that it is shit cool to be free." (single male)

Impact on family and social life

Few thought the impact on children, particularly young ones, was that great except for the obvious material disadvantages. Teenagers found it difficult accepting that they could not have what others their age had. Only one couple talked about children sensing the atmosphere after an argument although the man admitted to drinking more when unemployed ("well you don't have to get up in the morning", he explained). A single mum said her kids felt worse when she worked because she had so little time for them. The Somalian's children wanted to know why he wasn't out working when they came home from school. Two female partners implied that for them their children were always prioritised – their needs came first – so they wouldn't notice that much difference.

As unemployment went on, so for some it became more intolerable. One male respondent became angry, upset and when it came to criticism was "on a short fuse". One man's partner had given up looking for work and was frightened to go out. A single man felt broken down and lonely and had tended to get fixed in certain routines. Another felt isolated and had lost his self-respect. "You want to do something, to produce something, to get away", he said. While another respondent was happy to regard ALU projects as good as a 'proper' job and felt there were a lot of things the unemployed could do, such as caring for others, he too found that long-term unemployment brought on a crisis of identity.

However, this was not the case for one single woman, who painted and did creative needlework into the night. Nor for a male respondent who had lots to do around the house, saw himself as a homebody and didn't look for too many jobs since there was no point. Those who did, only became depressed, he claimed. One lone parent just "felt great".

It was the attitudes of strangers which upset unemployed people most. Their friends, neighbours and relatives seemed to be understanding but outsiders only condemned. One man (part of a couple with children) felt the authorities were difficult to handle. They didn't accept that his injuries were as bad as he maintained and he needed his wife to speak up for him and to help him deal with officials. "I can't defend myself", he claimed. "I feel insecure". A single man complained about the difficulties of getting credit to pay for goods by instalment. A single woman agreed and also rounded on people on TV and those "shit-cursed" writers to the press who said that the unemployed should be sent to the forests to cut timber. "They think you sit at home all day", she said. Her time was so taken up with her parents that she felt she needed a holiday! She said:

> "You know how it is in Sweden. 'Hi! What do you do for a living?' Your identity is your occupation, so it is. 'What do you do?' 'I'm unemployed.' I'm nothing.... Then they say, 'How long have you been unemployed?' and 'What's wrong with you?' They come right out with it. Some are smart and, just to continue the conversation, say, 'What did you do before?' Others are stumped and say 'Mmmmm'. They think you should do something for your unemployment benefit."

Four times in this section of her interview, she rhetorically asked the question "What do you do?" each time paraphrasing some angry reply. It was obviously a sore point.

A single man, the traveller, had had similar experiences:

> " 'I haven't seen you for ages', they say. 'Have you been abroad?' They expect me to say something adventurous like 'I've been fighting grizzly bears, photographing lions and elephants, parachuting, flying air balloons and diving'. They want to know what I'm doing now. Then they are silent. Typically Swedish."

Another single man was irritated when some people, with right-wing leanings, came to a party he held, looked around his flat and expressed astonishment that he had such a nice home. He said:

> "People talk of a two thirds/one third society. I think there is a three thirds society with a separate third at the bottom. There is more unemployment than people think. We're regarded as social parasites."

While there were those who, because of illness and injury, felt they could not hold down a job or felt they should be pensioned off, most respondents talked with verve about their need to work. Only one respondent, a single woman, said she would take any job, which, given her views on education and training, seemed a little contradictory. She was perhaps being more honest when she said, "I'm no workaholic. Work isn't me". Many mentioned money as an important motivation but most wanted more. Quite a few mentioned the social side of work, meeting people. It was particularly important to the Kurdish refugee, since he had few other ways of doing so. For a single mother it was the most important thing about work. For four others work had to be meaningful, useful and demanding. A single man put it succinctly when he said:

> "I'm no Lutheran. I don't want a job that is too demanding, too stressful.... Work for me is where I can do something good."

For one man it was the self-confidence and self-respect that being independent of the authorities would bring. His partner put it more simply when she said, "It is better to have something to go to than live off a mass of benefits".

Not many respondents had much to say about the future. One man felt that something had to be done to get him back to full employment. Another could only say he wanted something more than just a cleaning job. The single father, a Somalian refugee, simply wanted to become a qualified electrician. A single man wanted out. He was fed up with what he called the narrowness of Swedes, concerned only with running around cleaning and tidying. "It's all status", he said. For him, the labour market in Sweden and Europe seemed dismal. He wanted to get away to Australia or Canada.

All of the respondents at some point in their interviews expressed a hopelessness and frustration about the position of being a long-term unemployed person who bit by bit was being pushed, in middle age, to the point of being useless. One said that he felt he was "standing on the outside, looking in" (single male); another thought, "Many of us have been forgotten" (single female). A male refugee said he felt "thrown away and forgotten". Another respondent felt "locked out of the system" (male partner of a couple). Perhaps the most poignant statement came from a single man who had had an idyllic childhood, had always been in work as a young man and through his period of unemployment had kept in social contact with his workmates. He spoke highly of the work-orienteering course he had attended, praised his Af (Public Employment Service) advisor, was surviving financially and had enjoyed his ALU scheme. He was 43 and could see no chance of full employment returning to Sweden and knew that was the only solution to the problems of people like him. "I want", he said, "to come into the system again".

No one expressed severe criticisms about the areas in which they lived. There were the odd complaints about the neighbours or, as in the case of two single men, about the narrowness and intolerance of the people of Örebro but none of the respondents mentioned delinquent behaviour or examples of vandalism. People were pretty happy with the facilities on their estates and had good transport into Örebro city centre. One (single male) thought he lived in a "shit good" area, while the 'deprived' respondent (male partner of a couple with children) said they'd have to tear the area down before he would think of leaving. He had friends going back years, neighbours who looked after each others' kids and who sat outside chatting over coffee on summer evenings. For a single parent, who had no extended family, Örebro was her "security". For one respondent (male partner of a couple), there was no point in moving away from a city where all of his friends and family were living. Others commented on how peaceful their area was (usually in contrast to a previous bad experience). Two of the immigrants lacked social contacts but the four Africans spoke highly of their neighbours. One was pleased there were so many fellow Eritreans about.

While people might complain about the impact of unemployment or society's attitudes to those affected by it, their own social lives were often discussed in happy terms. One man (part of a couple with children), who at times became depressed and "drank his sorrows away", said people were always dropping in for a coffee and a chat. A single man belonged to an association of his old workmates. They played table tennis, formed a computer club and met socially for parties and at Christmas. A single parent, who had left the area in which her former partner had lived to move to Örebro, said that the social life she had with her local church – she herself was a scout leader – and with fellow students on her adult education course, was very fulfilling. Others mentioned the fact that so many in the city were unemployed now, there was no problem meeting people. If you went into town, there was always someone to talk to.

One respondent had held a party to which the neighbours were invited. His black immigrant neighbours came and had a great time but "the racialist" Swedes stayed away rather than have to mix. He complained that when you commented on the good weather to the locals they would grumble, "Today, yes". Most critical of the area were two single men, one who came from Stockholm and another who had spent much of his life living and working in Australia, Canada and the US. Perhaps Örebro could not fulfil their more cosmopolitan needs.

Material impact

Trying to manage on a low income was a challenge for some but for others it was a headache. Where possible, respondents went to supermarkets to do a big, cheap food shop – reckoning up what they were spending as they went round. Many said they bought second-hand clothes. They did not go out to the cinema, the pub or restaurants. Christmas for one single male was miserable – not being able to afford cards or presents. The biggest problem was a holiday; some had not had one for years. Others visited their relatives' country cottages (in Sweden, where land is relatively cheap and plentiful and the population small, it is not uncommon for families to have access to a small stuga [a country cottage] by a lake in the country). A few managed to sneak abroad for a foreign holiday without letting the authorities know (if you were on holiday, two respondents claimed, you were not entitled to benefit).

Respondents spoke of not being able to afford to buy expensive goods new and if furniture or the video went bust, not being able to replace them. Three respondents mentioned that they saved by not going to the doctor or the dentist. One said he preferred an extraction to a filling since it would save money in the long run. No one felt they could save, although one man's partner said you had to put something by for emergencies (couple with children). The biggest fear was the crown bailiff (kronofogden). If you got behind with loan repayments or hire purchase agreements, you could be in big trouble. People tried to juggle with repayment periods, adjust their loans over longer periods or seek permission from the bank for a postponement of repayment.

Asked what method existed in her household for managing the family finances, one man's partner said, "We beat each other to death." This 'joke' probably indicated some angry disagreements about money. A

Table 11: Reserve annual wage by household type for the Swedish unemployed respondents

Single (9 respondents)	£10-£16,000
Lone parent (3)	£8-£19,000
Couple (4)	£8-£14,000
Couple with children (2)	£9-£13,000

single woman was able to be resourceful because of her sewing skills but her well-off parents were able to lend or give her money from time to time. Others too were fortunate in having relatives of friends who could tide them over. One respondent's partner said they had relatives who would say they were going to clean their fridge and would they like to come over and help themselves to what otherwise would have to be thrown away (couple with children). Interviewees were only too aware that a loan could be the beginning of a vicious circle but some had past debts from banks or study loans hanging over them ranging from the equivalent of £400 to £6,300.

Given the level of financial problems, respondents were reluctant to take on work which left them worse off than when on benefit. A single parent said that if she was paid a wage she would lose free daytime care for her children and her housing benefit. While some simply said that they were willing to work for a little more than benefit, others put their reserve wage higher. Table 11 gives their responses. Given the relatively high cost of living in Sweden these amounts would not seem to be unreasonable.

Attitudes to benefits and other sources of income

Most of those interviewed were receiving earnings-related unemployment benefit administered by the trade unions (a-kassa). One, the Kurd, was receiving the flat-rate unemployment benefit (KAS). Two, a single man and a single mother, were in receipt of social assistance while two single mothers were receiving study assistance for unemployed adults (SVUXA). Two of the men's partners were on sickness benefit. One single man was receiving a social assistance supplement to his a-kassa from social services while other respondents had either applied for such supplements or were awaiting a decision on their application. Although most were receiving a-kassa, it left some of those interviewed near to or below the social assistance norm. A single man had opted for SA simply because his a-kassa fell well below what social services were prepared to give him. This type of situation arose when, for example, a person's full-time income had, prior to unemployment, been very low or they had only worked part time. In his case this left him with a 75% income replacement of a 75% (that is, part-time) job. Similarly, although the African refugees received a-kassa, it was based on the compensation they received for their ALU schemes.

For most respondents a-kassa amounted somewhere between SKr4,000 to SKr8,000 a month (equivalent at the time to around £400-£800 a month or £4,800-£9,600 a year). Some recipients also received a housing allowance as well as child allowances. These, in some cases, more than doubled the amount received in a-kassa. A small minority expressed satisfaction with the level of their main benefit, but most were dissatisfied. Many complained that the system functioned well when recipients received 80-90% of their previous income but the reduction to 75% in addition to cuts in other benefits, such as child benefit, was making life too hard. Dissatisfaction ranged from "it is not enough" to "it stinks".

Asked whether they thought, as critics had suggested, that a-kassa was too high and discouraged people from seeking work, some, such as one man's partner, agreed that it could make you lazy. She claimed that many signed on when they had worked for a year just to live on a-kassa. She'd done it herself. She said:

> "They should fix people up with jobs instead. Better to find jobs for young people than for older ones. Young people get loads of money. Instead of signing on at the age of 20 they should be starting work. It's dumb. They can see no way out. It's so easy to find yourself in a vicious circle and in bad company and you begin to drink. Some have been sacked or injured but others just lie on the sofa all day. They should be investigated."

Others vehemently denied that a-kassa was a disincentive. One man said he was used to working 15 hours a day and a-kassa could never give him the sort of income he was prepared to earn given the opportunity. A male respondent's partner wondered how benefits could be a disincentive when there were simply no jobs to seek.

One single man would rather a full-time job in preference to a 75% benefit of a 75% income. The trouble was that there were no decently paid full-time jobs on the labour market. "It is Christmas for employers. They can pick and choose," he said. A single woman implied something similar when she said she would go for a job if it were a good one and well paid, but otherwise the benefit enabled her to say, "Let me be. There's so bloody much to do that I'm always occupied."

Few talked about working on the side. One said he would if he could but there were no jobs anyway. Another said she had to from time to time in order to survive. Another had done so in the past but said he wouldn't do it anymore since, because you were exploiting the position of those in work who paid taxes, it undermined the operation of the labour market. One respondent, after checking that this research was going to someone in England for analysis and was entirely confidential, revealed that he had always worked on the side. It was, he said, the only way to have a normal life. His skill was only in demand on a seasonal basis. He could not afford not to qualify for a-kassa. He claimed, perhaps in self-justification, that not only were 50% of a-kassa claimants working on the side but that thousands of Polish migrant workers were claiming benefit using false addresses in Sweden.

By and large, applying for and receiving a-kassa was a relatively simple matter. Recipients thought of it as a right which they had earned through years of previous contributions (or in the case of one respondent through her parents' taxes). The real problems seemed to arise when benefits needed adjustment between different agencies. As one respondent said, when criticising "paper Sweden", things became complicated when one authority thought another should be paying the bill (couple with children). Those who complained of bureaucracy seemed to be those trying to get social assistance on top of a-kassa, or a disability pension instead of sickness benefit. When there was a change of circumstances things could become problematic with paper going backwards and forwards and delays created. A single man, on getting a social assistance supplement to his a-kassa, said:

> "There's a lot of pettiness. They adjust for every tiny change. You have to report every penny every month. Then your social worker changes and you begin all over again. They have to check with their head of department. Everything is delayed. Your bills aren't paid on time and you get charged extra."

Some were philosophical about this and said it tended to sort itself out in the end. Others were incensed. Only one respondent expressed himself politically when he complained that the cuts in jobs and welfare were not caused by high benefits but by those who had created Sweden's economic problems – the speculators, the rich, those who awarded themselves enormous golden handshakes. With all the money these people were being paid, thousands of jobs could be created, was his argument.

On one subject there was agreement among a number of the women – that a-kassa was preferable to claiming social assistance:

> "Go to social services? I've been there three times and it was a fruitless experience. It feels like a stigma." (female lone parent)
>
> "You feel as though you are begging." (single female)
>
> "I'd rather live on nothing than live on social assistance." (female lone parent)
>
> "I felt shat upon. I applied for emergency help and it took a whole month before I got any money." (single woman)
>
> "It makes you so angry when you go to social services." (female partner of a couple with children)
>
> "[A-kassa] feels better than to say I go to social services. Some aren't ashamed of it but I am. I haven't told my son that I go to the social. I keep it in the dark." (female lone parent)

Two of the single men expressed satisfaction with social services. One was happy with the suit and travel expenses they gave him for his partner's funeral and the other was very grateful for the way they dealt with his problems as a refugee.

Escaping unemployment

Attitudes towards labour market programmes and employment services

All of the respondents, with the exception of three of the female partners, had been on one or more labour market schemes; 19 had been on an ALU placement, 13 had received labour market training (AMU) while 11 had experienced relief work. Others had benefited from a variety of courses and work placements with AMK, work experience and the Temporary Replacement Scheme (substituting for a member of staff who is sick or on leave) and occupational guidance. Many of those interviewed had been on several programmes. They had received training in the 1970s or had been on the young people's programmes run by the commune in the 1980s and now in the 1990s were experiencing ALU.

The men seemed to have had more training opportunities in fields such as carpentry, sound technology, workshop mechanics, telecommunications and welding; a female refugee had had training in catering. Only one of these had continued to find work in their trade. Sometimes the explanation for this was the absence of jobs, a slump in demand or a surplus of trainees.

The ALU projects were very diverse – sorting clothes, security guard work, extending a sports pavilion, tree-felling. Two of the Africans worked on African cultural projects, while the Kurd spent time on a special programme for immigrant workers. In a significant number of cases individuals dreamed up their idea for an ALU and Af gave permission for it to go ahead. One single respondent was financed to run her local cultural association. It was a "rather good ALU" which involved a lot of responsibility and was "character-building". A single man had devised a nature preservation project; a single woman had run a rebate card scheme for the unemployed. One single parent had helped run a women's refuge; another had taught in her local school, and a male respondent had found some archival work which needed doing.

Of the 17 who commented on the value of the schemes they had been on, 13 were positive. Some simply said they were very good and/or enjoyable; others said how they had been strengthened as people as a result; others were pleased to have done something useful. Three people expressed mixed feelings: two women were worried about the displacement effects of ALU while a man thought labour market measures should be abolished altogether.

Given the criticisms of labour market measures mentioned in Chapters Three and Four, the picture that emerges from this sample of long-term unemployed people is that nearly all had been given some opportunity to improve or maintain work skills. A number of very vulnerable individuals had been given a lot of support, and many of those interviewed seemed to consider their training and work experiences worthwhile. However, in many instances, these unemployed people were taking up places either because they would lose benefit if they did not or because they would be entitled to a further period of a-kassa by doing so. This came across clearly from a number of the interviews. It was not resented, rather it was accepted as a reasonable condition of further benefit.

Seeking work

The interviews did not convey a feeling that either much was going on in terms of searching for jobs, or that those searching had much hope. Only one respondent, a single male, gave an impression of being very active, claiming to have applied for 103 jobs during his most recent spell of unemployment. Three people gave figures of 10 and one of seven job applications made. A few had had one interview and been unsuccessful. A number had been assured of a firm's interest but had heard nothing more. The next nearest sign of activity was visits to Af. While some did this on a regular basis to see if any jobs were being advertised in *Platsjournalen* (a newspaper produced by Af advertising job vacancies) or in any other form, little hope was expressed that anything positive would result. Two respondents complained that Af had encouraged them to apply for inappropriate jobs. Others conducted their searches through local newspapers, through friends or by direct approach to employers. Some were not searching at all. They were content to work on their present and future schemes. This would seem to be a reflection of the paucity of jobs on the labour market.

With the possible exception of one respondent, who wanted to train as an artist but did not know if there was such a thing as a beginner's course, and a refugee couple, who wanted to teach but had no training or prospect of it, most seemed to have realistic job ambitions. As one respondent said, "You should have dreams but not believe they are reality" (male partner of a couple). They either wanted jobs similar to ones they had held before or were prepared to consider anything they were capable of doing. One single woman had no idea of wanting to do anything – apart from a job; another wanted something sensible that would offer enough to live on but did not want to work in a munitions factory or be a manipulative salesperson. A lone parent wanted a permanent job, working with people, but not in a factory. A single man was critical of unemployed people who said they were prepared to do anything since this boosted the demand that the unemployed *should* be prepared to do anything. One lone parent admitted to turning down offers because the times of working were incompatible with her family responsibilities. No one else had had any offers to turn down.

Support for jobsearch

While many may have felt that AMS, Af and AMK had provided them with valuable opportunities, the attitude to attempts by Af and its job advisors to aid their search for employment was often criticised. Jobsearch schemes were regarded as "meaningless", "boring", and "foolish". Other opinions expressed were:

> "You just sit there and talk." (female lone parent)

> "I could run one with my experience. I know more than they do." (single male)

> "It was like sitting in school again." (female lone parent)

> "It did nothing for me." (partner in couple with children)

> "Not much help." (female lone parent)

Views were more mixed about employment services generally and their staff. Some said Af was very thorough, open and helpful; others that it was useless and "should be abolished" (single male), and that it was unselective (single female). Respondents could have a poor view of schemes such as jobsearch but be pleased with what individual advisors had done for them. Advisors seemed to see these clients once a month or every two months or keep contact on an informal basis. They were regarded highly by five respondents; uncooperative and insulting by two; good and bad by another.

Obstacles to employment

It was not surprising to find that many of the reasons which people gave for being restricted in terms of jobseeking had to do with their age and personal circumstances. All of the main respondents were between 30 and 45 (some of the partners were older). Inevitably, they had lost the flexibility they had when young. They were competing with young people who had more education and training than themselves; they had children or elderly parents to look after; they had health problems which were likely to get worse rather than better; they had partners to consider; they were settled in homes and areas which they were reluctant to leave. Being unemployed for a long time had sapped their motivation.

One single woman knew her eyesight would not improve but hoped that her self-confidence would and that she would "stick her nose out more" and "get on her feet". A male respondent said that before his injury he would have been prepared to do anything. He had had a highly-skilled job with ASEA, a large Swedish company, but was moved to a section where the work was much heavier. The resulting injury and his long periods of time off had greatly reduced his job prospects. His partner also saw herself as virtually unemployable.

Lone parents felt they could not take work in the evenings or at weekends because their children would suffer. One felt that a full-time job would leave her with neither the time nor strength to be of much use to her children. Childcare during the day was no problem. As an Eritrean refugee said, "In Sweden, if my wife gets a job as well, childcare will be automatic".

Apart from their own limitations and problems, respondents knew they were less attractive to employers. A single man felt that the age group 35-45 did not exist for employers. Another respondent said employers were not interested in you once they discovered that you had small children and were a single mother. They simply assumed you would take a lot of time off. One refugee, the male lone parent, was reluctant to accuse employers of racial discrimination but suspected it existed. He knew that the disadvantage of immigrants and refugees was compounded by not knowing what your rights were. Another refugee thought he didn't have a chance with so many educated Swedes unemployed. He said employers thought it was better to have a Swede. Although they claimed they gave jobs to those most able to do them, "They wouldn't give me one in any case", he said. One respondent had been subjected to a lot of sex discrimination in the jobs she had done previously and felt that being unemployed enabled different forms of discrimination to be exercised (she was part of a couple with children).

As to labour market policy itself, few were willing to accept that generous benefits of long duration prevented them from seeking work. However, a single man did think that the lack of contact between Af and employers made the whole point of visiting Af depressing. "A strange institution", he said. You went in, got your card stamped, looked at the ads and walked out again. Others felt that reducing benefits, increasing waiting days and insisting on claimants making a specific number of job applications would do nothing to increase motivation. They were motivated, it is just that there were simply no jobs. Another single man, when asked whether he felt that benefits and measures locked him into the system, replied that he felt "locked out of the system". A single woman expressed some of the frustrations felt by the unemployed when she exploded, parodying the demands of employment advisors:

"'It's all your fault! Go and hang yourself. Get out of our sight and come back when you have papers and can say, 'Look now I've had a face lift, so I look 25. And I've educated myself and got a driving licence. I've taken some pills to make me more lively'. They talk about us being a resource. But I'm not. For them I'm a problem that has to be solved and it isn't easy. That's why the whole time they're saying, 'Educate yourself, educate yourself, educate yourself. What do you want to be?.... You stand a better chance in the labour market if you go and study something'. Yes, say that I come back next year when I'm 46 and ready. What will it bloody well matter that I've become educated, what kind of chance will I have? When young educated men and women of the right age stand there and can't get a job."

Policy improvements

A number of respondents, mainly men, had a range of policy proposals of their own for dealing with unemployment. Some simply said they wanted to see more jobs. A refugee wanted grants for immigrants to start their own companies which would then employ people. One respondent proposed an overtime ban. Some saw the unemployed as a resource which could be used to satisfy a number of social needs. Unemployment centres, where the unemployed could meet and swap ideas, could be set up. ALU could be used to provide more meaningful placements, to form the basis of people's own projects not to provide something for people to do when their benefit ran out. ALU and schemes for young people often displaced real jobs and exploited people. This should be discouraged. There was a general feeling from a number of statements made that the unemployed should be treated as individuals who had something useful to give to society. Labour market measures too often "played to the gallery" said one single man. Another thought that people ought to look after themselves – like they did in Australia!

Proposals did not stop at the level of labour market measures. One male respondent thought government grants should not be given for acquiring labour-saving technology. Another said they should be cut in preference to cutting benefits. A third said there was too much concern with holding interest rates down. Dealing with the problem of unemployment was no longer a priority. Membership of the EU was to blame, said a fourth, claiming that Norway was ten-times better off than Sweden because it had stayed out. Buying foreign goods was also blamed for Sweden's problems.

A significant number of respondents thought that the interests of Swedes should be put before those of immigrants:

> "Sorry for saying it but instead of taking so many immigrants we should fix it so that there are a few more jobs for those who live in Sweden." (female partner of a couple)

> "I don't want to speak badly of those from other countries but I think that we should take care of ourselves in the first instance." (single male)

> "Foreigners shouldn't be blamed for coming here. It's clear that they've got to take their chances but I don't think we should take people when we can't offer them jobs or social security." (single male)

> "It's nothing to do with racism but if you come from another country you get all the help and education you need.... I've nothing against foreigners but you notice the difference." (female lone parent)

> "[Provide more help for the unemployed] above all for Swedes. That's what I think. Not that I'm racist in any way but...." (male partner of a couple with children)

What some of the unemployed had to say about the EU, foreign companies and immigrants merely illustrates that many unemployed people begin to blame the 'other' for what they are suffering.

Conclusions

Until recently, most of the Swedish interviewees had found it relatively easy to find work. They had not been ground down by poverty and a lack of opportunity in the past. *Marginal* best describes the situation of many of them, in that they have begun to lose a sense of worth and the hope of re-entering the world of work. Stigmatised by others, they have begun to blame outsiders for the problems they experienced. There seemed to be little point in looking for work as the jobs were simply not there. Employers discriminated against them because of their age, sex, ethnicity or health. Jobsearch activities were frowned upon, the usefulness of employment advisers criticised, the role of social services regarded with hostility, and the value of education questioned. However, most of them appreciated receiving a benefit by right and had gained valuable experiences and insights through the various labour market measures they had attended. Their homes and neighbourhoods, their friends and communities were valued and they managed reasonably well on the benefits they received

Sweden is a country in which more effort has been made than in many others to ensure that people, both nationals and immigrants, have a place in 'the people's home'. Sometimes these efforts have been misguided, ineffective or poorly implemented. However, they still prevent Swedish cities and estates from displaying the signs of deprivation and despair found so frequently in other Western countries. There can be little doubt that the social infrastructure and the active labour market policy help to resist the most damaging effects of long-term unemployment. While much was being done to help the unemployed and while the extremes of social exclusion were being kept at bay, these interviews have shown that the signs are there and are likely to grow unless a way can be found to make the unemployed not a problem but, in the words of one of those interviewed, "a resource".

TEN

Long-term unemployed people in Britain

Introduction

This chapter explores the experience of long-term unemployment in Britain. Between January and March 1996, 23 people were interviewed, all of whom lived in or near Lincoln, a British city chosen for its similarities to the German and Swedish cities in the study. The city is in the East Midlands; it has a travel to work area population of 160,000 and a workforce of 71,000. Its three dominant industrial sectors are: services, including public administration and tourism; retail and distribution; metal goods, engineering and vehicles. The travel to work area had one of the highest unemployment rates in the region, standing at 9.3% in 1994, 42% of whom had been unemployed for at least one year. The rate improved slightly in subsequent years to 8.3% at December 1995 and 7.2% in December 1996. Lincoln is disadvantaged by having one of the lowest skill bases in the region and a poor communications infrastructure.

The original intention was to recruit some respondents outside the Jobcentres. However, staff were on strike throughout the relevant period, so both Jobcentres were closed to all except new claimants. A local drive against fraudulent claiming meant that door-to-door recruitment was hampered since many people were unwilling to answer *any* questions about being unemployed. In the event, unemployed people were professionally recruited to participate in the interviews from Jobclubs, in the city centre, or by house-to-house calling in areas known to have high levels of unemployment. The recruitment criteria mirrored those in Germany and Sweden. Respondents were living in three household types, as shown in Table 12. It had been anticipated that interviews with partners would be conducted separately, but in practice this was possible for only two

Table 12: Household types of the British unemployed respondents

Single	8	(4 with children living with previous partners)
Lone parent	7	
Couple with children	8	
Total	23	

couples. In the other six interviews the partner responded to relevant questions during the interview. A total of 31 respondents was interviewed: 19 individually, and 12 in couples. It was also intended to interview couples without children, but it was not possible to contact any in the time available; nationally only a small percentage of long-term unemployed people are couples without children (see, for example, Dawes, 1993, p 80).

Half of the respondents lived in housing rented from the local council and one quarter were owner-occupiers. The rest rented from housing associations or privately. The length of time for which respondents had been out of work ranged from one year to 10 years; one third had been out of work between two and three years and a further third for more than five years. Three quarters of the respondents were male. Five had health problems; two of these were claiming Invalidity Benefit and one was in the process of applying. Three quarters of the people signing on as unemployed or claiming Invalidity Benefit had taken part in TfW or Jobclubs during their current spell of unemployment.

Education and employment histories

The respondents' educational backgrounds varied widely. Half left school with O-levels or CSEs: one third of these went on to in-work training – apprenticeships and college courses on 'day release' – and half of them continued into higher education. A feature of this British sample was that one quarter of the respondents, mostly single men, had university degrees or an equivalent qualification. One quarter of all the respondents left school with no qualifications; none of these undertook subsequent vocational training.

All of the respondents had been employed at some time, but some very infrequently and for relatively short periods of time. Previous jobs among those without qualifications included labouring, cleaning, factory work and clerical work. Those who had further training had worked, for example, in engineering, run a business or as a laboratory assistant.

Respondents with higher qualifications had worked in areas such as the civil service, accountancy and the armed forces.

This relatively heterogeneous sample enables us to compare the consequences of long-term unemployment for people with widely differing educational, labour market and personal histories.

Long-term unemployment and its impacts

Attitudes towards unemployment

All of the respondents, and all their partners except one who had recently had a baby, wished to stop living on benefit and to get back to work. They sought to alleviate the negative consequences of unemployment, believing that they would be better off financially, socially and personally when they were employed. They deplored the inactivity:

> "I want to work, I'm not one of these people who just wants to sit here and vegetate. I want to be able to buy nice clothes, I want to be able to go out drinking, nice holidays, you know." (single person)

People found it very difficult to live on benefit. They learned to adjust to a lower level of income as the length of unemployment increased and their savings were depleted, and to an ever lower standard of living:

> "I suppose you're always going to say (the levels are not adequate) but they're not going to give you loads and loads of money, but I don't think they give you enough to manage on. You survive, just. You're getting further and further into debt the more months go by. We exist, don't we." (couple with children)

Respondents wished for a job which would at least allow a less frugal lifestyle and get them out of debt. They wanted to earn enough to pay their bills and have a little more "to buy little extra bits for the kids or save up for a little holiday." However, they hoped to return to work for an income which would allow them to attain the standard of living they used to enjoy. Those with degrees and professional qualifications wanted salaries to match.

Respondents also deplored unemployment for its effects on their social life. They said that long-term unemployment is boring and restricts social life; in contrast, a job would provide money, interest and companionship. They found it difficult to occupy their days and missed the social contact and structured time which employment provides. Many had enjoyed work and missed the camaraderie.

> "... you've got too much time on your hands, you've got to occupy your time. It's hard to fill your time in during the day." (single male)

Parents with full-time childcare responsibilities looked forward to a change of environment and activity. They spoke of the need to "get out of the house, for money, and for me to get a bit of a life back ... to meet new people...."

Respondents also had more personal reasons for disliking unemployment. Half of them said they wished to work in order to gain a sense of pride and to regain their self-esteem. This was true for people experiencing their first period of unemployment and for those who had undergone long spells of unemployment before. They spoke of the difficulty of enforced inactivity, how they could not adjust to it and the strain it placed on relationships, and they spoke of the pride and independence of earning their own money:

> "I think when you're working and you pick up your wages on a Friday, you think ... that's mine. You sit there with pride and say I've earned that, the government ain't give it me. It [makes you] proud to work." (female lone parent)

These feelings were so strong that some respondents could not understand why anyone would not want to work: "I find it quite remarkable that someone can choose not to work" (single female).

Impact on family and social life

One positive aspect of unemployment, for many people the only positive aspect, was the extra time available to spend with their children:

> "With both partners working it creates difficulties at home. Can you remember when you had your night job and I was working and some of the times we had to leave them with [eldest daughter].... You used to get really depressed about it and she didn't want to leave them because she was coming home ... they hadn't done things or they hadn't looked after themselves and the house was a tip. They were up late. It creates all those sorts of problems." (male partner of a couple with children)

Parents were particularly constrained by living on benefit: they said they rarely, if ever, went out because of limited finances and childcare considerations. Most were restricted to free activities such as visiting friends and walking in the park. All parents regretted that they could not afford to take their children out more and worried that the financial consequences of their unemployment might have psychological and social implications for their children. Parents of school age children were particularly concerned that they could not provide the things their children wanted and their friends had, such as branded clothes, games and activities. Parents feared this could make them feel excluded. For example, a single mother was very upset she could not pay for ballet lessons for her daughter. Some children regularly saved for things or took part-time jobs.

Parents were worried that their children would be stigmatised. For example, several were unwilling to let their children have free school dinners which would label them as coming from a family claiming benefit:

> "The school meals and things like that, I don't let him have free school meals because they have to take tokens and present them." (female lone parent)

One father told how his 16-year-old daughter was ashamed that he was unemployed and lied about it. He said that he understood her feelings:

> "She actually makes things up, she feels embarrassed. When she's at school and she has to fill things in, what does your dad do and your mum, she writes things in.... I can understand it. I obviously don't tell her off or anything but it brings a bit of a wry smile.... I think if I was in her position I'd probably do the same thing.... Because you know what kids are like; 'your dad hasn't got a job' and 'you haven't got this and that'." (male partner of a couple with children)

Boredom was a common complaint among all respondents; they found it difficult to fill up the time available. One quarter of them were members of teams or societies, such as darts teams or local charities, which brought social contacts:

> "I'm in a marching band, I'm on the committee there, and they keep me going and the landlord, well he runs the band, so it keeps me going, gives me things to do, keeps me occupied." (single male)

Almost all the respondents had regular contact with a support network of friends and/or family living in the city. Those whose families were in employment often received financial help in the form of loans and gifts. Friends and family were also an important source of emotional support. Some believed such support had been vital to keep them going. However, respondents felt embarrassed because they could not 'pay their way' when they went out with friends. Two cases showed that neighbours could not be relied on to be sympathetic or supportive. In one, a couple became isolated because they were increasingly stigmatised by their neighbours as their spell of unemployment lengthened. The other, a recent immigrant to the city, had not spoken to his neighbours in three years, but had received valuable support from other family members who lived in the city and from his English tutor and fellow students.

Material impact

In contrast to Germany and Sweden, benefits in Britain are unrelated to the claimant's previous earnings or to average earnings among working people, and are set at comparatively low levels. While financial management is important for all adults, it takes on crucial importance in the lives of people on low incomes. Because respondents could not manage on benefit, expenditure was prioritised. Very basic and cheap foodstuffs were sought out, and the heating for the house was limited. Families, in particular, might go without even basic necessities such as food and warmth. Single people had not gone without heating or food, but they had little if any social life or things they had previously taken for granted, such as nice clothes or a hi-fi system.

> "... and if at the end of that week there isn't enough to get something, then we go without till the following week when I pay it first and then something else will probably be missing, [a] continual circle that you never actually catch up with everything, but you never get too far behind with 'em neither." (couple with children)

> "... I don't think it's enough to live on, to pay your food and your bills. I mean, basically, all my money could go, really, just on paying bills without eating, or eating without paying bills, it really could." (single male)

> "I just struggle, really. From week to week I just live off my book and I think I just can't wait until Monday and then I'll get paid and on Tuesday I say I just can't wait until Monday." (female lone parent)

Every respondent stressed the importance of planning their expenditure to try to keep within their income, and many believed they had got better at managing and 'juggling' during their spell of unemployment. They contrasted their present situation with their lives when in work. They had changed their approach to household management: they were more organised because there was no spare capacity, and they learned which were the cheap places to shop. A common strategy was to pay bills in small instalments, "a little bit here, a little bit there", either monthly or using meters and tokens. The DSS can arrange to make deductions from benefit for payment of overdue utility bills. Respondents who had such deductions felt it was a sensible system, and were happy to be relieved of the fear of having their utilities cut off. Research has shown that debt is common among recipients of Income Support (Shaw et al, 1996). The respondents in this study were no exception: excluding mortgages, three quarters of them had debts ranging from £30 to £3,000 which had been incurred during their spell of unemployment. Two thirds had found their debts difficult to handle during the previous year.

Respondents who needed to borrow used four providers of loans or credit: family and friends; the Social Fund; consumer credit, in particular catalogue companies; and credit companies. For many unemployed people, being in debt had become a way of life.

Two thirds of respondents received material or financial support from their families. For a small number with children, support was in the form of items such as clothing for the children or second-hand furniture. Two people ran cars that their families had given to them, and who also paid the car tax and insurance. Half the respondents borrowed money from their families, and all but one always repaid the loans. They acknowledged the difficulty of making repayments and living on even less money:

> "... and he takes it back off me so much a week. He's good, very good, he'll help me any way I want to. But the thing is I've got to be careful I don't overstep on withdrawing money because then I'm going to find that I can't afford to pay that back." (female lone parent)

For people unwilling or unable to borrow money from family members, the Social Fund was useful for emergencies, despite the difficulty of repaying loans. A common form of budgeting is to pay for items in instalments. Half the respondents regularly used catalogue shopping to spread the cost of items. However, as with Social Fund loans, respondents found the consequent reduction in their income difficult to manage.

> "They ... say don't get things on HP [credit].... The majority of people have to because it's the only way they can do it. If you don't have HP repayments to make you're going to be much better off per week, but if you don't have them on HP you'd never get them in the first place, so you don't have a choice." (partner of a couple with children)

Respondents reported that they had been excluded from forms of credit available to working people, such as interest free credit and overdrafts. A single professional man contrasted the current attitude of his bank manager with when he was working:

> "When I was successful and putting lots of money in the bank.... I was the best thing since sliced bread, but the minute it stops, they don't want to know.... It's got to a stage like before Christmas I went like to borrow a hundred quid and I had to plead for it ... whereas I used to be able to put a hundred a day in there...." (single professional male)

Several respondents still had access to the credit cards they had acquired when they were working, although two had cut theirs up so they couldn't use them. They were seen as a mixed blessing, providing a lifeline but also a considerable temptation. For most respondents, the only source of new credit was credit companies charging high rates of interest. A lone parent with two children used two such companies which charged more than 50% annual percentage rate. Only a minority used such companies for items the Social Fund would not cover such as children's birthdays and Christmas.

Attitudes to benefits and other sources of income

We have seen that, for families in particular, benefit levels are not adequate. Respondents also believed that their benefits were not increasing in line with inflation (although benefits are cost-of-living indexed) putting them in an ever worsening financial situation. The majority wanted a modest rise to allow them to live more comfortably and with less debt. In the meantime, they used a range of strategies, including using savings, strict budgeting, and supplementing income through borrowing and working part time.

The households in this study can be divided into two broad groups: those who had savings at the start of their spell of unemployment, and those who did not. Their spending priorities were different and altered over the lengthy spell of unemployment.

One third of the households started with either redundancy pay or savings accumulated during their employment. Almost all of these respondents used their savings at the start of their spell of unemployment to supplement their income and cushion the difficulties of living on benefit, at least temporarily. Only one, a lone parent, still had the majority of her savings left, and used them regularly for items such as quality toys for her son. She could not imagine how she would manage on benefit alone.

Benefit levels are constant and do not take account of sudden expenditure needs such as replacement of household items (White, 1991). The three households whose savings had 'dwindled' were now concerned to keep what was left for 'rainy days' and 'emergencies'. Two single men used their savings just for emergencies or paying the mortgage. A family who had been out of work for six years had recently received an addition to their reduced savings in the form of an inheritance of several thousand pounds. They planned to use it as before, to take a short holiday once a year and to meet unexpected needs, but, they said, these unexpected needs were becoming more frequent as household goods wore out.

Three households had used up all of their savings. Their spending priorities were the same as those households who had never had the cushion of savings. For families, these were buying food, paying essential bills, and paying for clothes for their children. One lone father had spent the last of his savings contributing to his daughter's school uniform, having to borrow from family to make up the difference.

Long-term unemployed people become adept at 'juggling' their money and finding ways to pay bills in small instalments. Respondents also sought additional sources of income. They borrowed and fell into debt; and some work while claiming. (At the time of the interviews, the 'disregard limit' – the amount which can be earned before benefit levels are affected – for unemployed Income Support recipients was £5, and £15 for couples who had both been unemployed for two years. Beyond the limit, a pound is deducted from benefit for each additional pound earned. Since April 1996 a proportion of the part-time earnings lost because the disregard limit has been exceeded is saved and returned to claimants who move off benefit and into work as the Back to Work bonus.)

One third of respondents had worked during the year but had not declared their earnings, even when they were lower than the disregard limit. The general feeling was that disregard limits were too low, and encouraged dishonesty. Only three respondents had regular, undeclared earnings, and only one of those was earning more than the disregard limit. However, even those with extra earnings found life difficult financially.

Everyone who did undeclared work was aware of, and worried about, the risk of being found out and sanctioned (losing part of their benefit) and told as few people as possible. Several who had worked in the past would no longer do so for fear of getting caught, although a few mentioned that there were fewer opportunities to work for "cowboys" or "on the quiet" than in the past:

> "I just couldn't take the risk of getting caught. You get caught and that's it. I mean, you struggle as it is." (male partner of a couple with children)

The issue of working for cash in hand to supplement benefits raised some strong feelings among respondents. All but three thought that small amounts of undeclared earnings were acceptable because of the low level of benefits. However, they also thought that high, regular wages, or claiming benefit without serious intention to work, was unfair and disadvantaged genuine claimants. This view was endorsed even by those who did regular undeclared work. Three respondents strongly disapproved of any undeclared work. One couple stressed the unfairness of the abuse which they believed to be going on:

> R:"It isn't fair, there's a lot of people round here who are abusing the system. It angers me when I see what they can get.... The thing was, like when we was working before, we've never had a car."
>
> P:"We could never afford it...." (couple with children)

Escaping unemployment

Research suggests that people are keen to stop living on benefit and to get back to work (Shaw et al, 1996; Dean and Taylor-Gooby, 1992). As we have seen, all the respondents wanted to work for positive reasons and to escape the negative consequences of unemployment. They wished to escape the financial, social and personal privations associated with unemployment, particularly in the long term. They believed that employment would bring an improved standard of living, and ideally a return to the lifestyle and standard of living they had previously enjoyed. They missed the social contacts, sense of purpose and structure to the day, and satisfaction they had gained from work. They wished to work in order to gain a sense of pride and to improve their self-esteem.

Attitudes towards labour market programmes

Many of the respondents perceived their lack of skills and/or experience as a barrier to work. One fifth had undertaken non-government training during their spell of unemployment to improve their chances of getting work. A lone parent with few CSEs had recently done voluntary training by attending a local care home at nights for seven months, until restricted by childcare responsibilities from continuing to do so. She found it beneficial and was sure that it would help her to find work once the more immediate barrier of childcare was overcome. The other four were all professionals who had updated or broadened their qualifications. Two used savings to fund their courses, while another received free tuition at a local college. Staff at the jobclub were giving a single man informal help in learning about computers to help him to update his skills.

Most respondents did not have the resources to fund their own training, or were not aware of training opportunities other than TfW. Unemployed claimants have a Restart interview every six months at which they may be offered TfW: trainees receive £10 on top of their benefit and are given job specific training, a course leading to an NVQ, or temporary work experience. They then have to wait six months for the next opportunity.

Opinion was divided about Restart interviews. Some respondents found them useful but others did not. One respondent believed they were to police the unemployed, rather than give information and advice. Only half of the respondents had participated in TfW. Most of those who had not were not eligible because they were not registered as unemployed. The lone parents had limited knowledge of their options or of the need to revise their claimant status to 'unemployed' and to fulfil the conditions attached to become eligible (to be available for work and actively seeking it). People registered as sick also do not attend Restart interviews, but they are eligible for TfW, without the six-month rule. However, only one of the two people registered as sick had participated. The other respondents who had no experience of TfW were all professional people. Most had not been offered it and none thought it would help them. However, all had used the Jobclub (see below).

Opinions varied among those who had experience of TfW. Five men, with diverse educational backgrounds, saw it as a positive step towards their reintegration into the labour market. Two had taken the initiative by requesting it. These participants were impressed by the quality of the training and educational elements, but only one was optimistic about the opportunities offered by the work experience component.

Eight respondents believed that, enjoyable or not, TfW was of no help in leaving long-term unemployment. Not one had noticed any improvement in their job prospects in the months following the scheme. They were sceptical about the quality of the training. An unskilled man's description of his job-related training with a poor supervisor was typical:

> "They said they'd had a lot of complaints about him. It was just rubbish really, they weren't trying to train you, they were just doing it so you got off the dole ... there wasn't any training involved whatsoever. Just digging holes, pulling up weeds, chopping brambles down.... That was all it was." (male partner of a couple with children)

The common view was that companies used TfW as a source of cheap labour, with no intention of offering people work at the end of the period. This opinion was shared by a man who was very pleased with the training he was receiving, but deeply cynical about the work placement side of the scheme.

> "Companies that just keep taking placement after placement is another thing that I don't agree on. If they're going to take somebody on after the placement, let them. If they do more than three placements the placements should stop. Because they're only screwing the system. They're paying a training agency £40 a week to have someone there full time. They're laughing, the money is in their pockets." (male partner of a couple with children)

Respondents wanted to see more effort put into finding them a job at the end of their six or 12-month course, rather than simply abandoning them. They also wanted to be offered courses of higher quality and wider range. This is demonstrated by the fact that of the eight respondents who were cynical about what they had achieved through TfW, six would be willing to do it again if there was a good quality course.

Several respondents criticised the six-month rule of eligibility. For example, an unskilled man had been on a scheme. Then within six months, a course providing training in fork-lift truck driving, with the chance of getting a licence, had become available, but he was not eligible since a claimant cannot take one then one course in a six-month period. He saw this as a missed opportunity. A further complaint about TfW was that it had too many regulations and that they were not always applied as they should be. One man had been 'sacked' for taking time off to visit his physiotherapist, and respondents were doubtful if participants would be given time off to attend interviews, as the rules allow.

Seeking work

The two most commonly used strategies for finding out about vacancies were the Jobcentre and newspaper advertisements. Lone parents and people registered as sick are not required to visit the Jobcentre, although several did so. A few who rarely went to the city centre and lone parents with pre-school age children did not. Respondents were critical of the range and quality of jobs advertised in the Jobcentre. They said there were too few jobs, "not enough to go round", and they tended to be unsuitable, to offer very low wages or to be temporary. One thought that only "the shittiest job at the end of the day is put in the dole office".

Local newspapers, including the free paper, were important to unskilled people while qualified people used the national papers and, sometimes, specific trade journals. Respondents remarked that the lack of suitable advertised jobs reflected the poor state of the labour market. A few emphasised the importance of informal, word-of-mouth information about local jobs.

Although all the respondents were strongly motivated to find work, they spent different amounts of time looking for and applying for jobs. Some had increased their efforts from personal resolution or, more usually, because of a change of circumstances such as acquisition of skills or removal of childcare barriers. Others had become despondent and effectively given up. Almost one third put a lot of effort into their jobsearch, applying for as many jobs as possible, in one instance more than a thousand in one year. This group was mostly professional or managerial people who were geographically mobile. None had had a previous long period of unemployment, although their current spells ranged from one to five years. Three had increased their jobsearch effort following a training course. Two of the respondents in this group were unskilled: both had experienced a very long period of unemployment and had made a conscious decision within the last year to do everything possible to improve their financial and social situations.

Although most of the other respondents regularly looked for vacancies, they applied for few jobs. Many of them faced temporary barriers to working, mainly from caring responsibilities for young children or elderly relatives, although also from sickness. Several were hopeful that a training course would put them in a better position to apply for more jobs. One man had stopped applying for jobs because he was trying to start his own business. Only two respondents made very few applications because they were disheartened and despondent. Both were unskilled with family commitments and long spells of unemployment. One had previously literally "got on my bike" and visited every possible employer in the city, but to no avail. The main barriers to their working were the lack of suitable jobs, their own lack of skills and the difficulty of earning enough to make them better off in work than receiving benefit.

Support for jobsearch

The Employment Service is responsible for providing support and advice to unemployed people. Respondents were dissatisfied with the vacancies displayed in the Jobcentre (see below) and thought that Jobcentre staff were not helpful: they were described as "not interested", "not there to help you", "they're selling jobs on behalf of companies, they're glorified reps [sales representatives]. It's because they're on a low wage" and "not useful at all".

One lone parent found herself being 'vetted' by the Employment Service officer, who then refused to submit her job application on the grounds that she did not have the qualifications required, although she maintained that she had enough experience. She felt humiliated:

> "He wouldn't submit my application form.... So I'd sat there and filled the application form in, handed it to this snip nosed young man of about 25 or 30 and been turned down, just there and then, and he ripped it up and threw it in the bin.... I felt very hurt by that, I suppose I am, I've got no qualifications, I know I'm nobody aren't I? But I know I could do the job.... He made me feel a couple of centimetres big, my face was bright red I was so angry. It's no wonder

> people get nasty in the Jobcentre.... There really is no wonder because they are so condescending." (female lone parent)

Employment Service staff were criticised because they did not provide useful information, but only responded to direct questions and because they were ignorant of the rules, so finding out about training and other schemes and entitlements was hit or miss. Respondents had mixed experiences of their six-monthly Restart interviews: some found them useful, and some did not. Similarly, jobclub provision appeared to differ in quality.

The city has several companies contracted to supply jobclubs. One of these was consistently praised for its facilities, staff and willingness to buy papers or magazines which contained job ads. Participants used it frequently. The only criticism was that attendance was limited to six months. However, another was criticised for failing even to buy a newspaper as requested. Several training agencies were running non-executive jobclubs at the time of the interviews.

Family Credit is an in-work, means-tested benefit to low paid workers with children, but awareness of it appeared patchy. Only half of the 15 families mentioned Family Credit, or used it to calculate their 'reservation wage' (lowest acceptable wage). Most of these knew of the benefit from previous experience, although one family had received an information pack. They thought it would allow them to accept a job they otherwise could not afford to do. However, there was some serious misinformation about the rules of entitlement to Family Credit, such as the numbers of hours worked. The policy response designed to help families with childcare costs is the Childcare Disregard introduced in 1996: up to £60 of childcare costs may be discounted when calculating entitlement to Family Credit. Only one parent appeared to be aware of the disregard.

Obstacles to employment

Respondents indicated various barriers to their return to work. These fell into four broad groups: shortage of jobs; personal circumstances; moving from benefit to employment; and employer prejudice.

Regardless of their skills, experience or occupation, respondents believed that the underlying obstacle to their employment was a general shortage of jobs. Firms were not taking on people, but were instead downsizing. These prevailing market conditions translated into increased competition for jobs, bringing the requirement for higher and higher qualifications. This acted as a barrier for professionals and non-professionals alike. However, two of the professionals had applied for jobs for which they were overqualified, and had been turned down on those grounds.

Many of the policy interviews (see Chapter Six) emphasised the need for employees to respond to a 'flexible labour market'. This requires individuals to reskill and retrain, be geographically mobile, and be willing to undertake less secure work of varying hours. It assumes that people will act in economically 'rational' ways and takes no account of personal circumstances, aspirations and desires. However, there were limits on the flexibility of respondents in this study.

One fifth were restricted by injuries, and could not consider all types of work. Only two were claiming Invalidity Benefit at the time of the interview.

Respondents largely accepted the need to update and increase their skills. However, their ability and willingness to retrain was limited by access to quality training and tempered by their opinions of its usefulness in the light of the lack of jobs. They had mixed experiences of training courses, and in any event were still unemployed at the end of them.

Few respondents were willing or able to be geographically mobile. Only four seriously considered moving for a job, and they were all professionals without family ties. However, even willingness to move did not guarantee success: one respondent had attended an interview 300 miles away, only to be told he had not got the job because he did not live within 18 miles. A few respondents could not leave because they had sick or invalid parents who needed their support. Most had grown up locally and were unwilling to leave their friends and social networks, or indeed the local football team. We have seen earlier how social networks and relying on material and emotional support from families and friends were crucial to helping respondents cope with long-term unemployment.

Respondents made it clear that there is a strong financial incentive to escape unemployment. However, the interviews suggest that they have to believe that the improvement in their finances is real, sufficient and secure before they will accept work.

Respondents took certain factors into account when calculating their 'reservation wage'. Non-professional parents considered the demands of their dependent children, and lone parents in particular needed to cover the costs of childcare. They wanted a wage that would allow them to be better off than when on benefit. Labour market decisions seemed to be taken not by individuals, but as a family, taking account of total income and the effect on benefits, including passported benefits. None of the respondents with absent children knew how maintenance would be calculated – although one thought his ex-wife would "take me to the cleaners".

Professional respondents tended to set their reservation wage in relation to their skills, experience and previous earnings rather than just what they needed to survive, although they were prepared to accept a little below the market rate, and a cut from their last job.

The risk of taking on insecure work worried several respondents, particularly those with mortgages. Similarly, they were unwilling to take temporary work, not just because of current difficulties associated with moving on and off benefits, but because of fear of future changes in the rules.

Four respondents had considered self-employment. One had pursued setting up his own business and was waiting for a planning decision. The others had been barred primarily by lack of capital: one offered the equity on his house as security against a loan for a franchise business, but was refused; another could not afford the fee for a JCB test, or even do labouring on a self-employed basis because he did not own the necessary tools and equipment.

The 'flexible labour market' does not take into account people's needs for job satisfaction. Work is a major part of life and one of the incentives to work is the pleasure it can bring. Respondents would rarely consider a job they could not enjoy, particularly if the wages were poor.

Many respondents believed that employers held negative preconceived ideas based on age and the very experience of being unemployed for a long period. They recounted their experiences of such discrimination. Most of those who felt they were "too old" were around 40, but one 30-year-old also felt "on the scrap heap". Although several admitted that keeping to a routine became harder as unemployment lengthened, they pointed out that they had not lost their qualifications, skills or ability to work. A single professional man was turned down by a recruitment agency for a job for which he had the relevant qualifications and experience. The agency said they were instructed not to forward the CVs of anyone who had been out of work longer than three months, "Because the guy in the company said anybody who has been out of work for more than three months is either bone idle and doesn't want to work, or is stupid."

Policy improvements

Particular policy changes which had been enacted or were widely discussed at the time of the interviews have already been discussed. In April 1996, a month or so after the interviews, payment of Housing Benefit and Council Tax Benefit was extended into the first four weeks of employment, to 'bridge the gap' until the first pay arrived. None of the respondents were aware that this would happen. Given the financial barriers they face, and the particular fears about the security of their homes, it is likely that knowledge of the scheme could positively influence their decision to take work.

The Jobseeker's Act was to come into force in October 1996. No respondent knew enough about it to hold detailed opinions, but there was concern about the element of coercion in the scheme.

As was found in the interviews with policy makers, opinions regarding the introduction of a minimum wage differed. Some respondents, skilled and unskilled, thought that if it were introduced in conjunction with changes to benefit levels it could greatly improve the financial incentive to work:

> "Yes, I think nobody should work for anything less than they need.... No one should work for less than £2.50 an hour, no one. We're reverting back to slave labour. For kids to work for £60 or £70, I was on that 20 years ago." (male partner of a couple with children)

> "It clarifies what people can or should be earning and then you can work from that to benefits and pay a certain amount which obviously won't match the minimum wage but would give someone, as a right, enough not to starve or enough to live on. But a minimum wage would give every incentive to look for a job and do some work to earn an amount that is not derisory." (professional male partner of a couple with children)

Other respondents were concerned that the introduction of a minimum wage would cause the loss of even more jobs:

> "I think that would cause more problems than it would solve. I mean, because it would force up the differentials from the minimum wage further up the scale and what few jobs would be created would be counterbalanced by a lot of people losing theirs." (single professional)

Several respondents wanted to see the (then Conservative) government encourage active job creation. However, they held little hope of improvement in the near future. A respondent said that, ideally, company profits should be shared equally between investment in the company and dividends for shareholders, but "nowadays it's the shareholders, everyone is greedy for money and they don't invest". He thought this was unlikely to change in the near future.

Respondents suggested the following changes to current provision:

- changing the six-month eligibility rule for access to jobclubs and training schemes;
- providing more quality training, and training to suit their needs;
- providing more active help in securing work following training courses;
- improving non-executive jobclubs to ensure they offer maximum help;
- helping with childcare costs and crèche provision alongside training places;
- providing more generous help to mortgage payers: the current system is a serious deterrent to accepting work which is not secure and permanent;
- improving dissemination of information about schemes available to help people off benefit and into work (Childcare Disregard, Family Credit, Extended Payment of Housing Benefit and Council Tax Benefit);
- improving the quality and range of jobs advertised in the Jobcentre;
- improving the training, professionalism and helpfulness of Employment Service Jobcentre staff.

Conclusions

The respondents' experiences of employment varied considerably, not least because of the wide differences among their levels of education and training. However, their views of long-term unemployment appeared more or less universal and differences, such as there were, seemed more of degree than of type. Respondents agreed about the personal, social and financial reasons for working. Employment was preferred over unemployment because work brought its own intrinsic pleasures and because it was 'normal' whereas not working was seen as disagreeable and painful, with the benefits system providing little comfort.

Long-term unemployment damaged family life, bringing constraints on living standards and social circumstances. Parents feared the effects of stigma and isolation on their children. All were dependent on family and friends for material and emotional support and such social life as they could manage. The single professionals felt they could move away for a job, but the others could not risk losing their local support. Lifestyles changed as living standards were eroded: going without and juggling debts became normal. Respondents felt that benefits were set at levels which made it impossible to manage: they had to use up their savings to survive, and many felt justified in working 'on the side' although none condoned systematic flouting of the rules.

Respondents had mixed experiences of the various Employment Service schemes and programmes intended to help them back to work. They faced formidable barriers to employment, not least because of the lack of jobs, or of work they could see as adequately paid and reasonably secure. They were limited by personal circumstances such as illness and disability, and caring responsibilities; by their mortgage repayments; by the difficulties of moving from benefit to paid employment and calculating when they would be better off in work, and by age barriers and employers' prejudices.

For this group of long-term unemployed people, the idea of a flexible labour market had manifested itself as a shortage of jobs, with acute competition for the few which became available in which they lost out to people who had been unemployed for a shorter time. For a variety of reasons, they feared taking temporary, part-time and insecure work; they were trapped by the lack of jobs and by low wages.

ELEVEN

Conclusion

Introduction

In the previous three chapters the financial consequences and social implications of long-term unemployment in three countries have been presented and reactions to benefits and services explored. This chapter seeks to highlight the main findings and cross-national similarities and contrasts. As in Chapter Seven, two further aims are to:

- discuss how far responses from long-term unemployed people reflect institutional aspects of unemployment and labour market policies and thus justify the conceptualisation of national unemployment support regimes outlined in the introductory chapter;
- assess responses in the light of the debate about long-term unemployment and 'social exclusion'.

Long-term unemployed respondents

The educational backgrounds of the respondents at least partly reflect national systems of education. Most German respondents had completed their basic education and gone on to apprenticeships. In Sweden, some had continued their education and taken vocational courses, while many took advantage of the extensive adult education system to improve their educational attainment. Roughly equal proportions of British respondents had: left school with no qualifications and had taken no training or education subsequently; taken up an apprenticeship or continued in further education; or a university degree or professional qualification (a peculiarity of the sample).

Nearly all of the German and Swedish respondents had been unemployed between one and three years. What is more, most of them had had relatively continuous work histories since completing their main period of education and training. The British respondents were different: on average, they had been unemployed longer and, although they had all been employed at some time, many had worked infrequently and for relatively short periods. This accords with differences in national labour market structures and a longer history of mass unemployment and shorter average job tenures in Britain (OECD, 1994).

In all the countries, the lone parents differed from the rest of the respondents. Many had been unemployed for prolonged periods. Ironically, while Sweden made the most generous childcare provision, Swedish lone parents were the most likely to say they had chosen not to seek full-time employment while their children were young.

Financial consequences and the impact of unemployment support regimes

Universally, and most importantly, long-term unemployment had an adverse effect on the living standards of respondents from all three countries. However, reflecting differences in both generosity and type of national unemployment support systems (Reissert, 1994; Ploug and Kvist, 1996), differences between as well as within countries became apparent. As discussed in Part One, benefits for the majority of registered (and even for many long-term) unemployed people in Sweden and Germany are insurance based and related to previous earnings, while benefits in Britain are not. While in theory earnings-related systems can be less generous than means-tested support, especially if the latter is supplemented with other types of transfers, in practice the systems in the three countries have been shown to cause different degrees of material hardship.

None of the respondents described living on benefits as problem free. All described the adjustments they had made to their lifestyles as a consequence of their depleted incomes, reporting a range of outcomes in which most had somehow learned to live on their available money and were managing. For many, unemployment meant being forced to look out for bargains and going shopping in special discount shops. All referred to the need to plan and monitor their expenditure and stick to a budget. However, on the whole it can be argued that German and Swedish respondents regarded themselves as better off than their counterparts in Britain. Only British respondents reported difficulties in affording even basic necessities such as buying food for the family, paying essential bills, and paying for clothes for their children.

The problem of debt illustrates national differences in the impact of long-term unemployment. Reflecting the general experience of Income

Support claimants in Britain (Kempson and Bryson, 1994), debts were more common among British respondents. Excluding mortgages, two thirds of them had debts. These debts were incurred during the spell of unemployment rather than originating from before unemployment, which was mostly the case for German and Swedish respondents.

However, such a comparison would be misleading if it did not account for intra-country differences. For example, while debts were much less common for German respondents on the whole, it was a different case for lone parents in that country. Long periods without employment meant that most were in debt to relatives, while some were also indebted to banks or mail order companies, and for past social security overpayments. On the other hand, one quarter of all German respondents even managed to make small but regular monthly savings. This more 'differential' picture of the impact of long-term unemployment on German respondents contrasts with the more 'universal' notion of financial stringency in Britain. It accords with the notion of the more 'selective' type of unemployment compensation in Germany compared with the 'egalitarian residual' form in Britain, as discussed in the introductory chapter.

Discussion of the interviews with long-term unemployed people, in the previous three chapters, has revealed that these institutional differences do not only have an impact on the degree of material deprivation experienced but also on the experience of long-term unemployment. National welfare arrangements influence the way in which unemployment is perceived. In general, respondents in all countries felt more comfortable with insurance-based rather than means-tested benefits. In Germany in particular, and Sweden to a somewhat lesser extent, it is not long-term unemployment per se which affects people's status and self-esteem, but the impact that joblessness and entitlement to particular types of benefit has on the perception of social status (Offe, 1991). This was particularly evident among German respondents. Those who claimed local social assistance were not only critical about the level of support they received but strongly disliked applying for it, feeling it raised the spectres of poverty, destitution and social stigma. This was in stark contrast to recipients of unemployment insurance benefit which respondents regarded as a more legitimate and acceptable form of public support. Similar, although perhaps less frequent and less pronounced, distinctions were made by Swedish respondents.

Regulations which allow or restrict options of supplementing benefit receipt with part-time earnings was another aspect which indicated the importance of national benefit regimes. For example, one third of German respondents relied on often small but generally regular and declared types of paid employment. While the same proportion of British respondents reported income from paid work in their case it was a more irregular, and precarious source of income, and was undeclared. These differences might be explained with the higher amount of earnings disregarded before benefits are reduced in Germany compared with Britain. This applies to both insurance as well as means-tested benefits for the unemployed (Evans, 1996). While it could appear that a more extensive use of insurance-based benefits facilitates a more lenient treatment of income from paid work within means-tested benefits this cannot be concluded from the evidence of this study.

Coping with long-term unemployment

Respondents differed in their initial responses to becoming unemployed. None anticipated that they would be out of work for such a prolonged period of time. Those who had worked continuously for many years recalled the shock of losing their job and feelings of worthlessness and inferiority. Others, who had been in and out of employment and especially those who had suffered a work-related accident or illness, were initially more relaxed, hoping that the interruption to work would be only brief.

Common experiences across countries manifested themselves in two ways. First, as time passed, respondents were caught between suffering the pains of unemployment and adjusting to their new status. For nearly all respondents, the adverse effects of the lack of paid work on self-esteem became more dominant the longer unemployment lasted. They referred to feelings of loneliness, isolation and loss of self-respect. The importance of regular work for social contact, interest and a structured daily life became more apparent. Boredom and inactivity were a burden. These impacts of lengthy absence from paid employment correspond with findings of previous studies (Hess et al, 1991; Engbergsen and Timmer, 1993).

Different coping strategies and forms of adapting became apparent within countries supporting earlier research which questioned the idea that the long-term unemployed form some part of a homogenous 'underclass' (Kronauer, 1993). Some respondents became resigned to their fate, others remained optimistic and continued to apply for jobs. Some worked on the side to maintain their standards of living, while others sought alternative ways to spend their time in the absence of real jobs. It would not be difficult to assign those interviewed for this study to the various typologies of adaptation constructed by other writers (White, 1991; Strittmatter, 1992; Engbergsen and Timmer, 1993).

A second common experience of respondents in all countries was a distinction between the response from friends, neighbours and relatives and that from outsiders. The former were perceived to be understanding, provided an important source of social support and gave financial assistance in the form of loans or gifts. In contrast, respondents felt that the societies in which they lived held unsympathetic and prejudiced views about unemployed people, believing that they could get work if they really wanted it. This became evident when respondents from all three countries described how they attempted to avoid admitting being unemployed.

However, national differences were noticeable. For example, while the lack of paid work led to similar processes of social retreat and perceptions of shame and stigma, the interviews demonstrated that in Britain these feelings were associated more with being without paid work per se. By contrast, the stigmatising effect of unemployment in Germany is reinforced for those claiming social assistance and weakened for those receiving insurance-based benefits, or training allowances.

The respondents' personal characteristics influenced their feelings and views about the effects of long-term unemployment on their close families. Cross-national similarities emerged: those with children tended to focus on the effects on them, while adults alone described their personal responses.

However, in all the countries, a positive impact of unemployment, for many people the only one, was the extra time available to spend with their children, compared with when they were working. Confirming previous studies, this was more frequently mentioned by women than men (Gallie, 1994; White, 1991). A small group of the Swedish respondents in particular spoke of the advantages and were happy to spend their energies in the confines of their homes. However, they were the exception. More common were descriptions of the adverse effects unemployment had had on family life. Reflecting findings of previous studies (for example, White, 1991) the long-term unemployed felt that the relationships with their partners and families were damaged because of a lack of material resources combined with the dislocation of normal patterns of behaviour and loss of social standing.

Parents were concerned that the financial consequences of their unemployment might have psychological and social implications for their children. This appeared to be a near universal concern for the British parents, but a minority one for German and Swedish parents. Parents of school aged children pointed out that they could not provide the things their children wanted and their friends had, such as brandname trainers and fashion items; nor could they take them on outings to the cinema or McDonalds. Parents emphasised the need to dress themselves and their children so that they were no different in appearance from others so that their children would not feel excluded.

British, and to a lesser extent German, parents expressed anxiety that their children would be stigmatised. Once again, cross-national differences became apparent. For example, the British respondent who described how his 16-year-old daughter was ashamed that her father was unemployed, and lied about it in public can be contrasted with the example of the German mother who admitted to her children that she was unemployed but not that she was receiving social assistance. This indicates that there are a number of aspects – being in receipt of social assistance, being poor and being unemployed – which need to be taken into account to understand the relative impact long-term unemployment can have on processes of social exclusion or marginalisation in a comparative perspective.

Beyond families, a common consequence of not having a job identified in all countries was the loss of social contacts. In part, this followed from no longer meeting colleagues as part of work life but also from financial stringency and changed spending patterns which limited unemployed people's participation in social activities. Many, but not all, found their ability to have a social life was severely constrained, although there were differences among the countries because of benefit levels, and among types of respondents, such as parents and single people. On the whole, the British respondents appeared to have suffered more in this respect than those in the other countries. But even German respondents, who had been least hit financially, had cut back social activities which cost money. The majority claimed their friendships had not suffered, although some said that they had retreated from friendships and had fewer friends than before.

Typically, respondents in all three countries were members of clubs or societies, such as sports teams or local charities, which provided some social contacts and helped to alleviate boredom and fill the time during the day. For example, many of the Swedes described an active social life built around informal and voluntary activities. However, it was striking that these activities were not regarded as equivalent to employment in any of the three countries: they did not provide a similar source of identity and status and did not hold the same meaning for participants.

In general, respondents in all of the countries did not like to rely on the generosity of others. They were embarrassed when invited for a meal by well-meaning friends or relatives, knowing they would not be able to return the favour. They also felt awkward at not being able to contribute to conversations which derived from events at work, making them feel particularly cut off. As a consequence, contacts with former colleagues were often lost. This illustrates once again how paid employment confers identity and social status in all three countries.

Escaping unemployment

One of the most striking features of the interviews was that no respondent can be said to have made a conscious decision in favour of an idle lifestyle. This held even for those who had suffered the least financial deprivation. All intended to return to regular employment if at all possible, even those who had most visibly adjusted to their new lifestyle. Unemployment was not considered to be a viable status because it brought adverse financial, social and personal consequences which could only be alleviated through finding work. This is supported by evidence from the British Social Change and Economic Life Initiative which has shown that, "the attitudes to work of the unemployed are not distinctive and are not an important factor accounting for people's vulnerability to unemployment" (Gallie and Vogler, 1994b, p 152).

Respondents from all the countries expressed similar reasons for wanting to work. They saw it as a matter of pride, self-esteem and independence. Work also gave a structure and a balance to the day, and provided interest and companionship. Employment was sought which would enable them to earn enough to have a reasonable standard of living for themselves and their families. The British respondents, who experienced the most difficulty managing on benefits, also expressed relatively modest aspirations. However, German and Swedish respondents were also prepared to accept that they would not regain their former standard of living; they wanted as much as their benefit with a little more to cover expenses.

Interviews with German respondents underlined another, often overlooked, aspect of welfare regimes, namely their capacity to weaken or, in this case, foster work incentives. Even the younger interviewees were concerned to get back to work so they could maintain their contributions to health and pension insurance and not be disadvantaged in the longer run.

Attitudes towards training and work programmes

Regime differences in unemployment support mechanisms extended to labour market programmes. In general, respondents in all three countries took one of two, opposed views on schemes. They either welcomed them as a positive step towards their reintegration into the labour market and significantly improving their job prospects or they were sceptical about their quality and cynical about the opportunities they gave. At the extreme, they saw such schemes as merely massaging the unemployment figures and participated only because they received enhanced benefit or so as to prevent benefit suspension. However, the balance of views differed among the countries: those in Britain were the most negative while respondents in Germany were most positive about schemes and their likely outcomes (although differences were noticeable between those receiving training allowances and those on programmes run by local authorities).

Respondents in all countries had taken part in training programmes. In the main, German and Swedish participants, receiving maintenance grants related to former earnings, were happy to receive enhanced income and status from participation and thought their job chances might be improved. The Germans also welcomed a three-month guaranteed work period. While many of the Swedish, and some of the German, respondents had taken up places because they would otherwise lose benefit, or because participation increased their period of entitlement to unemployment-related benefit, they accepted rather than resented these conditions. However, differences between the 'selective' German system of labour market support and the more 'comprehensive' support system in Sweden were apparent. Only those with a relatively strong labour market attachment and shorter spell of unemployment participated in German training or rehabilitation programmes whereas in Sweden a number of particularly vulnerable people received considerable support from the schemes.

Nearly all of the British respondents who had undertaken training praised the educational content of well-run courses. However, in contrast to both their Sweden and Germany counterparts, they were more negative and critical of their experiences and confirmed the notion that the training courses were of a more 'residual' nature. The range of courses available was said to be limited, the quality regarded as poor and the level of material support for participants criticised as insufficient. Overall, existing training schemes were not seen to bring long-term prospects for work.

Similar attitudes prevailed with regard to work experience schemes. Only one of the few British respondents who had taken part in such a scheme was optimistic about the opportunities it might offer. The common view was that companies used participants as cheap labour with no intention to offer them work at the end. In contrast, and reflecting national policies and provision, many more Swedish respondents had been on, or were at the time participating in, work placements and job creation projects. Mostly, they welcomed the opportunity to work and were not deterred by its temporary nature. Job creation projects were described as enjoyable and 'character building' and respondents were pleased to have done something useful. In the main, criticisms centred on the low level of payment and worries that job creation brought displacement effects. Some of the German social assistance claimants were about to start temporary work placements offered by their local authority. Responses to this prospect were mixed: some criticised the programme as compulsory work and as of little value to them, others were hoping that it would improve their job prospects.

Seeking work

Respondents appeared to place few restrictions on the jobs which they would be prepared to take and did not set a high reservation wage. The majority emphasised their readiness to earn wages much lower than they had earned previously. They were prepared to accept low hourly rates so long as their income allowed them to lead a 'normal life', covering their essential expenditure and saving a little for holidays.

Interviews with respondents confirmed that the widespread use of means-testing in Britain creates particular obstacles to moving from benefit into employment. Much more than in Germany or Sweden, claimants believed they would not be better off in a particular job once they took account of work-related costs such as travel, clothes and childcare and the loss of allowances 'passported' through Income Support. There appeared to be little knowledge about the availability of in-work benefits. British respondents were also more likely than those in Germany or Sweden to own their homes and have a mortgage. Consequently, they faced particular difficulties because they had to find a job in which they would earn enough to make repayments on the mortgage; they could not risk taking insecure work.

Most of the respondents were also prepared to be flexible about the type of work they would do, their working hours and the time spent travelling to work. In Britain, it appeared that the (few) professionals without family ties were prepared to move away from the city for a job, although they expected to earn professional rates of pay for doing so. However, they constituted a small minority among the respondents as a whole; mostly, respondents were limited by the availability and cost of public transport.

Most of those interviewed can be said to have experienced what Gallie and Vogler (1994b, p 334) have called "a process of cumulative disadvantage". A substantial proportion of respondents in each country suffered from work-related accidents or injuries. Respondents with these problems could undertake only a restricted range of tasks; despite (universal) anti-discrimination legislation they found employers were "not interested" as soon as they mentioned they were not fully fit. There were national differences with perceptions concerning disadvantages and these broadly matched particular national obstacles identified in Part One. For example, German respondents in particular thought that they faced difficulties because of age barriers. However, rather than an age barrier at 45 which could have been expected according to interviews with the German policy community respondents believed that employers discriminated against people who were aged 40 or just over and had been out of work for a considerable length of time – and some had direct experience of this. Respondents also highlighted their personal circumstances, such as caring responsibilities and disabilities, as limiting their job chances. Similar worries were expressed by Swedish respondents who saw themselves as disadvantaged by competition with young people with better education and training or by having to care for children or elderly parents and be settled in homes and areas which they were reluctant to leave. Being unemployed for a long time had sapped their motivation. The immigrants in Sweden and in Germany, and also one British respondent, faced the additional problems of prejudice against them; more recent arrivals also had language difficulties, compounded, in their view, by their ignorance of their rights.

Again, lone parents constituted a particular group. In Britain and Germany, they faced barriers because of their caring responsibilities and the lack of provision of childcare facilities. The 'disregard' for childcare costs in the calculation of in-work benefit was mentioned by only one (British) parent; ignorance of the benefit limits its usefulness. In accordance with the 'weak male breadwinner' model (Lewis, 1992) adopted in Sweden the availability of public childcare was much less of an issue there.

Support for jobsearch

Respondents followed a variety of jobseeking activities. An option pursued in all the countries was newspaper advertisements. Most people looked at local papers, and qualified people who were prepared to move for a job also used the national press and, sometimes, specific trade journals. In Germany and Britain, speculative applications, phone calls or visits to potential employers were also made. However, a shortage of suitable jobs because of the poor state of the labour market was a common perception.

There were real differences among the respondents in the use they chose to make or were required to make of their employment offices. Respondents in Sweden appeared relatively inactive; some visited the office to see if any jobs were advertised, but little hope was expressed that anything positive would result. In Germany, all respondents were registered with the public employment office which is also the unemployment benefit office. Some had given up any attempt to find work with the help of the office but most were still in regular contact, hoping to be offered suitable vacancies. Compared with Germany, registered unemployed people in Britain are required to make more regular and frequent contact with the Jobcentre to sign on for their benefit and to provide evidence of activity in search of a job. Lone parents and people registered as sick are not compelled to visit the Jobcentre, but several did when they were in the city centre.

The Swedes also appeared the least active in searching and applying for jobs. In Britain, almost one third of the respondents were actively looking and applying for as many suitable jobs as possible. They were mostly the professional or managerial people who were geographically mobile, but also included others who had either undertaken extra training and felt their chances were enhanced, or, after a very long and disheartening period of unemployment, had decided to do everything possible to improve their situation. The German respondents as a whole were consistently active in their search, but not to the extent of this small group of British respondents. Some stressed the importance of local networks and word of mouth, a perception which corresponds with research by Morris (1992) which found that these were the most likely avenues for a return to paid employment. This can create a dilemma for long-term unemployed people who are expected to be flexible and mobile in their jobsearch behaviour, since it suggests that their best hope is to remain well connected to people, especially those who have jobs, in their own locality.

Policy improvements

Respondents in this study offered suggestions aimed at increasing the availability of jobs and improving local services. Overall, the British respondents had the most to say and the German respondents the least. No clear direction for policy can be found on most of the issues on which respondents expressed a view because they took different positions. However, respondents from all countries tended to agree on improvements to local employment office provision. This could be achieved by:

- increasing staff numbers;
- developing a more sensitive service especially for those with medical problems;
- providing a more helpful staff;
- widening the range of jobs advertised.

The country specific suggestions included British respondents referring to their fears about the element of coercion which they believed to be in the JSA (yet to be introduced when the interviews were undertaken). They wished to see improved availability of information, more quality training and changes to benefit rules which would help with the move into employment, referring specifically to childcare costs and mortgage interest payments. German respondents believed that training courses would be valued more highly if they ended with a test and a certificate for those who passed.

On a broader level, several Swedish and British respondents wanted to see the government encourage active job creation. Swedish criticism centred on economic policy: holding down interest rates, being a member of the EU and buying foreign goods. A significant number thought the interests of Swedes should be put before those of immigrants.

Other respondents were critical of measures which had been taken. Swedish respondents proposed an overtime ban and the use of unemployed people as a resource to satisfy a number of social needs. However, while some criticised schemes which merely provided something for people to do and wanted more meaningful placements, others were concerned about schemes which displaced real jobs and exploited people. A few German respondents referred to 'social companies' (soziale Betriebe) and other initiatives of that type as a positive attempt to find work for some long-term unemployed people, but hardly any had been in contact with such an organisation or were clear what they were.

Only the British respondents discussed the introduction of a minimum wage. As was found in interviews with policy makers, opinions differed:

some thought that it was a matter of right to earn "enough not to starve or enough to live on" and that it could greatly improve the financial incentive to work; others were concerned that it would cause the loss of even more jobs.

Conclusions

It would be misleading to suggest that the samples in this study allow a definitive statement to be made on the degree of marginalisation and exclusion associated with each of the three welfare states. All the respondents, by definition, suffered what Rodger (1992) has called the *principal* form of exclusion, that is, exclusion from the labour market. Many in each of the three countries also experienced *derivative* exclusion whereby they were excluded from those benefits which derive from employment such as pension plans or health insurance. Others suffered from *contingent* exclusion, which refers to the stigma and disadvantage experienced by the long-term unemployed. This often arose in interaction with employed individuals but also, importantly, through discrimination by employers or the hostility of public officials.

However, national differences became apparent. Most Swedish and many German respondents received more generous, earnings-related benefits or training allowances; they were able to manage, although on depleted incomes. For British respondents, long-term unemployment was also associated with financial privation to the extent that basic needs could not be met. This indicates a link between the policies of the different countries and the degree of marginalisation experienced by its people. On the whole the Swedish respondents were the most satisfied with the benefits they received and the labour market schemes in which they participated. The same attitude was adopted by many Germans, but a more differentiated picture emerged. The experiences of many of the social assistance claimants were closer to those of their British counterparts, who all were dependent on means-tested benefits, than those of their fellow Germans on insurance-based schemes. Based on the differential extent to which each welfare state relies on social assistance as a means to provide the long-term unemployed with a cash benefit, it seems justified to characterise unemployment support systems in the three countries as 'residual', 'selective' and 'comprehensive' models of unemployment compensation (Ploug and Kvist, 1996).

However, the interviews demonstrated that such a characterisation can be enhanced due to the impact of different benefit regimes in other respects, such as conferring social status, reinforcing social divisions, facilitating or blocking options to supplement benefits with earned income or fostering or weakening work incentives. This was one important outcome of this comparative study. The perspective from the outside, that of long-term unemployed people themselves, did not merely confirm the importance of the nature of regimes but also revealed additional dimensions which are not captured in the characteristics of welfare regimes offered by insiders. Such conceptualisations are based on descriptions of administrative rules and benefit arrangements and are shown to be partial.

Although the interviews suggested that policy responses in Germany and Sweden mitigated the effects of long-term unemployment, this does not mean that long-term unemployed people in a particular country face less problems to overcome obstacles on the way back into employment than in another. The study has shown that, when there are too few jobs, specific difficulties are encountered to different degrees in each country. A common experience seems to be that long-term unemployed people who are older, and those who in addition are not physically fit or have caring responsibilities, face particular barriers. These people are not convinced that welfare and labour market institutions as currently constituted will assist them in regaining paid secure employment and thus a social status which is generally perceived as crucial to be fully integrated in all three societies. This study has shown that paid work is a dominant part of people's daily life in all three countries. Even, or perhaps especially, for those who have been unemployed for long periods of time, it seems that employment continues, for better or worse, to be closely associated with an individual's position and status as a citizen.

Part Three

Overall findings

TWELVE

Comparing responses from within and without

Introduction

A central aim of this study has been to explore problems of long-term unemployment from a cross-national perspective, focusing on the perceptions of policy communities and unemployed people themselves. Many of the findings confirm those of previous single-country research, based on large and representative samples of unemployed people, for example Morris (1992) and Gallie (1994). The approach adopted in this study, however, was to examine in depth the views of respondents who could represent particular positions and experiences in countries chosen for their contrasting welfare state regimes and provision for unemployed people. While long-term unemployment in all three countries affects people disproportionately late or early in their working life (although the latter less so in Germany), this study has deliberately focused on those out of work for long periods during their 'mid-career' years. It was assumed that labour market entry or exit programmes would be less available for them, and that the social impact of long-term unemployment would be perhaps particularly evident because this age group is 'expected' to be at work.

Given that the three countries studied represented each of Esping-Andersen's welfare state regimes, it was intended to see whether there were also three corresponding unemployment support regimes. Previous chapters have already shown that while there is some evidence of a convergence of ideas concerning labour market policies and employment rights, there is little movement towards similar unemployment compensation systems.

This final chapter will make comparisons between the responses of long-term unemployment which emerged from the literature and members of policy communities and the responses from those who have experienced long-term unemployment first-hand – between those within the policy-making process and those outside. It will then discuss implications for the future in the light of more recent policy developments.

Similarities and differences

A concern expressed by many sources in Part One about long-term unemployed people was that there was a danger that they would give up the search for work, that they would become uninterested in employment, become resigned to their situation, accept 'alternative' roles and be content to live on benefit. Little evidence for such an attitude emerged from the interviews with the long-term unemployed. While jobsearch activities varied a great deal, the importance of employment to people's lives was stressed time and again for a variety of reasons. For some, employment was important because of the implications for their future pension, for others, there was the desire for greater material advantage, while others expressed their need for the social status and social fulfilment that employment provided. Lack of work was associated with boredom, feelings of worthlessness and a lack of structure. The unemployed respondents in all three countries feared social disapproval to the extent that some hid their present status, while those who were parents feared that their children would be stigmatised.

The reluctance of unemployed people to move to 'where there are jobs' is sometimes cited by their critics as evidence of their willingness to live on benefit. This study suggests that one of the reasons long-term unemployed people are not more adventurous is because their only security is their locality, the wider family and established social networks they have there. They see no point in risking a move to a distant area, for a job with little security and low pay. Local social networks, where unemployed people may still have some contact with employed friends, will continue to be a source of job information since word-of-mouth is often the way in which people find employment. For these reasons it may not be appropriate to see mobility as the solution to the problem of long-term unemployment.

It was the very strength of people's social lives that made it difficult to describe the long-term unemployed people interviewed for this study as socially-excluded. The literature and policy interviews indicated a greater degree of marginalisation than was actually the case in the experience of the long-term unemployed. However, people did feel marginalised by public officials, by employers, by the media and by the wider society.

Both the policy interviewees and the unemployed respondents showed a recognition that certain groups were much more likely to remain unemployed for longer periods due to employer prejudice. Age was seen as a barrier to gaining work. The main difference between the 'responses from above', from the policy communities, and the experiences of those on the ground was the position of the age barrier. The literature and the consensus among the policy respondents tended to put it above 45. The interviews with the long-term unemployed suggested that people around the age of 40 feared that they might never again be employed.

Not surprisingly, there was agreement that employers probably discriminated against applicants on grounds of race and ethnicity. Language skills and qualifications were often used as rationalisations for preferring 'native' employees. Lone parents also complained of discrimination, even in Sweden, where the opportunities for childcare are widespread. What clearly emerges from Parts One and Two is that mass unemployment makes it relatively easy for employers to discriminate. Both the policy interviews and the unemployed themselves revealed a twin recognition that while employers created a barrier to employment for all vulnerable groups, their behaviour was rational and almost acceptable in the circumstances. So long as there was a plentiful supply of labour, employers did not have to take risks with those who had been unemployed for a long time, had family or caring responsibilities, had serious health or social problems, were seen as too disabled or too old. Only with a return to full employment would members of such groups again be sought by employers in the labour market.

Unemployment support regimes

In all three countries, but particularly in Germany and Sweden, there was a widespread view that labour market programmes needed to be tailored to the diverse needs of the long-term unemployed. This was stated explicitly in many of the policy interviews, but was reinforced implicitly by the negative comments of the unemployed respondents when they complained about the anonymous treatment they received and the inappropriateness of some of their training. This reflects findings of the EU first and second ERGO programmes which stressed the need for local actions and a more 'holistic' approach to reintegrating long-term unemployed people – "concentrating on individuals' needs, personal development and capacity building by customising actions of different types into packages" (ERGO, 1996, p 6). These packages may involve training and work experience programmes but also counselling, debt advice and help with psychological and social problems. This is needed in particular for those long-term unemployed people who suffer from a multitude of disadvantages (such as medical problems, qualification deficit, psychological problems, being the 'wrong' age).

Policy respondents in all three countries expressed a concern about organisational issues. In Sweden and Germany, it was felt that labour market policy needed to be decentralised and more effectively coordinated. This implied a criticism of their centralised labour market boards. It was thought that greater efforts should be made to cooperate with, and involve, local authorities and the private sector. In Britain, the concern was aimed more at the relationship between the DfEE and local provision by the TECs. The unemployed themselves had little to say about such organisational issues, apart from those in Germany who felt that experience on placements in private companies would be more beneficial than those in public sector organisations.

Unemployed people made a clear distinction between what they saw as the positive aspects of labour market schemes and those which they saw as degrading or a waste of time. On the whole, it was the British respondents who were critical of the poor quality of training provision while their Swedish and German counterparts were more likely to express satisfaction with the range of opportunities on offer. This would suggest that active labour market policies are not only valued by the German and Swedish authorities but appreciated by those for whom they are designed.

This study has also demonstrated that more generous welfare provision weakens the link between long-term unemployment and poverty. The policy communities in Germany and Sweden were confident that, overall, social security and labour market programmes were still effective in preventing processes of deprivation, social exclusion and ghettoisation. In Britain, by contrast, the policy experts commented on the clear link between long-term unemployment and poverty. This was, in turn, reinforced by the perceptions of the unemployed whose living standards were considerably lower than those of their continental counterparts.

The German welfare state has placed considerable importance on maintaining status differentials through a variety of income-related, social insurance and assistance schemes. In contrast, the British, in the last 15 years, have reverted to a historical preference for means-tested flat-rate benefits. The Swedes have built up an earnings-related system of benefits, like the Germans, but with a state-managed, universalistic approach, characteristic of British welfare. These differences were reflected in the standards of living as well as in the responses of the unemployed people interviewed. Greater differentiation was found in both German benefits and labour market programmes with stigma attached to local means-tested benefits. The status achieved when participating in federal training programmes, as opposed to those which were managed by local authorities, underlines this differentiation. Compared with Germany, unemployment benefit in Sweden has certain advantages. The income replacement rate is higher and the benefit includes a minimum level. Access to labour market programmes is guaranteed and participation extends the right to benefit. As a consequence, fewer people have to resort to local social assistance schemes. In Britain, there was very little differentiation, with everybody receiving the same low benefits and often poor quality schemes. For many of the Swedish and German respondents, there was an opportunity to maintain some self-respect and to take part in worthwhile programmes.

The very structure of benefits seemed to influence the attitudes expressed in the policy interviews and by the unemployed themselves. In Germany and Sweden there was an acceptance of the principle of the right to insurance-based benefits. Politicians were not so concerned about their abuse nor the unemployed about their receipt. While there was some concern about the abuse of social assistance and stigma did attach to claimants, in Britain, where insurance-based benefits were short-lived and reliance on social assistance more widespread, there was, ironically, an even greater official concern about the disincentive effect of benefits.

Despite the apparent focus in this research on the micro level (individual perceptions, labour supply programmes, barriers to employment) this should not be taken as an endorsement of the view that long-term unemployment is largely a problem of labour supply. A recent study (Webster, 1997) found that many of the theories which suggest that high levels of long-term unemployment have something to do with characteristics of the long-term unemployed themselves (lack of skills, demotivation, declining productivity the longer unemployment lasts) are highly questionable. Instead, a stable relationship was found between unemployment and long-term unemployment over time and in geographical terms. This reinforces a view, frequently reported in this study, that policies towards long-term unemployed people which adopt an exclusively supply-side focus (such as training and work experience placements) must be an inadequate response to the problem of long-term unemployment. While training and other measures may be beneficial for some groups of long-term unemployed people, long-term unemployment as such – and unemployment generally – needs also to be seen as a demand-side problem, affecting some areas more than others. Labour market programmes will remain insufficient unless there is targeted urban investment which leads to the creation of "blue collar jobs in areas which have lost them most" (Webster, 1997, p 51).

Macroeconomic policies which foster labour demand are crucial for preventing long-term unemployment, despite the fact that this view is not very fashionable in Britain – or in the EU and OECD for that matter. This point was made by many respondents within the German and Swedish policy communities, and even in Britain, although to a lesser degree. It was also made by the unemployed respondents who emphasised the need to create real jobs for which training and other schemes were not regarded as an adequate substitute.

Implications for the future

None of the three countries can be said to provide a model for others to follow. None has tackled the problem of long-term unemployment in a way that suggests they have solved the problem. However, the findings do suggest that providing decent benefits and labour market schemes significantly alleviates the sense of exclusion and marginalisation which the long-term unemployed feel.

Unfortunately, it is these very characteristics of the German and Swedish systems which are coming under domestic criticism and scrutiny. Germany and Sweden are beginning to accede to pressures for a more deregulated labour market and to adopt more decentralised, flexible labour market programmes, trends which British Conservative governments, like the Republican counterparts in the US, embraced with enthusiasm for more than a decade. The commitment to monetarism and supply-side measures in the early 1980s had initially resulted in an increasing number of people losing their jobs. Subsequently, they were deprived of decent benefits and labour market schemes. This was accompanied by the weakening of the very institutions which were there to help protect them – trade unions and local authorities. Germany and Sweden have so far resisted this process but as time goes on their governments may be tempted. So far it can be said that the institutional strength of countervailing power in the more corporatist countries has prevented them from going down the neo-liberal path (Clasen and Gould, 1995).

The results of this study would suggest that for the long-term unemployed this can only be beneficial. However, the conflict between and debate about the relative merits of these two models, the neo-liberal and the corporatist, has recently taken a new twist. The American economist Robert Reich, in an interview in the British weekly, *New Statesman*, has suggested that Britain has the opportunity to chart a course between the cheap labour route of the US and the corporatism of continental Europe:

> The continental European approach – shorter work weeks, the maintenance of rigid labour market rules, very high security against dismissal – is not the right way to go. It slows you down too much and makes the transition even more difficult. It creates a zero-sum game of the most pernicious kind. A 35-hour week as they've announced in France and are talking of in Italy is not going to help. (Lloyd, 1997)

While Reich's optimism about British policy may reflect his close association with leading figures in the New Labour government elected in 1997, his pessimism about continental polices may be partly a consequence of other recent developments.

At the time of writing (late 1997), the relative unemployment rates in Germany, Sweden and Britain had changed from those quoted in the introductory chapter for 1995. Germany's rate, by September 1997, had risen to 10.0%, Sweden's had also risen to 8.8% while the figure for Britain had dropped to 7.2% (*Eurostat*, 1997). There can be little doubt that the British trend was exaggerated by concentrating solely on the number of people claiming benefit since broader definitions of unemployment were falling at a much slower pace (Convery, 1997c). Nonetheless the trend was real and is reflected in the *Eurostat* figures above. However, because the three countries were at different stages in their respective economic cycles it would be premature to suggest that each of the trends would continue or that they constituted evidence of the effectiveness of labour market strategies. Nevertheless, the loss of public revenue and increased expenditure associated with mass unemployment places a strain on the maintenance of existing labour market policies in Sweden and Germany.

Prior to the British General Election in May 1997, the Conservative government had claimed that the downward trend in unemployment was due to deregulation, a commitment to labour market flexibility and its reluctance to accept the social chapter provisions in the Maastricht Treaty. With the advent of a Labour government, it was hoped that a more sympathetic view would be taken of the unemployed and a more constructive approach adopted towards benefits and labour market programmes. Certainly, Labour's New Deal (funded by a windfall tax on the private utilities which had made considerable profits under the Conservatives) was intended to create substantially improved opportunities for the young unemployed. More than £3 billion was to be devoted to a package of measures for more than 350,000 long-term unemployed between the ages of 18-24. Less than 11% of the sum devoted to the young unemployed was to be made available to long-term unemployed adults above the age of 25 living in areas of high unemployment. Private employers would be encouraged to provide employment and training in return for a job subsidy and a fee to cover the costs of training. Full-time education and training places would be provided while allowing the unemployed to continue to receive benefit and stimulus to self-employment was created with a business enterprise subsidy (Convery, 1997b). These measures were a marked improvement to British labour market provision, and there was the possibility that the new government would try to improve the genuinely advisory role of the Employment Service and get away from the obsession with simply removing people from the claimants' register. In other respects too – in its commitment to the social chapter and the minimum wage – the government indicated a change of direction. Social exclusion was recognised as a serious and complex issue and long-term unemployment a major component of the concept (DSS, 1997). However, there was still an insistence on the need for a flexible labour market and a tendency to regard any increases in social benefits as an incitement to dependency.

In Sweden, government attempts to reduce benefits and to have a more flexible labour market faced political and institutional obstacles. Trade union pressure forced the government to reverse its decision to lower a-kassa from 80% to 75% of income. Attempts to limit the merry-go-round which would have resulted in more unemployed people having to live on social assistance continued to face considerable hostility from trade unionists and social democrats (*Dagens Nyheter*, 1996a; 1996b). The government faces similar difficulties in trying to change employment protection laws (*Riksdag och Departement*, 1996a). On another front, a reluctant government was forced to accept that the Social Democratic Party, and the women's section in particular, believed a reduction in working hours would alleviate unemployment (*Dagens Nyheter*, 1996c).

Only in the reform of labour market policy was there the basis for a reasonably broad consensus. The committee which investigated the work of AMS proposed a more limited set of aims and tasks and more individually-orientated action plans for the unemployed (*Riksdag och Departement*, 1996b).

In Germany, the record unemployment figures provided the background for the government to implement a new Employment Promotion Act in 1997. However, this did not imply a fundamental change in policy direction. The measure simplified regulations, allowed for a higher degree of decentralisation, introduced new instruments, such as benefits for the part-time unemployed, and improved others, such as options for women returnees. The age threshold for receiving benefit for longer than one year was raised and, as far as other changes for the long-term unemployed people are concerned, the new legislation introduced incentives for labour market integration, including new forms of wage subsidies in the new Länder as well as 'integration contracts' (Sozialpolitische Umschau, 1997:16). The latter rewarded employers who offered a job to a long-term unemployed person by transferring some of the costs to the FLO and suspending certain labour law regulations. For example, employers were not obliged to continue paying wages to employees appointed under such a contract who were sick, on a training course or on holiday, and restrictions on redundancy were lifted. The Act also put pressure on the unemployed though by, for example, lowering the threshold of what were regarded as suitable job offers which unemployed claimants could reasonably be expected to accept.

Not surprisingly, in these circumstances, the new British government is claiming that there is a middle way between the neo-liberal and corporatist employment policies. The Luxembourg summit of EU heads of state held in November 1997 provided a forum for such a case to be argued. The outcome would seem to lend support to the argument made in Chapter Seven that a degree of convergence was already taking place. Unemployment was firmly on the agenda, thus reassuring trade union anxiety that the priority given to monetary union might impose budgetary constraints which would bring "Thatcherism to Europe by the back door" (*The Guardian*, 1997). Individual countries would remain responsible for their own labour market policies – enabling France, and Italy to experiment with 35-hour weeks – but would be expected to submit "national action plans to cut unemployment and present them for peer review once a year" (*Financial Times*, 1997). Sweden and Britain proposed programmes to guarantee long-term unemployed people work experience and training placements. A further proposal, to increase the percentage of unemployed people on training schemes from 10% to 25%, was finally agreed when a compromise level of 20% was proposed by the German government. Guidelines on the need for more flexible labour markets, lower statutorily-imposed labour costs and less stringent employment regulations for small businesses were also accepted (*Financial Times*, 1997).

The resulting compromise was one which reflected a new willingness on the part of the British to accept the need for a more interventionist approach and on the part of countries such as Sweden and Germany to accept that some aspects of their previous policies might actually be making matters worse.

Conclusions

Long-term unemployment should be of greater public concern. The effects on the long-term unemployed themselves, their families and particularly their children, are considerable. Western economies should pursue a policy of full employment more vigorously and find more dignified ways to help and protect the vulnerable. Long-term unemployment does increase the threat of social exclusion not just for young and elderly workers but also for adults in the age range of the respondents in this study. Exclusion from the labour market automatically marginalises the long-term unemployed but for many it begins to weaken their social ties. Social and labour market policies can play an important part in minimising the threat, by providing the long-term unemployed with adequate benefits and opportunities to maintain and improve their skills and morale. While German and Swedish policies leave much to be desired, they do seem to provide their citizens with the means to resist the threat of social exclusion more effectively than have British policies in the past. At least the new government in Britain accepts that social exclusion exists and that labour market policy can alleviate some of the effects of long-term unemployment. However, ultimately the problems of long-term unemployed people can only be addressed satisfactorily when the member countries of the EU – individually and collectively – begin to prioritise the expansion of employment.

Bibliography

Adnett, N. (1996) *European labour markets: Analysis and policy*, London: Longman.

Agell, S. (1995) 'Swedish labour market programmes: efficiency and timing', *Swedish Economic Review*, vol 2, no 1, Stockholm.

Agell, S., Björklund, A. and Harkman, A. (1995) 'Unemployment insurance, labour market programmes and repeated unemployment in Sweden', *Swedish Economic Review*, vol 2, no 1, Stockholm.

Albert, F. (1989) 'Arbeit für erwerbslose Hilfeempfänger – Grundlagen und Ergebnisse des Berliner Modells', *Nachrichtendienst des Deutschen Vereins für öffentliche und private Fürsorge*, no 69, pp 228-33.

AMK (Arbetsmarknadskontoret) (1996) 'Jobb till tusen', Örebro: Örebro Kommun.

ANBA (Amtliche Nachrichten der Bundesanstalt für Arbeit) (1994) *Arbeitsmarkt 1993*, no 42, special issue, May.

ANBA (1995) *Arbeitsmarkt 1994*, no 43, special issue, June.

ANBA (1997) *Arbeitsmarkt 1996*, no 45, special issue, June.

Andreß, H.-J. (1989) 'Instabile Erwerbskarrieren und Mehrfacharbeitslosigkeit – ein Vergleich mit der Problemgruppe der Langzeitarbeitslosen', *Mitteilungen aus der Arbeitsmarkt- und Berufsforschung*, no 1, pp 17-32.

Arbeitskreis AFG Reform (1994) *Memorandum für ein neues Arbeitsföderungsgesetz*, Düsseldorf: Arbeitskreis AFG Reform.

Arbetsmarknadsverket (1994) *Årsredovisning 1993/1994*, Solna.

Ashworth, K. and Walker, R. (1994) 'Measuring claimant populations', in N. Buck, J. Gershuny, D. Rose and J. Scott (eds) *Living in Britain*, Colchester: ESRC/RCMC.

Auer, P. and Riegler, C.H. (1994) 'Sweden: the end of full employment', *Employment Observatory*, no 46, Berlin.

Bach, H.-U., Brinkmann, C. and Spitznagel, E. (1994) 'Individuelle und gesellschaftliche Belastungen durch Arbeitslosigkeit', *Arbeit und Sozialpolitik*, vol 48, no 5-6, pp 15-24.

Bäcker, G. (1995) 'Soziale Sicherung bei Arbeitslosigkeit', in H. Seifert (ed) *Reform der Arbeitsmarktpolitik*, Cologne: Bund Verlag.

Baldwin, P. (1996) 'Can we define a European welfare state model?', in B. Greve (ed) *Comparative welfare systems: The Scandinavian model in a period of change*, Basingstoke: Macmillan.

Berglind, H. (1972) *Utslagningen på arbetsmarknaden*, Lund: Studentlitteratur.

Bergmann, C. (1993) *Initiative für einen öffentlich geförderten Beschäftigungssektor (Zweiten Arbeitsmarkt)*, Berlin: Senatsverwaltung für Arbeit und Frauen.

Bergmann, C. (1994) *Berliner Erklärung. Zur Halbierung der Arbeitslosigkeit bis zum Jahr 2000*, Berlin: Senatsverwaltung für Arbeit und Frauen, Grundsatzreferat Arbeitsmarktpolitik.

Blanke, B., Evers, A. and Wollmann, H. (eds) (1986) *Die Zweite Stadt. Neue Formen lokaler Arbeits- und Sozialpolitik*, Opladen: Westdeutscher Verlag.

Blanke, B., Heinelt, H. and Macke, C.-W. (1987) *Großstadt und Arbeitslosigkeit*, Opladen: Westdeutscher Verlag.

BMAS (Bundesministerium für Arbeit und Sozialordnung) (1990) 'Arbeitsvermittlung zwischen Arbeitslosigkeit und Fachkräftemangel', *Forschungsbericht Nr 167*, Bonn: BMAS.

BMAS (1995) *Gegen Langzeitarbeitslosigkeit. Ein Leitfaden für Arbeitgeber*, Bonn: BMAS.

Bogai, D., Hess, D., Schröder, H. and Smid, M. (1994) 'Binnenstruktur der Langzeitarbeitslosigkeit älterer Männer und Frauen', *Mitteilungen aus der Arbeitsmarkt- und Berufsforschung*, no 2, pp 74-93.

Bonoli, G., George, V. and Taylor-Gooby, P. (1996) 'Politics against convergence? Trends in European social policy', *Swiss Political Science Review*, vol 2, no 3, pp 1-17.

Bosch, G. (1995) 'Beschäftigungsgesellschaften in den alten und neuen Bundesländern', in H. Seifert (ed) *Reform der Arbeitsmarktpolitik*, Cologne: Bund Verlag.

Bottomley, D., McKay, S. and Walker, R. (1997) *Unemployed and job seeking: A national survey in 1995*, DSS Research Report No 62, London: HMSO.

Bradshaw, J. and Lynes, T. (1995) *Benefit operating policy and living standards*, York: Social Policy Reports, SPRU.

Brinkmann, C. (1984) 'Die individuellen Folgen langfristiger Arbeitslosigkeit. Ergenbisse einer repräsentativen Länggsschnittuntersuchung', *Mitteilungen aus der Arbeitsmarkt – und Berufsforschung*, no 4, pp 454-73.

Brinkmann, C. and Wiedemann, E. (1994) 'Individuelle und gesellschaftliche Folgen von Erwerbslosigkeit in Ost und West', in L. Montada (ed) *Arbeitslosigkeit und soziale Gerechtigkeit*, Frankfurt: Campus Verlag.

Bryson, A. and McKay, S. (eds) (1994) *Is it worth working? Factors affecting labour supply*, London: Policy Studies Institute.

Budd, A., Levine, P. and Smith, P. (1987) *Unemployment, vacancies and the long-term unemployed,* Discussion Paper No 154, London: Centre for Economic Forecasting, London Business School.

Burchell, B. (1994) 'The effects of labour market position, job insecurity and unemployment on psychological health' in D. Gallie, C. Marsh and C. Vogler, *Social change and the experience of unemployment*, Oxford: Oxford University Press.

Calmfors, L. and Herin, J. (1993:52) 'En ny arbetslöshetsförsäkring', *Ersättning vid arbetslöshet*, Stockholm: SOU.

Castels, R. (1990) 'Extreme cases of marginalisation: from vulnerability to deaffiliation', Paper presented to conference, 'Poverty, marginalisation and social exclusion in the Europe of the 1990s', organised under the auspices of the European Commission, Alghero, Sardinia.

Castles, F. and Mitchell, D. (1992) 'Identifying welfare state regimes: the links between politics, instruments and outcomes', *Governance*, vol 5, no 1, pp 1-26.

CBI (undated) *Tackling long-term unemployment: A business agenda*, London: CBI.

Christe, G. (1995) 'Wie erfolgreich können Soziale Betriebe sein?', extended version of a paper presented to the conference 'Auf dem Weg in den Markt – Perspektiven Sozialer Betriebe', Hanover, 14 March.

Clasen, J. (1994a) *Paying the jobless: A comparison of unemployment benefit policies in Great Britain and Germany*, Aldershot: Avebury.

Clasen, J. (1994b) 'Social Security – the core of the German employment-centred social state', in J. Clasen and R. Freeman (eds) *Social policy in Germany*, Hemel Hempstead: Harvester Wheatsheaf.

Clasen, J. and Gould, A. (1995) 'Stability and change in welfare states: Germany and Sweden in the 1990s', *Policy & Politics*, vol 23, no 3, pp 189-202.

Commission (Commission of the European Communities) (1988) *Very long-term unemployment*, Luxembourg: DG for Employment, Industrial Relations and Social Affairs.

Commission (1992) *Employment in Europe 1992*, Luxembourg: DG for Employment, Industrial Relations and Social Affairs.

Commission (1994) *Social protection in Europe 1993*, Luxembourg: DG for Employment, Industrial Relations and Social Affairs.

Commission (1995) *Employment in Europe 1994*, Luxembourg: DG for Employment, Industrial Relations and Social Affairs.

Commission (1996) *Employment in Europe 1995*, Luxembourg: DG for Employment, Industrial Relations and Social Affairs.

CSJ (Commission on Social Justice) (1988) *Social justice: Strategies for national renewal*, London: Vintage.

Commission on Urban Priority Areas (1985) *Faith in the city: A call for action by Church and nation*, Report of the Archbishop of Canterbury's Commission, London: Church House.

Convery, P. (1997a) 'Unemployment', in A. Walker and C. Walker (eds) *Britain divided: The growth of social exclusion in the 1980s and 1990s*, London: CPAG.

Convery, P. (1997b) 'The New Deal gets real', *Working Brief*, Issue 97, London: Unemployment Unit.

Convery, P. (1997c) 'JSA is responsible for half of fall in unemployment', *Working Brief*, Issue 82, London: Unemployment Unit.

CRG (1996) *Evaluation of the self-employed option within Training for Work*, Department of Education and Employment Research Studies RS35, London: The Stationery Office.

Dagens Nyheter (1994a) 'AMS får samköra dataregister', 16 September, p 7.

Dagens Nyheter (1994b) 'Skärpta krav på arbetslösa' [by J. Schück] 6 December, p 7.

Dagens Nyheter (1994c) 'Avskaffa rätten till arbete' [by A. Isaakson] 6 September.

Dagens Nyheter (1995a) 'Regeringen hoppas på fp' [by A. Sundström] 29 January.

Dagens Nyheter (1995b) 'Felinriktat anställningstöd' [by S. Agell] 21 February, p 4.

Dagens Nyheter (1995c) 'Lägg ner AMS' [by L. Calmfors] 19 July.

Dagens Nyheter (1995d) 'Ambitionen har fått sänkas' [by G. Bernhardsson] 13 September.

Dagens Nyheter (1995e) 'Forskarfel I AMS rapport', 11 November.

Dagens Nyheter (1995f) 'Full sysselsättning avslutad epok', 13 January, p 3.

Dagens Nyheter (1995g) 'Var tredje arbetslös har gett upp helt' [by S. Agell], 27 January, p 15.

Dagens Nyheter (1995h) 'Det finns ingen arbetsminister', 11 February, p 15.

Dagens Nyheter (1995i) 'Tre vägar till framtiden', 9 February, p 15.

Dagens Nyheter (1995j) 'Arbetslösheten minskar', 8 February, p 3.

Dagens Nyheter (1995k) 'Arbetslösheten fortsätter minska', 8 March, p 3.

Dagens Nyheter (1995l) 'Allt tuffare på arbetsmarknaden', 9 July, p 3.

Dagens Nyheter (1996a) 'Regeringens politik buades ut', 18 October.

Dagens Nyheter (1996b) 'Persson hårt ansatt', 19 October.

Dagens Nyheter (1996c) 'Partistyrelsens linje segrade', 17 March.

Davies, R., Elias, P. and Penn, R. (1994) 'The relationship between a husband's unemployment and his wife's participation in the labour force', in D. Gallie, C. Marsh and C. Vogler (eds) *Social change and the experience of unemployment*, Oxford: Oxford University Press.

Dawes, L. (1993) *Long-term unemployment and labour market flexibility*, Leicester: University of Leicester, Centre for Labour Market Studies.

Dean, H. and Taylor-Gooby, P. (1992) *Dependency culture*, Hemel Hempstead: Harvester Wheatsheaf.

Department of Employment (undated) *Policies and programmes for employment in the UK*, London: HMSO.

DfEE (Department for Education and Employment) (1996a) *Shepherd sets out 'devastation' caused by minimum wage*, Press Release 128/96, 16 April.

DfEE (1996b) *Expenditure plans, 1996/97-1998/99*, London: HMSO.

DfEE (1996c) *Eric Forth: Employment legislation – less is more*, Press Release 136/96, 24 April.

DfEE (1996d) *Employment Service to target those most in need*, Press Release, 104/96, 28 March.

Deregulierungskommission (1991) *Marktöffnung und Wettbewerb. Bericht 1990 und 1991*, Stuttgart: Deregulierungskommission.

Deutscher Städtetag (1994) 'Kommunale Beschäftigungsförderung. Ergebnisse einer Umfrage über Hilfen zur Arbeit nach BSHG und Arbeitsbeschaffungsmaßnahmen nach AFG', Cologne: Deutscher Städtetag.

Diderichsen, F. (1994:148) 'Arbetslöshetens effekter på friska och sjuka – konsekvenser för sjukförsäkringen', in *Förtidspension – en arbetsmarknadspolitisk ventil*, Stockholm: SOU.

Dobson, B.(1994) *Diet, choice and poverty*, Working Paper 227, Loughborough: Centre for Research in Social Policy.

Dobson, B., Beardsworth, A., Keil, T. and Walker, R. (1994) *Diet, choice and poverty: Social, cultural and nutritional aspects of food consumption among low income families*, London: Family Policy Studies Centre.

Donnelly, C. (1997) *The chance of a lifetime: How the benefit system creates barriers to lifetime learning for the unemployed*, London: Unemployment Unit.

Ds (Department of Employment) (1991:52) *Arbetsmarknad och arbetsmarknadspolitik 1990*, Stockholm: Arbetsmarknads-departementet.

Ds (1994:108) *Arbetsmarknad och arbetsmarknadspolitik 1993*, Stockholm: Arbetsmarknadsdepartement.

Ds (1995:12) *Kommunernas ansvar för ungdomar under 20 år*, Stockholm: Arbetsmarknadsdepartement.

DSS (Department of Social Security) (1996a) *DSS publishes spending plans for next three years*, Press Release 96/056, 20 March.

DSS (1996b) *Peter Lilly outlines radical reform of social security administration*, Press Release 96/035, 28 February.

DSS (1997) *Harman sets out Government's priorities for tackling social exclusion*, Press Release, 13 November.

Duffy, K. (1997) *Review of the international dimensions of the thematic priority on social integration and exclusion: A report to the United Kingdom Economic and Social Research Council*, Leicester: De Montfort University.

Dyson, K. (1989) 'Long-term unemployment: the ideological perspective', in K. Dyson (ed) *Combating long-term unemployment: Local/EC relations*, London: Routledge.

Employment Gazette (1995) 'New development in the pattern of claimant unemployment in the United Kingdom', September, pp 351-8.

Employment Observatory (1995) 'East Germany: labour market developments and policies in the new German Länder', No 14, Brussels: European Commission, DG-V.

Engbergsen, G. and Timmer, J. (1993) 'The heterogeneity of unemployment', *International Journal of Political Economy*, vol 23, no 3.

Enheten för Regional Utveckling (1993) 'Vad gör kommunerna åt arbetslösheten?', Rapport no 20, Stockholm: Länstyrelsen i Stockholms Län.

ERGO (1996) *ERGO final report: Action and research programme on long-term unemployment*, European Commission, Directorate-General V.

Esping-Andersen, G. (1990) *The three worlds of welfare capitalism*, Cambridge: Polity Press.

Esping-Andersen, G. (1996) 'Welfare states without work: the impasse of labour shedding and familialism in continental European social policy', in G. Esping-Andersen (ed) *Welfare states in transition: National adaptations in global economies*, London: Sage.

Esping-Andersen, G., Assimakopoulou, Z. and von Kersbergen, K. (1993) 'Trends in contemporary class structuration: a six nation comparison', in G. Esping-Andersen (ed) *Changing classes*, Cambridge: Polity Press.

Eurostat (1997) Current figures on EU unemployment obtained from the Internet, November, Luxembourg.

Eurostatistics (1997) May, Luxembourg: Eurostat.

Evans, M. (1996) 'Means-testing the unemployed in Britain, France and Germany', Discussion Paper 117, London: Welfare State Programme, STICERD, London School of Economics and Political Science.

Fawcett, H. and Papadopoulos, T. (1997) 'Adequacy of support for the unemployed in the EU', *West European Politics*, vol 20, no 3, pp 1-30.

Field, F. (1989) *Losing out: The emergence of Britain's underclass*, Oxford: Basil Blackwell.

Financial Times (1997) 'EU agrees new-style drive to cut jobless', 22 November.

Finn, D. (1997) *The stricter benefit regime and the New Deal for the unemployed*, Paper presented at the Social Policy Association Annual Conference, Lincoln, 15-17 July.

Finn, D., Murray, I. and Donnelly, C. (1996) *Unemployment and training rights handbook*, London: Unemployment Unit.

Fryer, D. (1992) 'Psychological or material deprivation: why does unemployment have mental health consequences?', in E. McLaughlin (ed) *Understanding unemployment*, London: Routledge.

Furåker, B. (1995) 'Vad händer på arbetsmarknaden?', in *I marginalen: att ställas utanför*, Stockholm: Rapport från forskarseminariet i Umeå, Försäkringskassan.

Gallie, D. (1994) 'Are the unemployed an underclass? Some evidence from the social change and economic life initiative', *Sociology*, vol 28, no 3, pp 737-57.

Gallie, D. and Vogler, C. (1994a) 'Labour market deprivation, welfare and collectivism', in D. Gallie, C. Marsh and C. Vogler (eds), *Social change and the experience of unemployment*, Oxford: Oxford University Press.

Gallie, D. and Vogler, C. (1994b) 'Unemployment and attitudes to work', in D. Gallie, C. Marsh and C. Vogler (eds), *Social change and the experience of unemployment*, Oxford: Oxford University Press.

Gallie, D., Marsh, C. and Vogler, C. (eds) (1994) *Social change and the experience of unemployment*, Oxford: Oxford University Press.

Gaß, G., Krömmelbein, S. and Schmid, A. (1995) 'Internationale Maßnahmen zur Bekämpfung der Langzeitarbeitslosigkeit', *WSI Mitteilungen*, no 12, pp 792-800.

Gaß, G., Klems, W., Krömmelbein, S. and Schmid, A. (1997) *Strategien gegen Langzeitarbeitslosigkeit. Strukturen, Ursachen und Maßnahmen*, Berlin: Edition Sigma.

Geers, F., Neilson, S. and Darlin, S. (1992) *Strategies to combat long-term unemployment in Belgium, Denmark and the UK Synthesis*, Berlin: European Centre of the Development of Vocational Training.

Ginsburg, N. (1997) 'Housing', in A. Walker and C. Walker (eds) *Britain divided: The growth of social exclusion in the 1980s and 1990s*, London: CPAG.

Goodman, A. and Webb, S. (1994) *Far richer, far poorer: The UK income distribution, 1961-91*, London: Institute for Fiscal Studies.

Gould, A. (1983) *MEGA: A minimum educational grant for all*, Occasional Report, Nottingham: Association for Recurrent Education.

Green, A. (1994) *The changing geography of unemployment and non-employment in Britain*, in S. Hardy, G. Lloyd and I. Cundell (eds) *Talking unemployment and social exclusion: Problems for regions, solutions for people*, Proceedings of the Regional Studies ASSOC Annual Conference, pp 12-24.

Gregg, P. and Wadsworth, J. (1994) *More work in fewer households?*, Discussion Paper No 72, London: National Institute of Economic and Social Research.

Gregg, P. and Wadsworth, J. (1995) 'A short history of labour turnover, job tenure and job security, 1975-93', *Oxford Review of Economic Policy Unemployment,* vol 11, no1, pp 73-90.

Gröbner, G., Lang-Neyjahr, R. and Weber, A. (1995) 'Langzeit-arbeitslosenprogramm: Mit verstärkter Kraft', *Bundesarbeitsblatt*, no 4, pp 5-13.

Guardian, The (1997) 'EU gets to work on jobs', 21 November, p 14.

Gustafsson, U. (1994) *Från låg till hög arbetslöshet*, Working Paper No 15, Stockholm: Arbetslivscentrum.

Hammarström, A. (1995) 'Ung och arbetslös', in *I marginalen: att ställas utanför*, Stockholm: Rapport från forskarseminariet i Umeå, Försäkringskassaförbundet.

Hansen, H. (1997) *Elements of social security in six European countries*, Copenhagen: The Danish National Institute of Social Research.

Häntsch, U. and Mirbach, T. (1994) 'Kommunale Beschäftigungsgesellschaften als Instrument zur Bekämpfung von Arbeitslosigkeit und sozialer Ausgrenzung', *Zeitschrift für Sozialreform*, vol 40, no 9, pp 577-94.

Hardes, H.-D. (1988) 'Langzeitarbeitslosigkeit und Arbeitsbeschaffungsmaßnahmen', *Wirtschaftsdienst*, pp 463-9.

Harkman, A. (1994) *Unemployment, labour market policy measures and their influence on the probability of gaining employment*, Solna: Arbetsmarknadsstyrelsen.

Hedborg, A. and Meidner, R. (1984) *Folkhems modellen*, Borås: Rabén and Sjögren.

Hedges, A. (1993) *In-work benefit project*, London: DSS, Social Research Branch.

Hess, D., Hartenstein, W. and Smid, S. (1991) 'Auswirkungen von Arbeitslosigkeit auf die Familie', *Mitteilungen aus der Arbeitsmarkt- und Berufsforschung*, no 1, pp 178-92.

Hills, J. (1995) *Joseph Rowntree inquiry into income and wealth, vol 2*, York: Joseph Rowntree Foundation.

HMSO (1994) *Jobseeker's Allowance*, Cm 2687, London: HMSO.

HMSO (1995) *Competitiveness, forging ahead*, Cm 2867, London: HMSO.

Howard, M. (1997) 'Cutting social security', in A. Walker and C. Walker (eds) *Britain divided: the growth of social exclusion in the 1980s and 1990s*, London: CPAG.

Howell, R. and Frank, F. (1995) *Right to Work Bill*, presented July.

Huebner, M., Krafft, A. and Ulrich, G. (1992) *Das Spektrum kommunaler Arbeitsmarktpolitik*, Berlin: Edition Sigma.

ISA (Informationen zur Sozial- und Arbeitsmarktpolitik) (1995) 'Arbeitslosigkeit und Sozialhilfe Ausgrenzung stoppen', *Deutscher Gewerkschaftsbund*, Bundesvorstand, June.

Jacobs, H. (1995) *Evaluierung von Maßnahmen der 'Hilfe zur Arbeit' in Bremen*, Bremen: Centre for Social Policy Research.

Jaedicke, W., Ruhland, K., Wachendorfer, U., Wollmann, H. and Wonneberg, H. (1991) *Lokale Politik im Wohlfahrtsstaat. Zur Sozialpolitik der Gemeinden und ihrer Verbände in der Beschäftigungskrise*, Opladen: Westdeutscher Verlag.

Lloyd, J. (1997) 'Interview: Robert Reich', *New Statesman*, 14 November.

Lorenz, W. (1994) 'Personal social services', in J. Clasen and R. Freeman, *Social policy in Germany*, Hemel Hempstead: Harvester Wheatsheaf.

Marsh, D. and Vogler, C. (1994) 'Labour market deprivation, welfare and collectivism', in D. Gallie, C. Marsh and C. Vogler (eds) *Social change and the experience of unemployment*, Oxford: Oxford University Press.

Martin, R (1994) 'Regional inequalities, income and poverty: the North–South divide lingers on', in S. Hardy, G. Lloyd and I. Cundell (eds) *Talking unemployment and social exclusion: Problems for regions, solutions for people*, Proceedings of the Regional Studies ASSOC Annual Conference.

McKay, S. and Marsh, A. (1994) *Lone parents and work*, London: HMSO.

McLaughlin, E. (1994) *Flexibility in work and benefits,* London: Institute for Public Policy Research.

McRae, S. (1987) *Young and jobless: The social and personal consequences of long-term youth unemployment*, London: Policy Studies Institute.

Meadows, P., Cooper, H. and Bartholomew, R. (1988) *The London labour market*, London: HMSO.

Millar, J. (1994) 'Understanding labour supply in context: households and incomes', in A. Bryson and S. McKay (eds) *Is it worth working?*, London, Policy Studies Institute.

MISSOC (1995) *Social protection in the member states of the European Union*, Luxembourg: Office for Official Publications of the European Communities.

Morgan, C. (1994) *Family resources survey statistics 1993-4*, Government Statistical Series. London: HMSO.

Morris, L. (1992) 'The social segregation of the long-term unemployment in Hartlepool', *The Sociological Review*, vol 40, no 2, pp 345-69.

Morris, L. (1994) *Dangerous classes*, London: Routledge.

Motion till Riksdagen (1994/95a) no A274, Stockholm: Riksdag.

Motion till Riksdagen (1994/95b) no A55, Stockholm: Riksdag.

Murray, C. (1990) *The emerging British underclass*, London: Institute for Economic Affairs.

Murray, C. (1994) *Underclass: The crisis deepens*, London: Institute of Economic Affairs.

Murray, I. (1994) 'Unemployment benefits in Europe: UK bottom of "social insurance" league', Working Brief, October, London: Unemployment Unit.

Murray, I. (1996) *Compulsion is not working*, Working Brief, Issue 71, London: Unemployment Unit.

Myles, J. (1996) 'When markets fail: social welfare in Canada and the United States', in G. Esping-Andersen (ed) *Welfare states in transition: National adaptations in global economies*, London: Sage.

Nilsson, A.-S. (1995) *Kamp för samvaro: en studie av långtidsarbetslöshetens sociala konsekvenser för individen*, Socologiska institutionen, Umeå: Umeå Universitet.

Nord (1994) *Vad kan göras åt arbetslösheten?*, no 17, Stockholm: Nordstedts.

Nyberg, E. (1987) *Långtidsarbetslöshetens individuella karaktäristika*, Växjö: Rapporter från högskolan i Växjö.

OECD (1968) *The long-term unemployed*, Paris: OECD.

OECD (1988) *Measures to assist the long-term unemployed: Recent experience in some OECD countries*, Paris: OECD.

OECD (1994) *The OECD jobs study*, Paris: OECD.

OECD (1995) *Employment outlook*, Paris: OECD.

Offe, C. (1991) 'Smooth consolidation in the West German welfare state: structural changes, fiscal policies and populist politics', in F.F. Piven (ed) *Labour parties in postindustrial societies*, Cambridge: Polity Press.

ONS (Office for National Statistics) (1996) *Labour force survey historical supplement*, London: HMSO.

Philpott, J. (1993a) 'Working towards full employment', *Economic Report*, vol 7, no 8, Employment Policy Institute.

Philpott, J. (1993b) 'Making Workstart work', *Economic Report*, vol 7, no 8, Employment Policy Institute.

Ploug, N. and Kvist, J. (1996) *Social security in Europe*, The Hague: Kluwer Law International.

Regeringens proposition (1994/95:218) *En effecktivare arbetsmarknadspolitik*, Stockholm.

Reissert, B. (1994) 'Unemployment compensation and the labour market: a European perspective', in S. Mangen and L. Hantrais (eds) *Unemployment, the informal economy and entitlement to benefits*, Cross National Research Papers, Third Series, Loughborough: European Research Centre, Loughborough University.

Riksdag och Departement (1993) *Bra arbetsmarknadspolitik ersattes med inflationsbekämpning*, no 21, Stockholm: Riksdag.

Riksdag och Departement (1994) *Kortare arbetstid ska utredas igen*, no 30, Stockholm: Riksdag.

Riksdag och Departement (1995a) *Fortsatt goda villkor till exportindustrin*, no 2, Stockholm: Riksdag.

Riksdag och Departement (1995b) *RAS hejdades*, no 8, Stockholm: Riksdag.

Riksdag och Departement (1995c) *RAS klart!*, no 10, Stockholm: Riksdag.

Riksdag och Departement (1995d) *Medelålders kan ta ledigt för ge arbetslösa jobb*, no 4, Stockholm: Riksdag.

Riksdag och Departement (1996a) *Arbetsrättskommissionen har 'strandat'*, no 17, Stockholm: Riksdag.

Riksdag och Departement (1996b) *Arbetsförmedlingen bör fömedla jobb*, no 8, Stockholm: Riksdag.

Robinson, P. (1988) 'Why are the long-term unemployed locked out of the labour market and what can be done about it?', *Campaign for Work Research Report*, vol 1, no 2.

Robinson, F. and Gregson, N (1992) 'The "underclass": a class apart?', *Critical Social Policy*, vol 12, no 1.

Rodger, J. (1992) 'The welfare state and social closure: social division and the "underclass"', *Critical Social Policy*, vol 12, no 2.

Room, G. (ed) (1995) *Beyond the threshold: The measurement and analysis of social exclusion*, Bristol: The Policy Press.

Rosenbladt, B.v. (1991) 'Arbeitslose in einer properierenden Wirtschaft', *Mitteilungen aus der Arbeitsmarkt- und Berufsforschung*, no 1, pp 146-56.

Schmid, A. and Gaß, G. (1995) 'Langzeitarbeitslosigkeit', in H. Seifert (ed) *Reform der Arbeitsmarktpolitik*, Cologne: Bund Verlag.

Schmid, A., Krömmelbein, S., Klems, W. and Gaß, G. (1994a) 'Neue Wege der Arbeitsmarktpolitik: Modellarbeitsämter und Modellprojekte', *WSI Mitteilungen*, no 2, pp 84-94.

Schmid, A., Krömmelbein, S., Klems, W. and Gaß, G. (1994b) *Neue Wege der Arbeitsmarktpolitik für Langzeitarbeitslose*, Berlin: Edition Sigma.

Schmid, G. and Reissert, B. (1996) 'Unemployment compensation and labour market transitions', in G. Schmid, J. O'Reilly and K. Schömann (eds) *International handbook of labour market policy and evaluation*, Cheltenham: Edward Elgar.

Shaw, A. and Walker, R. (1996) 'Disjoined interaction: the labour market and the benefits system', in P. Meadows (ed) *Work out – or work in? Contributions to the debate on the future of work*, York: YPS, pp 87-105.

Shaw, A., Walker, R., Ashworth, K., Jenkins, S. and Middleton, S. (1996) *Moving off Income Support: Barriers and bridges*, DSS Research Report No 53, London: HMSO.

Silver, H. (1994/95) 'Social exclusion and social solidarity: three paradigms', *International Labour Review*, vol 133, no 6.

Social Rapport (1994:10) Stockholm: Socialstyrelsen.

SOU (1995:7) Stockholm: *Obligatoriska arbetsplatskontakter för arbetslösa*, Arbetsmarknadsdepartementet.

SOU (1996:51) Stockholm: *Grundläggande drag i en ny arbetslöshetsfösäkring*, Arbetsmarknadsdepartementet.

Soydan, H. (1995) 'Ung och invandrare', in *I marginalen: att ställas utanför*, Umeå: Rapport från forskarseminariet i Umeå.

Sozialpolitische Umschau (1995:60) *Presse und Informationsamt der Bundesregierung*, Bonn: Sozialpolitische Umschau.

Sozialpolitische Umschau (1996:7) *Presse und Informationsamt der Bundesregierung*, Bonn: Sozialpolitische Umschau.

Sozialpolitische Umschau (1996:9) *Presse und Informationsamt der Bundesregierung*, Bonn: Sozialpolitische Umschau.

Sozialpolitische Umschau (1997:12) *Presse und Informationsamt der Bundesregierung*, Bonn: Sozialpolitische Umschau.

Sozialpolitische Umschau (1997:16) *Presse und Informationsamt der Bundesregierung*, Bonn: Sozialpolitische Umschau.

Statistisk Årsbok (1994) Stockholm: Statistiska Centralbyrån.

Stephens, J.D. (1996) 'The Scandinavian welfare states: achievements, crisis, and prospects', in G. Esping-Andersen (ed) *Welfare states in transition: National adaptations in global economies*, London: Sage.

Strittmatter, F.-J. (1992) 'Langzeitarbeitslosigkeit im Wohlfahrtstaat', no 157, *Beiträge zur Arbeitsmarkt und Berufsforschung*.

Svedberg, L. (1995) *Marginalitet: Ett socialt dilemma*, Lund: Studentlitteratur.

Swedish National Labour Market Board (1995) *Increased cooperation between trade union organisations (LO, TCO, SACO) and the Swedish Labour Market Administration*, 9 May, Solna.

Taylor-Gooby, P. (1991), 'Welfare state regimes and welfare citizenship', *Journal of European Social Policy*, vol 1, no 2, pp 93-105.

Taylor-Gooby, P. (1996) 'Eurosclerosis in European welfare states: regime theory and the dynamics of change', *Policy & Politics*, vol 24, no 2, 109-23.

The European Foundation for the Improvement of Living and Working Conditions (1992) *Counselling and long-term unemployment: Report on Phase 1 of the EUROCOUNSEL Action Research Programme*. Luxembourg: Office for Official Publications of the European Communities.

TUC (1995) *Budget submission*, London: TUC.

Unemployment Unit (1994) *Working Brief*, Issue 51, London: Unemployment Unit.

Unemployment Unit (1995) *Annual Report 1994-95*, London: Unemployment Unit.

Unemployment Unit (1996) *Working Brief*, Issue 76, London: Unemployment Unit.

Vincent, J. and Dobson, B. (1997) *Jobseeker's allowance evaluation: Qualitative research on disallowed and disqualified claimants*, Research Report No 15, London: Department for Education and Employment.

Vincent, J., Leeming, A., Peaker, A. and Walker, R. (1995) *Choosing advice on benefits*, DSS Research Report No 35, London: HMSO.

Wagner, A. (1995a) 'Langzeitarbeitslosigkeit: Vielfalt der Formen und differenzierte soziale Lage', *WSI Mitteilungen*, vol 48, no 12, pp 739-59.

Wagner, A. (1995b) 'Zweiter Arbeitsmarkt mit neuem Anspruch?', in H. Seifert (ed) *Reform der Arbeitsmarktpolitik*, Cologne: Bund Verlag.

Walker, A. (1997) 'Introduction: the strategy of inequality', in A. Walker and C. Walker (eds) *Britain divided: The growth of social exclusion in the 1980s and 1990s*, London: CPAG.

Walker, A. and Walker, C. (eds) (1997) *Britain divided: The growth of social exclusion in the 1908s and 1990s*, London: CPAG.

Walker, R. (1994) 'Springing the poverty trap', *New Economy*, September, pp 113-17.

Walker, R. (1995) 'The dynamics of poverty and social exclusion', in G. Room (ed) *Beyond the threshold: The measurement and analysis of social exclusion*, Bristol: The Policy Press, pp 102-28.

Walker, R. (1996) 'Unemployment, welfare and insurance', Talk given to the Geneva Association Seminar on Employment and Insurance, London.

Walker, R. (1997a) 'Rethinking poverty', in H. J. Andress (ed) *Empirical poverty research*, Aldershot: Ashgate.

Walker, R. (1997b) 'Poverty and social exclusion in Europe', in A. Walker and C. Walker (eds) *Britain divided: The growth of social exclusion in the 1908s and 1990s*, London: CPAG.

Walker, R. and Ashworth, K. (1998) 'Welfare benefits and recession in Britain', in L. Leisering and R. Walker (eds) *The dynamics of modern society*, Bristol: The Policy Press.

Walker, R., Shaw, A. and Hull, L. (1995) 'Responding to the risk of unemployment', in Association of British Insurers (eds) *Risk, insurance and welfare*, London: Association of British Insurers, pp 37-52.

Wallace, C. (1994) 'Education and training', in J. Clasen and R. Freeman (eds) *Social policy in Germany*, Hemel Hempstead: Harvester.

Walsh, K. (1987) *Long-term unemployment*, London: Macmillan.

Warr, P.B. and Jackson, P. (1985) 'Factors influencing the psychological impact of prolonged unemployment and re-employment', *Psychological Medicine*, no 15, pp 795-807.

Warr, P. and Jackson, P.R. (1987) (cited Bryson and McKay [eds], 1994) 'Adapting to the unemployed role: a longitudinal investigation', *Social Science and Medicine*, no 25.

Webster, D. (1997) *The 'L-U curve'. On the non-existence of a long-term claimant unemployment trap and its implications for policies on employment and area regeneration*, Glasgow: Centre for Housing Research and Urban Studies, University of Glasgow.

White, M. (1983) *Long-term unemployment and labour markets*, London: Policy Studies Institute.

White, M. (1991) *Against unemployment*, London: Policy Studies Institute.

White, M. and Lakey, J. (1992) *The Restart effect: Evaluation of a labour market programme for unemployed people*, London: Policy Studies Institute.

White, M. and McRae, S. (1989) *Young adults and long-term unemployment*, London: Policy Studies Institute.

Zimmermann, K.F. (1994) 'Labour responses to taxes and benefits in Germany', in A.B. Atkinson and G.V. Mogenson (eds) *Welfare and work incentives: A North European perspective*, Oxford: Clarendon Press.

Appendix: Principal social security support for unemployed people in Germany, Sweden and Britain in 1995

Germany

	Responsible authority	Condition	Level	Duration
Unemployment benefit (*Arbeitslosengeld*)	Federal Labour Office	Contributory	60% of standardised net earnings (67% for those with children)	12 months (longer for older workers with longer contribution records)
Unemployment assistance (*Arbeitslosenhilfe*)	Federal Labour Office	Contributory and means-tested	53% of standardised net earnings (57% for those with children)	a) unlimited in principle for those who exhausted Arbeitslosengeld; b) one year for others
Social assistance (*Sozialhilfe*)	Local authorities	Household needs, means-tested	Standard allowances for claimant, additions for dependants, other costs (rent, heating) covered; additions to cover other expenses (eg, repairs, grants for clothes)	Indefinite in principle

Sweden

	Responsible authority	Condition	Level	Duration
Earnings-related unemployment benefit (*a-kassa*)	Trade Union Unemployment Benefit Societies	Contributory/member of trade union for 12 months who has worked at least 17 hours a week for four months	75% of usual income (between minimum and maximum levels)	14 months (21 months for those older than 55); renewable by five months' employment or participation in the labour market programme
Cash labour market assistance (*Kontant Arbetsmarkndsstöd*)	Labour Market Board	Contributory/member of trade union for less than 12 months who has worked for less than four months	Flat rate (based on a-kassa's minimum level)	Seven months (14 months for those older than 55); renewable by five months' employment or participation in a labour market programme
Social assistance (*Socialbidrag*)	Local district authorities/ municipalities	Means-tested allowances for claimant and dependants, based on the national norm; additional allowances for housing		Indefinite in principle

Britain

	Responsible authority	Condition	Level	Duration
Unemployment benefit	The Employment Agency	Contributory	Flat-rate benefit amounting to 23% of average earnings	12 months
Social assistance (Income Support)	The Benefits Agency	Means-tested and dependent on fulfilling eligibility conditions	Means-tested allowance for claimant and dependents; additional allowances for housing; passported health-related benefits and free school meals	Indefinite in principle

For more details see MISSOC (1995) and Hansen (1997)

Index